THE DESIGN OF THE
FACTORY WITH A FUTURE

McGraw-Hill Series in Industrial Engineering and Management Science

Consulting Editors:

Kenneth E. Case, Department of Industrial Engineering and Management, Oklahoma State University
Philip M. Wolfe, Department of Industrial and Management Systems Engineering, Arizona State University

THE DESIGN OF THE FACTORY WITH A FUTURE

J T. Black

Director, Advanced Manufacturing Technology Center
Professor of Industrial Engineering
Auburn University

McGraw-Hill, Inc.
New York St. Louis San Francisco Auckland Bogotá
Caracas Lisbon London Madrid Mexico City Milan
Montreal New Delhi San Juan Singapore
Sydney Tokyo Toronto

This book was set in Times Roman by Publication Services.
The editors were Eric M. Munson and John M. Morriss;
the production supervisor was Annette Mayeski.
The cover was designed by Ted Bernstein.
Project supervision was done by Publication Services.
R. R. Donnelley & Sons Company was printer and binder.

This book is printed on acid-free paper.

THE DESIGN OF THE FACTORY WITH A FUTURE

4 5 6 7 8 9 0 DOC DOC 9 5 4

ISBN 0-07-005551-3 {hard cover}

ISBN 0-07-005550-5 {soft cover}

3 4 5 6 7 8 9 0 DOC DOC 9 5 4

Library of Congress Cataloging-in-Publication Data is available: LC Card # 90-19991.

ABOUT THE AUTHOR

J T. Black is a professor of industrial engineering at Auburn University, where he also serves as the director of their Advanced Manufacturing Technology Center. He was born in Rahway, N.J., and has lived in New York, Ohio, Pennsylvania, and Delaware. He graduated from high school in Edgewood, Pennsylvania, and attended Lehigh University (B.S.I.E.), West Virginia University (M.S.I.E.), and the University of Illinois at Urbana (Ph.D.). He has been teaching manufacturing engineering since 1960 and is the author of over 70 technical papers and numerous books on manufacturing processes and systems. He resides in Auburn, Alabama, with his wife, Carol. His other interests include tennis (he's the number two ranked 50 and over doubles player in the state) and writing music and poetry.

CONTENTS

11 Automation of Manufacturing Cells

Introduction Automation in IMPS Decouplers in Manufacturing Cells
Automating the IMPS Robot Process Capability Definition of Process
Capability Improvement and Measurement Techniques Contact Sensing
Devices Noncontact Sensing Devices Process Capability Versus Calibration
Measurement Equipment Requirements Final Assembly Summary

12 Computerization of IMPS

Introduction Integral Elements of CIMPS Computer-Aided Design (CAD)
Computer-Aided Manufacturing (CAM) Computer-Aided Process Planning
(CAPP) Computer Network and Interface Cell with Hierarchical Control
Cell with Heterarchical Control Local Area Networks (LAN) Manufacturing
Automation Protocol (MAP) Computerizing the Unmanned Manufacturing
Cell Cell Host Problems A Proposed Manufacturing System Design of the
Data Communication Architecture Discussion of UMC Design-Manufacture
Integration Man-Machine Interfaces A Factory with a Future

PREFACE

The use of integrated manufacturing production systems (IMPSs) is a strategy for the factory with a future (FWAF). This strategy is based on a linked-cell manufacturing system (L-CMS). The L-CMS provides for a continuous flow (or smooth movement) of materials through the plant. The L-CMS was invented at the Toyota Motor Company by the vice president for manufacturing, Taiichi Ohno, but he never gave it a name. He simply referred to it as Toyota's production system. Ohno was the inventor of a new kind of manufacturing system that was simple and very flexible. The strategy was brought to the United States by Toyota and many other companies and has been implemented in various forms in many companies in the United States.

Other names for IMPSs are

- JIT/TQC (just-in-time/total quality control) — many companies
- ZIPS (zero inventory production system) — Omark Industries
- MAN (material as needed) — Harley-Davidson
- MIPS (minimum inventory production system) — Westinghouse
- Ohno system (after Toyota's Taiichi Ohno) — many companies in Japan
- Stockless production — Hewlett-Packard
- Kanban — many companies in the United States and Japan

I have examined the implementation experiences of many companies, both the successes and the failures. The IMPS strategy stands in marked contrast to the well-advertised computer-integrated manufacturing (CIM) approach. The CIM strategy is an effort to get the automated elements (sometimes called *islands of automation*) of the traditional types of manufacturing systems to communicate with one another by computer. Extensive efforts to automate the processes and the material handling, including robotization to replace workers on the factory floor, have taken place in many companies. Reams of information have been generated on flexible manufacturing systems (FMSs) and robotics. However, the Toyota revolution was accomplished without computers, AGVs (automated guided vehicles), robots, and the like.

This book takes the experience of companies that have successfully implemented some version of the Ohno system and presents that experience in a logical, step-by-step strategy.

The 10 steps to a redesigned factory are outlined in Chapter 1 and detailed in subsequent chapters. The strategy embodies just-in-time (JIT) manufacturing, setup reduction, and "pull" production control methodology (kanban links). Quality control, production control, inventory control, and machine tool maintenance are readily integrated into the linked-cell manufacturing system. An IMPS produces superior quality at low cost with minimum throughput time (minimum time as work-in-process [WIP]) and provides the proper structure for automation—automation to solve quality or capacity problems. Automation and robotization can be used to remove variability from the process or operations or to remove people from dangerous or boring tasks. Computerization of the integrated system completes the strategy.

I believe that L-CMSs are the manufacturing systems of the future. Common practice in the future will be to link manufacturing and assembly cells. In the 1990s, we will see more companies implementing manned cells that use multifunctional workers who walk from machine to machine. Cells are designed to be flexible so they can readily adapt to changes in product design and product demand. Cells can readily be integrated with the critical control functions. Cells that make families of parts using a set (or group) of manufacturing processes replace the functional job shop structure.

The last time a revolution happened in manufacturing systems, the world came to Detroit to see Henry Ford's assembly line, circa 1913. The L-CMS system Taiichi Ohno invented is a logical extension of the Ford system. Ohno studied and understood how the current system of mass production functioned. However, he recognized that the Ford system was designed to handle large volumes of the same parts—no variety. The Ohno system is designed to handle large or small volumes of a variety of parts using the *same* economies of volume as the Ford system. Many people are now saying Ford invented JIT. This is simply not so; the "inventor" of JIT manufacturing was Taiichi Ohno, and he should be so recognized.

Ohno got the idea for his kanban system after visiting an American supermarket, where he observed people pulling stock from the shelves to fill their shopping carts to order. The empty space on the shelf was the signal for the stocker to restock. Empty storage areas in the back of the store provided signals to the storeroom clerk to reorder cases of the depleted item. In effect, the shopper provided a totally flexible final assembly of the order. In applying this idea to manufacturing, Ohno developed a system whereby downstream usage of parts dictated upstream production rates. The materials were pulled through the factory by the usage of parts in final assembly. Ohno quickly discovered that it was more efficient to move the machines closer together so that the workers could "make one, check one, and pass it on" to the next machine. Thus cells evolved through the factorywide desire to eliminate waste. There is no record of Toyota's using group technology, a well-known method for finding families of parts around which cells can be designed.

It has become apparent that no industry is immune to this strategy. Figure P-1 shows a matrix of product type versus manufacturing system type. The industries

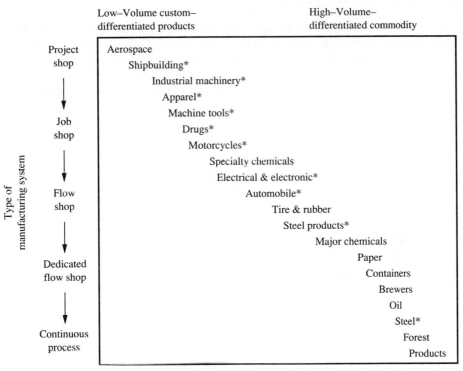

Type of industry by product

FIGURE P–1
Product type versus manufacturing system.

represent a broad spectrum of products and manufacturing systems. At least one company within each of these industries has already completed the conversion to L-CMS, so that virtually the entire spectrum of piece-part manufacturing industries has been affected by some version of IMPS and cell formation. Because the revolution began in Japan, many of the leading IMPS companies are Japanese. The good news is that the revolution is not culturally based. The bad news is that the key to this revolution lies in *redesigning* the existing manufacturing system. Many decision makers will resist this conversion because it is not very high-tech and because it severely impacts the social structure of the entire company—middle management will suffer the most and will be the greatest deterrent to the change.

There are many reasons for a company to undertake such an effort and many excuses for not doing it. However, this much is clear: companies that have the courage to undertake this change will be the survivors—the factories with a future (FWAFs). Those who resist will become history.

ACKNOWLEDGMENTS

There are many people who made significant contributions to this book. I hope I don't forget someone. Let's start with my wife, Carol, who did all the typing and editing of the first and second drafts. She also made many suggestions that greatly improved the readability of the final manuscript. Thanks to Angeline Honnell who read and edited many sections of this book. Dan Sipper, Steve Hunter, and Brian Paul provided many suggestions for improvement. Mark Lawley read it all for content and provided excellent editorial comments and corrections. Lynn Paul found some errors that even Mark missed.

Space does not permit naming all of the students of my IMPS course here at Auburn University and at the University of Alabama in Huntsville who contributed to the book with their questions and discussions, both in and after class. Some of the students, Dave Hanning, Steve Hunter, Yen Shi "Hopper" Tsai, Doris Lizotte, Jill Williams, Alice Carter, and Jack R. "Rick" Wade, provided written contributions. Jason Wang and Allen Chen used AUTOCAD to do original drafts of most of the figures. My special thanks to them. Naturally, I am indebted to Ed Unger and Dayne Aldridge (my department head and associate dean) for their continued support. Chapter 3 was extracted from the unpublished work of Nam Suh, a professor at MIT whose work on axiomatic design I have long admired. The chapter on setup reduction came easily after a face-to-face meeting with Shigeo Shingo. This book was inspired by Tom Gelb, an engineer at Harley-Davidson, who described with great passion the conversion of HD to IMPS. He was like the battle-scarred soldier returning from the great war.

J T. Black

THE DESIGN OF THE
FACTORY WITH A FUTURE

CHAPTER 1

INTRODUCTION/
BACKGROUND

The external customer decides the price. The internal customer decides the cost. The managers look to the difference (the profit).

INTRODUCTION

We are now entering a new era in the industrial world. It can, I believe, be quite reasonably termed a revolution, our third industrial revolution.

The first industrial revolution began with the advent of powered machine tools, the creation of factories, and a movement (a megatrend of the first industrial revolution) of people from the farms to the factories in the cities. Now only about 2 percent to 3 percent of the people work directly on farms, but their productivity continues to increase even today (see Figure 1-1). The measures of farm productivity are numerous, ranging from increased output per acre to increased number of people fed per farmer. As Figure 1-2 shows, the number of farmers (direct laborers in agribusiness) has reached an all-time low. The number of direct laborers in factories is continually decreasing in the same fashion. This does not mean that fewer people work in the entire agriculture or food production industry; it means that the number of direct laborers has been significantly reduced because of large, often automated, special purpose farming equipment.

The second industrial revolution began in the early 1900s with the advent of assembly lines and the Ford concept of mass production. Large, expensive manufacturing systems, called transfer lines, were part of this trend. These systems, fully developed in the 1940s, had large automatic material-handling mechanisms from which the term

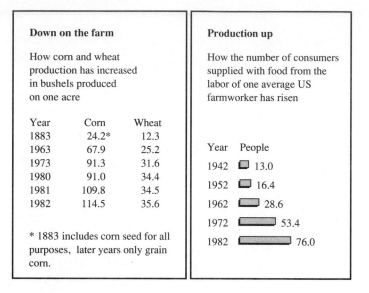

FIGURE 1-1
Productivity in farming has continued to improve with fewer people producing
more food. *(Source: U.S. Department of Agriculture)*

automation evolved. The objective was to develop "islands of (rigid) automation."
This kind of automation is today called *fixed* to contrast it with flexible automation,
which features programmable machines.

In recent years a third industrial revolution has evolved, every bit as dramatic
as its forerunners. This revolution features computers for control of both processes
and entire systems, including the information system. The same trend is happening
in the factories that happened on the farms. Over a period of time, fewer people will
work on the factory floor itself, but more people will be involved in the production of
goods. Remember that value is added and wealth created only through the conversion
of materials by manufacturing (or agriculture).

We are still creating more jobs every year than we eliminate with automation.
The factory worker of today is equivalent to the farmer at the turn of the century.
Farm work is hard duty, with long hours. Farm modernization freed many people to
work elsewhere (the factories). Now the trend is for people not to want the hard, dirty,
often boring, even dangerous, jobs in the factories. Thus, the trend is moving away
from an industrial-based society. This does not mean that we will abandon the factory,
for to abandon manufacturing would soon result in our demise as a world power.

The factory of tomorrow will require greater levels of knowledge and more
effective modes of information transfer about the quality and quantity of goods manufactured. The knowledge base of factory workers must be increased to improve their
productivity, and, ultimately, the productivity of the company. Knowledge has a market value, particularly technical knowledge, but we in the United States tend to give it
away or sell it to the lowest bidder. Japan purchased much of the technical knowledge
it needed to build cars, electronics, machine tools, and even electron microscopes.

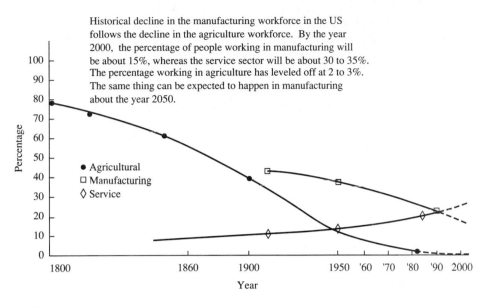

Historical decline in the manufacturing workforce in the US follows the decline in the agriculture workforce. By the year 2000, the percentage of people working in manufacturing will be about 15%, whereas the service sector will be about 30 to 35%. The percentage working in agriculture has leveled off at 2 to 3%. The same thing can be expected to happen in manufacturing about the year 2050.

- Agricultural
- Manufacturing
- Service

FIGURE 1-2
Historical trends in agricultural, manufacturing, and service industries.

The early Japanese transmission electron microscopes were essentially duplicates of the precision-made Siemens instruments. A common thread ties all Japanese product areas together—high (sophisticated) technology. For example, the precision machining of the magnetic lens and the fabrication of high-voltage electronics were key to the construction of quality electron microscopes.

Information (high-tech knowledge) has value because people are willing to pay for it. Information also has cost because it costs something to produce. This is especially true for technological information.

The factory of the future will need superior information systems and many people who can analyze, program, and otherwise deal with the information flowing to and from the factory floor. The unique aspect about knowledge and information is that, unlike energy, it does not follow the laws of conservation. Knowledge and information are synergistic, each promoting growth in the other. Thus, as the factory worker becomes better educated and more knowledgeable about how the entire manufacturing production system works, the system will work better.

Manufacturing processes and systems must become simpler as they become more automated. Often products are redesigned so that they can be automatically processed or assembled. By the next century, we will see significantly fewer workers on the plant floor. These workers will be better educated and involved in solving daily production problems, in working to improve the entire system, and in making decisions about how to improve their jobs and the manufacturing system.

What spurred this revolution was the competition provided by the Japanese in a wide variety of products and markets. Their prices are competitive and their quality superior. They have been able to finance this remarkable transformation through low-interest government and private loans. More significantly, they have developed techniques to reduce inventory levels, which result in a better cash flow because of the increased frequency of inventory turnover.

Many people in the United States believe that the Japanese success was due to excess products dumped into U.S. markets, or governmental support given to targeted industries, or cultural differences. The Japanese are a hard-working, industrious people, but so are Americans. The notion that this success was simply the result of working long hours for substandard wages does not hold water when complex, quality products are being built. The truth is that the Japanese developed *a new manufacturing system that is functionally and operationally different from ours*. At the outset, we must understand the significant factors of this new system so that we can determine which elements must be implemented in our systems.

Consider the following evidence. In 1977 a Japanese company named Matsushita purchased a Quasar television plant in Chicago from Motorola. The plant had been a consistent money loser. In the purchase contract, Matsushita agreed that all the hourly personnel would be retained. The first changes the new owners implemented were to clean up the plant and paint the floor. They also promoted the manager of quality control to plant manager, thus taking the first step in integrating the quality control function into the manufacturing system. Two years later they still had essentially the same 1,000 hourly employees but had reduced the indirect staff by 50 percent. During that period, daily production doubled. The quality, as measured by the number of repairs done in-house, improved more than twentyfold. Outside quality indicators also improved. Whereas Motorola had spent an average $16 million a year on warranty costs, Matsushita's expenditures were $2 million. (That's for twice as many TV sets, so it's really a 16-to-1 ratio.) These are big differences, achieved in the United States with American workers.

The Japanese have had one fundamental economic goal since the end of World War II: full employment through industrialization. They sought to obtain market dominance in selected product areas. The common thread in selecting these areas was technology. Japanese tactics were fourfold:

1. They concentrated on products that required high technology to achieve quality.
2. They imported their technology from all over the world rather than developing it themselves. For example, the entire Japanese semiconductor industry was built around a $25,000 purchase from Texas Instruments for the rights to the basic semiconductor process. Examples of this sort are numerous.
3. They developed a new and different manufacturing system that was flexible and delivered products on time, at the lowest possible cost on a continuing basis. They educated their work force and placed their best engineering talent on the production floor rather than in the design room. Those who say that the Japanese are not inventive or ingenious have simply looked in the wrong places for evidence. Rather than invent a new mousetrap, they developed a better way to make mousetraps of superior quality at lower cost.
4. They developed a system that produced superior quality products. They believed in total quality control and taught it to everyone, from the company president on

down to every production worker. They were able to change from a country that made junk to a nation that could give customers products of high reliability.

Implementation of these tactics was governed by two fundamental concepts. Most manufacturers agree with these tactics in principle, but the difference is the degree to which the Japanese practice them: (1) The Japanese firmly believe that industry must *eliminate waste*, and (2) they practice a great *respect for people*.

IMPS FUNDAMENTAL CONCEPTS

Elimination of Waste (Nonvalue-Adding Elements)

Focused factories or factories within a factory
Continuous flow manufacturing (the L-CMS)
Reduction/elimination of setup time
Integrated quality control (elimination of defects)
Integrated inventory control (kanban)
Just-in-time manufacturing
Mixed-model manufacturing/assembly

Respect for people

Attitude of management toward workers
Automation/robotics to solve problems
Consensus management
Vendor programs
Methods of compensation

By *waste*, we mean anything other than the *minimum* amount of equipment, materials, parts, and workers (working time) that is *absolutely essential* to production. Storage and banking must be minimized. If it cannot be used now, it is not made now because it would be waste. The other basic element, aside from the restructuring of the manufacturing system, is *respect for people*. All these elements go together to define the IMPSs. They are all applicable to American manufacturing companies.

Redesigning the manufacturing and production system requires a change in philosophy within the company. Employee involvement and teamwork are rooted in the idea that no one employee is better than another. Everyone is called an associate. There are no private offices. There is no executive lunch room. There are no preferred parking places (except for the associate of the month). The old system in which management tells workers what to do and how to do it must change. However, this change usually requires that the CEO have the courage to shift some of the decision-making power from management to the people on the factory floor. Restructuring the manufacturing system and the production system helps this most difficult transition. The biggest change is psychological—convincing the workers on the factory floor that nothing is more important than what they think and how they feel about the manufacturing system. For this to work, achievement must be tracked closely and rewarded. People are not going to "bust their guts" unless there is a strong reward system.

INTRODUCTION TO IMPS

IMPS implementation requires a systems-level change for the factory—a change that will impact every segment of the company, from accounting to shipping. Ten steps outline the IMPS methodology (see Figure 1-3). Before a company embarks on these 10 steps, all levels—from production workers through top management—must be educated in IMPS philosophy and concepts. Top management must be totally committed to this venture. Every employee must be involved and motivated and ultimately committed to the change.

The conversion to linked-cells is a *systems-level change* affecting the factory environment and the functional relationships within it. This is a long-term strategy. Changing the manufacturing system is equivalent to heart transplant surgery. It is major surgery and it usually is not elective.

Changing the manufacturing system is very difficult. It is the manufacturing system that produces the goods the customer wants or buys. There are two groups of people the manufacturing system must satisfy: the people who use the products and the people who use the system that makes the products. The second group, consisting of the *internal* customers is usually the smaller of the two groups. The *external* customers of the manufacturing system buy or use the products made by the internal customers. The manufacturing system must be *restructured* for the *benefit of the internal customer*, the users of the manufacturing system. Job satisfaction for the internal customer includes monetary rewards plus a good working environment. The external

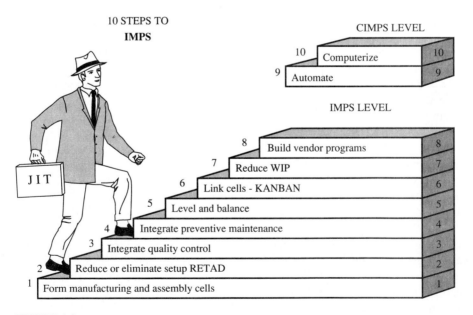

FIGURE 1-3
Ten Steps to integrated manufacturing production systems (IMPSs).

customers of the manufacturing system must also be satisfied. The external customers, those who buy the products, determine price. Everyone in the plant must understand that cost, not price, determines profit. The external customer wants low cost, superior quality, and on-time delivery. "Reduce cost by eliminating waste" is the operational motto of IMPS. Waste is viewed as anything done to the product that does not add value and quality.

THE 10 STEPS TO IMPS

The next generation of factories in the United States will be designed with a new kind of manufacturing system called cellular or linked-cell manufacturing system (L-CMS). This new kind of manufacturing system is an integral part of a 10-step strategy, developed by the author, to convert an existing factory into a factory with a future (FWAF).

After the first eight steps, the manufacturing system has been redesigned and infused (integrated) with the critical production functions of quality control, inventory control, production control, and machine maintenance. Automation and computerization then follow.

Step One: Form Cells—Build the Foundation

Creating cells is the first step in designing a manufacturing system of which production control, inventory control, and quality control are integral parts. The existing manufacturing system is systematically restructured and reorganized into a factory of manned manufacturing and assembly cells. The cell is a group of processes designed to make a family of parts in a flexible way. One-piece movement of parts occurs within cells. Small-lot movement of parts occurs between cells. The workers in the cells are multiprocess: they can run more than one process, and they can run different kinds of processes.

Step Two: Implement a RETAD System

By RETAD, we mean the rapid exchange of tooling and dies to reduce or eliminate setup. Forming cells for families of parts forces everyone to address the problems in setup time. The changeover time from one part to the next within the cell must be as short as possible. Everyone on the plant floor must be taught how to reduce setup time using SMED (single-minute exchange of dies) (see Figure 1-4). This is the key. *Everyone* on the factory floor works at reducing setup using the simple four-stage SMED system. The system works for any process. In the first stage, the current method is studied and analyzed. In stage two, internal setup is distinguished from external setup. In stage three, internal setup is converted to external setup. The intermediate jig concept is explained in Chapter 5. In stage four, all aspects of the setup are examined and adjustments are eliminated. This is the first step in the operator training program that develops multifunctional workers. A blue ribbon setup reduction team is developed to assist production workers with problems, demonstrate a project on the plant's "worst" setup problem, and train workers in the SMED approach.

Step Three: Integrate Quality Control

The design of the cell creates an environment that is conducive to quality control. Defective parts cannot be allowed out of the cell. The one-at-a-time system within the cell means make one, check one, pass one on. Thus, besides being multiprocess, operators in the cells are also multifunctional. They know how to reduce setup and organize their workplace. They also perform other functions including quality control and process improvement. Every worker has the responsibility and the authority to make the product right the first time and every time. Giving workers the necessary quality control tools integrates quality control into the manufacturing system, resulting in a marked reduction in defects. More details on this are found in Chapter 6.

Step Four: Integrate Preventive Maintenance/ Machine Reliability

An integrated preventive maintenance program can be installed by giving workers the training and tools to properly maintain equipment. Excess processing capacity obtained by reducing setup time allows the operators to reduce the speed of equipment and to

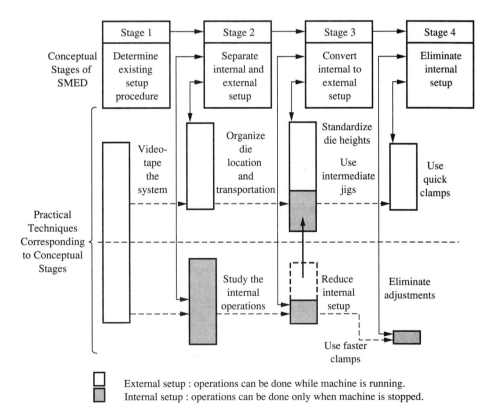

FIGURE 1-4
Conceptual stages and practical techniques of the SMED system. (*Developed by S. Shingo, 1985.*)

run the process at less than full capacity. Reducing pressure on workers and processes to produce a given quantity is part of the strategy to produce perfect quality. Part of making the factory floor safe includes two housekeeping rules:

1. Have a place for everything and put everything in its place so it is ready to use next time.
2. Each worker is responsible for the cleanliness of the workplace and the equipment.

Total preventive maintenance is discussed in Chapter 7.

Step Five: Level and Balance Final Assembly

The entire manufacturing system is leveled (each process made to produce the same amount) and balanced by manufacturing in small lots to reduce the shock of change. A simplified and synchronized system is used to produce the same number of everything, every day, as needed. The conversion can begin with mixed-model sequencing final assembly and progress back through subassembly and manufacturing cells. Long setup times in the subassembly or manufacturing flow lines must be eliminated, as discussed previously. In mixed-model final assembly, it is important to make at least one of each product every day so the production workers do not forget how to do it correctly. Leveling and balancing will be discussed in Chapter 8.

Step Six: Integrate Production Control—
Link the Cells with Kanban

Linking the cells integrates production control. Downstream processes dictate the production rates of upstream processes. Only final assembly is scheduled. *The structure of the layout of the manufacturing system now defines paths that parts can take through the plant.* This step begins with kanban links (see Figure 1-5). The kanbans are cards that control the movement of material between the processes. There are two basic kinds of kanbans. The withdrawal kanban (WLK) pulls material downstream from one cell to the next. The production-ordering kanban (POK) acts as the dispatcher for the cells, scheduling what to make, what order to make it in, and how many to make. Route sheets are eliminated. The material flows within the structure. This is integration of the production control function. What is unique about the system is that information about the material movement flows in the opposite direction to the material. Thus, downstream usage dictates upstream production volumes. Integration of production control is discussed in Chapter 9.

Step Seven: Integrate Inventory Control—
Reduce Work-in-Process/Expose Problems

The integration of inventory control into the system systematically reduces lot sizes and work-in-process (WIP). The people on the plant floor directly control the inventory levels in their areas. The kanban links serve as controllable inventory buffers, protecting downstream elements from upstream problems. Controlled reduction in the

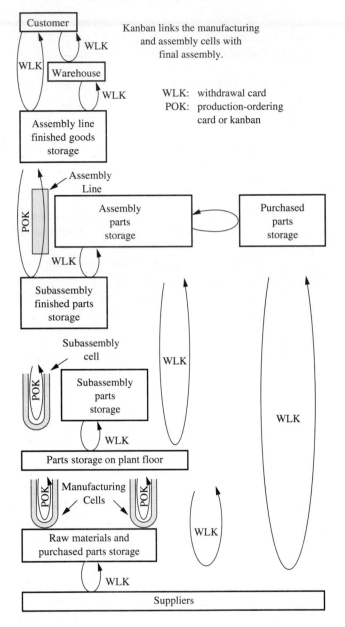

FIGURE 1-5
The manufacturing and assembly cells are linked to the final assembly
area with kanban inventory links or loops.

level of inventory in the links reveals the problems in the cells (see Figure 1-6). The system therefore uses inventory control (reduction) to expose problems rather than inventory excess to cover up problems. Integration of inventory control is discussed in Chapter 9.

Step Eight: Extend IMPS to Include Vendors

The final conversion step is to educate and encourage suppliers of the IMPS company to develop superior quality, low cost, and rapid delivery manufacturing systems. Vendors must be able to deliver material when needed, where needed, without incoming inspection. The "linked-cell" network eventually must include every vendor. Vendors eventually become remote cells (see Chapter 10).

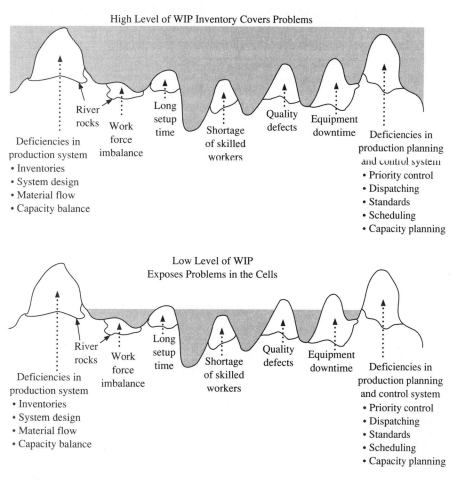

FIGURE 1-6
The rocks-in-the-river analogy.

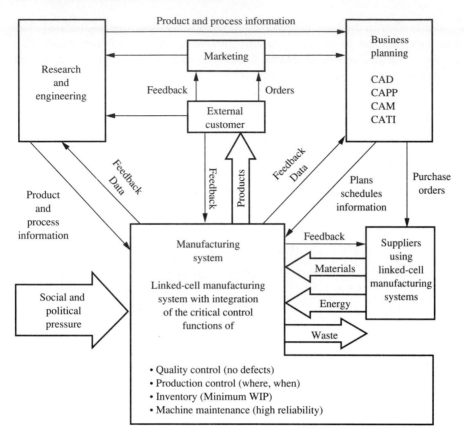

FIGURE 1-7
Simplified production system model of the intelligent factory with a future.

Step Nine: Automate and Robotize to Solve Problems

This step involves the conversion of manned cells to unmanned cells. It is an evolutionary process initiated by the need to solve problems in quality or capacity (to eliminate a bottleneck). It begins with the mechanization of operations such as loading, clamping, unloading, inspection, and setup and moves toward the automation of human thinking and the automatic detection and correction of problems and defects. The author has developed a new class of devices called *decouplers* to perform such functions. See Chapter 11 for a discussion of unmanned cells.

Step Ten: Computerize to Link the Linked-Cell Manufacturing System to the Production System

Total computerization of the integrated linked-cell manufacturing system is the last step in the conversion. At this point, the manufacturing system is simple and flexible enough for efficient computers to control. The computer communications for computer-aided design (CAD), computer-aided manufacture (CAM), and direct numerical control (DNC) arrangements can use manufacturing automation protocol/technical office protocol (MAP/TOP) strategies (see Figure 1-7). The secret here is not to computerize the existing job shop (functionalized) manufacturing system. Computerizing the integrated system is easier, and causes the company to become a factory with a future. Integrating the manufacturing system results in computerized IMPSs (CIMPSs). See Chapter 12 for introduction to computer-aided integrated manufacturing production systems.

IMPS IN SUMMARY

Every manufacturing system has certain control functions that must be performed. Table 1-1 summarizes eight functions and lists the tools that both the IMPS system and the job shop use to aid these functions.

Regardless of the type of manufacturing system, the same control functions are performed by every manufacturing system. However, the tools used by IMPS differ greatly from the job shop tools. Under IMPS, many of the tools are manual—kanban cards, andon lights, pokayoke checks, and oral orders. Under MRP, the most important tool is the computer. If the system being computerized is good, the computerized version has a chance to succeed.

TABLE 1-1
How eight manufacturing functions are controlled

Functions	Categories	IMPS	Job shop
Rate of output	Families of products	Leveling the manufacturing system	Production plan
Products to be built	Finished goods for make-to-stock, customer orders for make-to-stock	Master production schedule	Master production schedule
Materials required	Components—both manufactured and purchased	Pull system WLK cards	Push system— material requirement planning (MRP)
Capacity required	Output for key work centers and vendors	Controlled by number of workers	Capacity requirement planning (CRP)
Executing capacity plans	Producing enough output to satisfy plans	Meet downstream needs	Input/output controls, route sheets
Executing material plans—manufactured items	Working on right priorities in factory	POK cards— pull system	Dispatching reports, route sheets
Executing material plans—purchased items	Bringing in right items from vendors	Kanban cards and unofficial orders	Purchasing reports, invoices
Feedback information	What cannot be executed due to problems	Immediate	Anticipated delay reports

BACKGROUND ON MANUFACTURING SYSTEMS

Human history has been linked with the ability to convert raw materials into usable goods. This began with the Stone Age and continued through the Copper and Bronze Ages into the Iron Age. The Age of Steel, with our sophisticated ferrous and nonferrous materials, has dominated the material world for the past 100 years. We are now entering an era of tailor-made materials such as plastic composites and ceramics, but metals still represent a significant portion of usable (and reusable) materials.

As material variety expands, so does the variety of processes. Manufacturing processes are developed to add value to the materials as efficiently as possible. Advances in manufacturing technology often account for improvements in productivity. Even when a manufacturing technology is proprietary, the competition often gains quick access to it.

Materials, people, and equipment are interrelated factors in manufacturing that must be combined properly in order to achieve low cost, superior quality, and on-time delivery. Typically, as shown in Figure 1-8, 40 percent of the selling price of a product is manufacturing cost. Since the selling price is determined by the market, maintaining the profit often depends on reducing manufacturing cost. Direct labor, usually the target of automation, accounts for only about 12 percent of manufacturing cost even though many view it as the main factor in increasing productivity.

The IMPS strategy attacks material costs, indirect costs, and general administration costs in addition to labor costs. Material costs include capital cost and the cost of storing and handling materials within the plant. The IMPS strategy eliminates material handling, except as needed to make the products. (Eliminating material handling is not the same as automating it.)

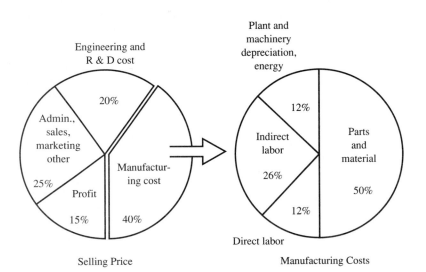

FIGURE 1-8
Manufacturing cost is the largest cost in the selling price. The largest manufacturing cost is material cost, not direct labor.

Of the total expense (selling price less profit), about 68 percent of dollars are spent on people: about 15 percent for engineers, 25 percent for marketing, sales and general management people, 5 percent for direct labor, and 10 percent for indirect labor (55/80 = 68.75 percent). The average U.S. labor cost in manufacturing was around $10 to $11 per hour for hourly workers in 1986. Reductions in direct labor will have only marginal effects on the people costs. A systems approach, taking into account all the factors, must be used. This requires a sound and broad understanding of materials, processes, and equipment by the decision makers followed by an understanding of manufacturing systems.

CHANGING WORLD COMPETITION

In recent years, major changes in the world of goods manufacturing have taken place. Some of these are

1. Worldwide competition by first class companies
2. Advanced manufacturing process technology
3. New manufacturing systems structure, strategies, and management

Worldwide competition is now a fact of manufacturing life. In automobile manufacturing, the foreign competition is relocating on American soil, demonstrating beyond a shadow of a doubt that the new system works just as well here as it does in Japan or Korea. The future will bring more (not less) world class competitors into the market. Everyone with enough capital has access to new manufacturing process technology: Technology can always be purchased. Thus, the secret to success in manufacturing is to build a company that can deliver on-time (short throughput time), superior quality products to the customer at the lowest possible cost (least waste) and still be flexible.

MANUFACTURING AND PRODUCTION SYSTEMS

Manufacturing is the economic term for making goods and services available to satisfy human wants. Manufacturing implies creating value by applying useful mental or physical labor.

Manufacturing processes are combined to form a *manufacturing system*. The manufacturing system takes inputs and produces products for the customer. The *production system* includes the manufacturing system and services it. Thus, *production system* refers to the total company and includes the manufacturing systems as shown in Figure 1-9. The following football analogy helps to distinguish between manufacturing systems and production systems.

College football is an example of a service industry. Football players are equivalent to manufacturing machine tools (see Figure 1-10). The things that they do, such as punt, pass, run, tackle, and block, are equivalent to operations. Different machines do different operations, and some machines do operations better than others.

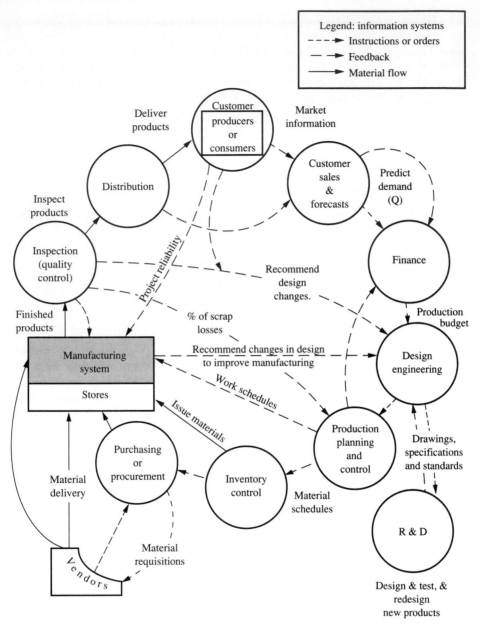

FIGURE 1-9
The functions and systems of the production system, which includes (and services) the manufacturing system.

FOOTBALL	VS	MANUFACTURING
Football players		Manufacturing proceses or machine tools
Operations Things football players do Run, punt, pass, block tackle, catch		Operations Things machine tools do Turning, drilling, boring, tapping
Offensive and defensive plays Single wing Pro-tee I back Wish bone		Manufacturing systems Job shop, flow shop Project shop Continuous Processes Cellular
Designing the plays or formations 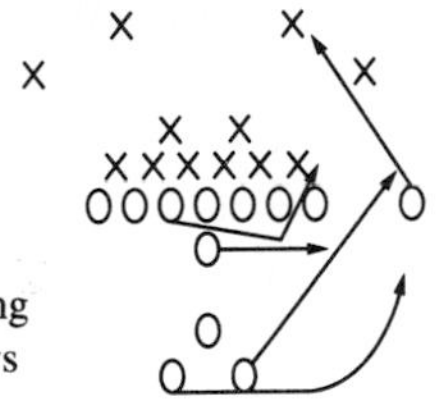		Design or layout of manufacturing system Functional layout Product layout Process layout
Athletic department Coach the players Recruit players Maintain field Sell tickets Print programs Training room		Production system Design Personnel Accounting Sales/ marketing Quality control Maintenance

FIGURE 1-10

Analogy of football to manufacturing and production system terminology.

The arrangement of machines (often called the plant layout) defines the basic design of the manufacturing system within the company. In football, this arrangement is called an offensive alignment or defensive formation. Modern teams use pro-Tee sets and I formations, but many U.S. factories are still using the "single-wing" version called the job shop.

The job shop (with some elements of the flow shop when the volume is large enough to justify special purpose equipment) is common practice in the United States. The job shop is a functionally designed manufacturing system where like processes are put together. The same organization occurs in football, with all the linemen segregated from the backs. Coaches are equivalent to foremen, and the head coach is the supervisor.

In the football analogy, the production system would be the athletic department that sells tickets, runs the training room (machine maintenance and repair), raises operating capital, arranges material handling (travel), and does whatever is needed to help keep the manufacturing system operating. The production system does not do any manufacturing. No one in the athletic department ever plays in the football game. They are all indirect, managerial, and staff employees. In the plant, the production system *services* the manufacturing system. This division is called *staff*, while people who work in manufacturing are called *line*.

The production system therefore includes the manufacturing system plus all the other functional areas of the plant that provide information, design, analysis, and control. When the manufacturing system is a job shop, the production system will also be functionally designed.

These subsystems are somehow connected to one another to produce either goods, services, or both. Goods refer to material items. Services are nonmaterial. We buy services to satisfy our wants, needs, and desires. *Service production systems* include transportation, banking, finance, insurance, utilities, health care, education, communication, entertainment, sporting events, and so forth. They are useful labors that do not directly produce a product or create wealth.

Production terms have a definite rank of importance somewhat like grades in the Army. Confusing *system* with *station* is similar to mistaking a colonel for a corporal. In either case, knowledge of rank is necessary (see Table 1-2). The terms tend to overlap because of the inconsistencies of popular usage.

PRODUCTION SYSTEMS

The highest-ranking term in the hierarchy is *production system*. A production system includes people, money, equipment, materials and supplies, markets, management, and the manufacturing system. In effect, all aspects of commerce (manufacturing, sales, advertising, profit, and distribution) are involved.

Much of the information given for manufacturing production systems is relevant to the service production system, which, by design, is usually a job shop. Most manufacturing systems require a service production system for proper product sales. This is particularly true in industries such as the food (restaurant) industry where customer service is as important as quality and on-time delivery.

MANUFACTURING SYSTEMS

A manufacturing system is a collection or arrangement of operations and processes used to make a desired product(s) or component(s). The *manufacturing system* includes the actual equipment composing the processes and the arrangement of those processes. Control of a system applies to total control of the whole, not of the individual processes or equipment. All the users of the manufacturing system must understand how it works (behaves). The entire manufacturing system must be controlled in order to regulate levels of inventory, movement of material through the plant, production (output) rates, and product quality.

There are many hybrid forms of these manufacturing systems, but the job shop is the most common system.

Because of its design, the job shop has proven to be the least cost efficient of all the systems. Component parts in a typical job shop spend only 5 percent of the time

TABLE 1-2
Production terms for manufacturing production systems

Term	Meaning	Examples
Production system (the whole company)	The entire company: all aspects of people, machines, materials, and information considered collectively.	Company that makes engines, assembly plant, glassmaking factory, foundry.
Manufacturing system (collection of processes)	A series of manufacturing processes resulting in specific end products; the arrangement or layout of all the processes, equipment, people.	Series of connected operations or processes; a job shop, flow shop, a continuous process, a project shop, a linked-cell system.
Manufacturing process (machine or machine tool)	A specific piece of equipment designed to accomplish specific processes; often called a machine tool; machine tools link together to make a manufacturing system.	Spot welder, milling machine, lathe, drill press, forge, drop hammer, die caster. These are all manufacturing processes.
Job (sometimes called a station)	A collection of or sequence of operations done on machines or a collection of tasks performed by one worker at one location on an assembly line.	Operate machine, inspect part, assemble A into B. The machine tool operator has the job of running the machine.
Operation (sometimes called a process)	A specific action or treatment, the collection of which makes up the job of a worker.	Drill, ream, bend, solder, turn, face, mill, extrude. Things done by/on a milling machine.
Tools or tooling (cutting tools, workholders)	The implements used to hold, cut, shape, or form the work materials; called *cutting tools* if referring to machining; can refer to *jigs* and *fixtures* used for workholding and *punches* and *dies* in metal forming.	Grinding wheel, drill bit, tap, end milling cutter, die, mold, clamp, three-jaw vise, plate jig.

in machines and the rest of the time waiting or moving from one functional area to the next. Once the part is on the machine, it is being processed (i.e., having value added by changing its shape) only 30 to 40 percent of the time (see Figure 1-11). The rest of the time the part is being loaded, unloaded, inspected, and so on. The advent of numerical control machines has increased the percentage of time the machine is making chips because tool movements are programmed and the machines can automatically change tools or load and unload parts. But the fact that these machines are still used in a job shop environment means that there is still a high percentage of waiting and delay.

The bottom line on these numbers is as follows. The percentage of time making chips (40 percent) times the percentage of time on the machine (5 percent) yields 2 percent productive time for an eight-hour shift. Suppose it is recommended that the process be

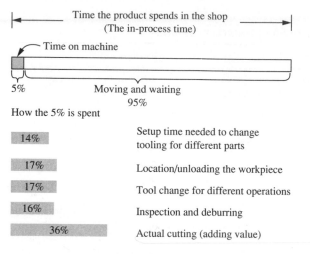

Time the product spends in the shop
(The in-process time)

Time on machine

5%   Moving and waiting
                     95%

How the 5% is spent

14%	Setup time needed to change tooling for different parts
17%	Location/unloading the workpiece
17%	Tool change for different operations
16%	Inspection and deburring
36%	Actual cutting (adding value)

FIGURE 1-11
The typical utilization of production time in metal removal operations with conventional tool handling, workpiece loading, setups, and inspections.

upgraded, increasing the percentage of time making chips to 50 percent, (using a faster machine) or even 60 percent. Such a process improvement might cost $300,000. But if no change in the manufacturing system takes place, the effect on the bottom line will be small, about 1 percent. However, if the manufacturing system is restructured to raise the time on the machine to 50 percent of the time the product spends in the factory, improvements in unit process will result in significant improvements in overall productivity.

UNDERSTANDING THE COMPANY'S BUSINESS

Understanding the unit process technology of the company is very important for everyone in the company. Manufacturing technology affects the design of the product and the manufacturing system, the way the manufacturing system can be controlled, the types of people employed, and the materials that can be processed. Table 1-3 outlines the process technology characteristics. One valid criticism of American companies is that their managers seem to have an aversion to understanding their companies' manufacturing technologies. This is no doubt related to the argument presented in the previous section: Why worry about unit processes or their improvement when they have such a small impact on the bottom line?

However, failure to understand the company's business (i.e., its fundamental process technology) can lead to the failure of the company. The way to overcome the aversion that many company executives have to manufacturing technology is to run the process and study the technology. Only someone who has run a drill press can understand the sensitive relationships between feed rate and drill torque and thrust. All processes have these "know-how" features. Those who run the processes must take part in the decision making for the factory. The CEO who takes a vacation working on the plant floor learning the processes will be well on the way to being the head of a successful company.

TABLE 1-3
Characterizing a process technology

Mechanics (statics and dynamics of the process)
How does the process work?
What are the process mechanics?
What physically happens, and what makes it happen?
  (Understand the physics)

Economics/costs
What are the tooling costs; engineering costs?
Which costs are short term and long term?
What are the setup costs?

Time spans
How long does it take to set up?
How can this time be shortened?
How long does it take to run a part, once set up?
What process parameters affect the run time?

Constraints
What are the process limits?
What cannot be done?
What constrains this process (size, speeds, forces, volumes, power, cost)?
What is very hard to do within an acceptable time/cost frame?

Process capability
What are the accuracy and precision of the process?
What tolerances does the process meet? (What is the process capability?)
How repeatable are those tolerances?

Uncertainties/process reliability
What can go wrong?
How can this machine fail?
What do people worry about with this process?
Is this a reliable, stable process?

Skills
What operator skills are critical?
What is not done automatically?
How long does it take to learn to do this process?

Flexibility
Can this process easily do new parts of a new design or material?
How does the process react to change in part design and demand?
Which changes are easy to do?

PRODUCT LIFE CYCLE

Manufacturing systems are dynamic and change with time. There has been a general, classical relationship between a product's life cycle and the kind of manufacturing system that produces it. Figure 1-12 simplifies the life cycle into these steps:

Start-up   New product or new company, low volume, small company.

Rapid growth   Products become standardized and volume increases rapidly. Company's ability to meet demand stresses its capacity.

Maturation	Standard designs emerge. Process development is very important.
Commodity	Long life, standard-of-the-industry product.
Decline	Product is slowly replaced by improved products.

The horizontal axis here is time, usually years. Preceding start-up will be initial design and prototyping that may take more years.

The maturation of a product in the marketplace generally leads to fewer competitors, with competition based more on price and on-time delivery than unique product features. As the competitive focus shifts during the different stages of the product life cycle, the requirements placed on manufacturing—cost, quality, flexibility, and delivery dependability—also change. The stage of the product life cycle affects the product design stability, the length of the product development cycle, the frequency of product design changes, and the commonality of components—all of which have implications for the manufacturing processes and system. The first line of Figure 1-12

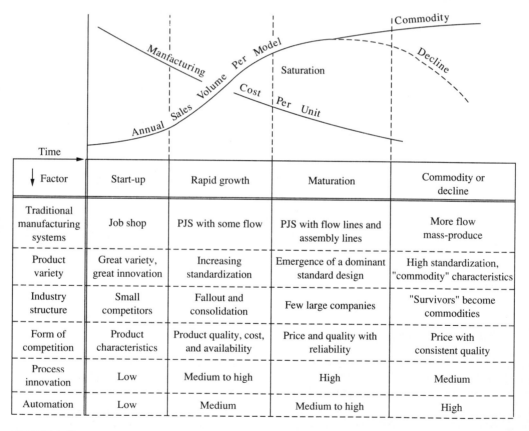

Factor	Start-up	Rapid growth	Maturation	Commodity or decline
Traditional manufacturing systems	Job shop	PJS with some flow	PJS with flow lines and assembly lines	More flow mass-produce
Product variety	Great variety, great innovation	Increasing standardization	Emergence of a dominant standard design	High standardization, "commodity" characteristics
Industry structure	Small competitors	Fallout and consolidation	Few large companies	"Survivors" become commodities
Form of competition	Product characteristics	Product quality, cost, and availability	Price and quality with reliability	Price with consistent quality
Process innovation	Low	Medium to high	High	Medium
Automation	Low	Medium	Medium to high	High

FIGURE 1-12
Traditional relationship between product life cycle and manufacturing system development/evolution.

shows that the manufacturing system is changed during the life cycle of the product. These manufacturing systems will be discussed in Chapter 2.

The product life cycle concept provides a framework for thinking about the product's evolution through time and the kinds of market segments that are likely to develop at various times. The different designs of manufacturing systems reflect the ability of the company to manufacture at various volumes while decreasing the cost per unit over time.

The linked-cell approach has changed this classic concept because linked-cells enable a company to decrease cost per unit significantly while maintaining flexibility and make smooth transitions from low-volume to high-volume manufacturing. That is, the same flexible system can accommodate large changes in volume without having to make major changes in the design of the manufacturing system. This will become clearer after Chapters 2, 3, and 4 have been examined in detail.

In terms of bringing new designs on stream, Toyota and Honda are examples of companies who are years into the development of IMPSs. They are able to introduce new models (new designs, styles) every three years, and they believe a two-year styling change is within reach. Detroit is trying to whittle the four-to-six-year product life cycle down to three years.

A NEW MANUFACTURING SYSTEM

Many countries have about the same level of process development in manufacturing technology. Much of the technology that exists in the world today was developed in England, Germany, and the United States. Japan, and now Taiwan and Korea, are making great inroads into American markets, particularly in the automotive and electronics industries. What many people have failed to recognize is that methodology is as powerful as technology, that a different kind of *manufacturing system* that permits functional integration of critical elements of the production system has evolved. In future years, this new system, based on linked-cells, will take its place with the Taylor system of scientific management and the Ford system of mass production. The original working model for this new system is the Toyota Motor Company. The system is known as the just-in-time system, the Toyota production system, or the Ohno system, after its chief architect, Taiichi Ohno. In this book, it is called the *integrated manufacturing production system (IMPS)*.

Many American companies have successfully adopted some version of the Toyota system. The experience of dozens of these companies is amalgamated into 10 key steps, which, if followed, can make any company a factory with a future.

Quality is the critical step. For the IMPS system to work, 100 percent good units flow rhythmically to subsequent processes without interruption. In order to accomplish this, an integrated quality control (IQC) program has to be developed. The responsibility for quality will be given to manufacturing people, and there is a company-wide commitment to constant quality improvement. The goal is to make it right (perfect) the first time by making quality easy to see, stopping the line when something goes wrong, and inspecting items 100 percent if necessary to prevent defects from occurring. The results of this system are astonishing. Six of the ten problem-free automobile models for 1985 were Toyotas. The Japanese, led by Toyota and Honda, had an average of 169 problems per car versus American cars with 268 and European cars with 267.

The Japanese became world class competitors by developing superior design and process technology. Now, Japan is concentrating on new product innovation with the emphasis on high value-added products. Japan spends as much as 14 percent of each sales dollar for research and development (R&D). The typical American company spends less than 5 percent for R&D. Many Japanese (and other) firms are now forming joint R&D ventures with American companies. Think about this! If the Japanese are able to utilize American (R&D) as well as they were able to commercialize the design and process technology brought from the United States, many more American companies will be in serious trouble.

HIGH TECHNOLOGY NEEDS
A HUMAN TOUCH

The most important factor in successful (economical) manufacturing is the manner in which the resources of workers, materials, and capital are organized and managed to provide effective coordination, responsibility, and control. Part of the success of the IMPS can be attributed to a different management approach. This approach is characterized by a holistic approach to people and includes

1. Consensus decision making by management teams coupled with decision making at the lowest possible level
2. Mutual trust, integrity, and loyalty between workers and management
3. Working in teams or groups, a natural outgrowth of linked-cells
4. Incentive pay in the form of bonuses for company performance
5. Elimination of hourly wages and piecework
6. Stable, even lifetime, employment for all full-time employees coupled with a large pool of part-time temporary workers

Many companies in the United States employ some or all of these elements, and a company can be organized and managed in many different ways. The real secret of IMPSs lies in designing a simplified manufacturing system in which everyone understands how it works and how it is controlled, and the decision making is placed at the correct level. In the manufacturing game, low-cost, superior-quality products are the result of teamwork within an integrated manufacturing production system. This is the key to producing superior quality at less cost with on-time delivery.

MANUFACTURING SYSTEMS, NEW AND OLD

In manufacturing systems, as in life, timing is everything.

INTRODUCTION

Significant changes are taking place in the design of manufacturing systems, fueled by the following trends:

1. Proliferation of the number and variety of products will continue, resulting in a decrease in quantities (lot size) as variety increases.
2. Requirements for closer tolerances (more accuracy and precision yielding better quality) will continue to increase.
3. Increased variety in materials, composite materials, with widely diverse properties will cause further proliferation of the manufacturing processes.
4. The cost of materials, including material handling and energy, will continue to be a major part of the total product cost, and direct labor will account for only 5 to 10 percent of the total and continue to decrease.
5. Product reliability will increase in response to the excessive number of product liability suits.
6. The time between design concept and manufactured product will be reduced through the efforts of concurrent or simultaneous engineering efforts.
7. Global markets will be served by global products.

25

These trends will require the following kinds of responses in terms of the manufacturing system:

- Continuous improvement of the product means continuous redesign and improvment of the manufacturing system.
- The system must be able to produce superior-quality products with reduced (unit) cost and on-time delivery in response to customer demands.
- The system must be designed to be flexible and understandable (simpler and more focused) as well as more reliable.

The recognition that manufacturing and assembly cells are the key first step to converting a system to JIT is critical. Many U.S. companies still cling to a wasteful (heavily buffered) manufacturing system that depends on large stocks of parts and work-in-process, so that faulty items are replaced and sizable rework areas fix defects day after day.

OPTIMIZATION OF MANUFACTURING SYSTEMS

In general, a manufacturing system should be an integrated whole, composed of integrated subsystems, each of which interacts with the whole system. The system will have a number of objectives, and its operation must optimize the whole. Optimizing pieces of the system (i.e., the processes or the subsystems) does not optimize the whole system.

The daily operation of the system requires information gathering and communication with decision-making processes integrated into the manufacturing system. The decisions about what is to be made, when it is to be made, where it is to be made, and how it is to be made are all critical to the health and well-being of the company. These decisions involve the control of the system. Without control, there is no optimization.

Each company will have many differences resulting from differences in subsystem combinations, people, product design, and materials. Differing interactions within the social, political, and business environments make each company a unique (manufacturing production) system with its own set of problems. Clearly, there is a danger in grouping all companies on a functional basis (calling them all job shops), but this is the most common design.

EVOLUTION OF THE FUNCTIONAL STRUCTURE

In the first industrial revolution, basic machine tools were invented and developed. With them came the first levels of mechanization and automation. Factories developed along with the manufacturing processes. These factories focused the resources (materials, workers, and processes) at the site where power was available. For the most part water power was used, so the early factories were placed near streams. Water turned waterwheels that drove overhead shafts running the length of the factory. A belt from the main shaft powered each machine.

The grouping of like machines that needed to run at about the same speed was logical and expedient. Factories were therefore laid out fuctionally according to the kinds of machines used. The machines were extensions of some human capability or attribute. A machinist developed different skills from a leather worker, or an iron worker, or a foundry worker. The processes were divided according to the kinds of skills needed to operate the processes.

When steam engines and, later, electric motors replaced other types of machine power they greatly increased manufacturing system flexibility; however, the functional arrangement persisted and became known as the job shop.

As product complexity increased and the factory grew larger, separate functional departments evolved for product design, accounting (bookkeeping), and sales. Later in the scientific management era of Taylor and Gilbreth, (F.W. Taylor and Frank and Lillian Gilbreth are generally recognized as the founders of the industrial engineering profession) departments for production planning, work scheduling, and methods improvement were added. Today these functions compose the *production system*. The production system services the manufacturing system. Because the production system was composed of functional areas to serve the functionally designed job shop, the production system evolved with a functional structure.

SYSTEMS DEFINED

The word system is used to define abstractly a relatively complex assembly (or arrangement) of physical elements characterized by measurable parameters (Rubinstein, 1975) and is quite appropriate for manufacturing systems (see Figure 2-1). The important physical elements for all manufacturing systems are people, processes, and material-holding and -handling equipment. Raw materials and products are inputs/in-process materials/outputs of the system. Some of the more common measurable parameters for a manufacturing system are listed in Figure 2-1. These parameters are very different from those for individual machines. These parameters are to be used as measures of effectiveness during the implementation stages of IMPSs. The user of the system is the internal customer. The user of the products from the system is the external customer. An efficient manufacturing system has satisfied customers, both internal and external. Conflicts between these two groups of customers must be resolved (See discussion of design in Chapter 3).

In order to model and control the system,

1. The system's boundaries or constraints must be defined.
2. The system's behavior in response to excitations or disturbances from the environment must be predictable through its parameters.

In general, models are used to describe how the system works or behaves. Mathematical models for control purposes generally require a "theory" or equations that describe the system's boundaries and behavior through its input parameters. In short, if no theory exists, the model is not viable and the system is not controllable.

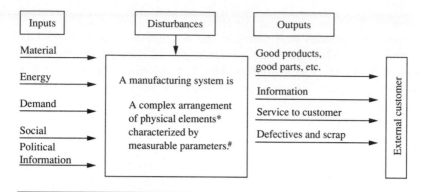

* Physical elements:
  △ Machine tools for processing
  △ Tools and tooling
  △ Material handling eqipment
  △ People (internal customers)

#Measurable parameters of system:
  △ Throughput time
  △ Production rate
  △ Work-in-process inventory
  △ % defective
  △ % on-time delivery
  △ Daily/weekly/monthly production
    volumes
  △ Total cost or unit cost

FIGURE 2-1
Definition of a manufacturing system with its inputs and outputs.

Manufacturing systems are very difficult to model, and thus their design, analysis, and control are difficult. Why?

1. System size and complexity may inhibit modeling, analysis, and control due to implied time expenditures.
2. Systems are always dynamic. The environment can change the system and vice versa.
3. Relationships may be awkward to express in analytical terms, and interactions may be nonlinear. Thus, well-behaved functions often do not apply.
4. The data or information may be difficult to secure, inaccurate, conflicting, missing, or even too abundant to digest.
5. Objectives are difficult to define, particularly in systems that have an impact on social and political issues. Goals may conflict.
6. The act of observing and trying to control the system will change the behavior of the system.
7. All analysis and control algorithms for systems will be subject to errors of omission and commission. Some of these will be related to breakdowns or delays in feedback elements because manufacturing systems included people in information loops.

Because of these difficulties, the technique of *digital simulation* of manufacturing systems is widely used for modeling and analysis of manufacturing systems, as well as for systems design. Whether or not simulation can be used for system control is the subject of much research.

MANUFACTURING VERSUS PRODUCTION SYSTEMS

In general terms, a manufacturing system inputs material, information, and energy into a complex set of elements (machines and people) that can be characterized. The materials are processed and gain value. Manufacturing system outputs may be either consumer goods or inputs to some other process (producer goods).

The production system services the manufacturing system. The manufacturing system pumps the blood (the material flow) and the production system checks the blood pressure and pulse rate (controls the flow). The material control functions are critical to the performance of the manufacturing system. A linked-cell manufacturing system permits, even invites, the integration of the critical control functions into the system. These critical control functions are

- Quality control (no defects in the material)
- Production control (when, where, and how many)
- Inventory control (how much work-in-process — optimum amount of blood)
- Machine tool reliability (keep the material flowing — no blood clots)

Figure 2-2 gives a general picture of the manufacturing system versus the production system. Observe that many of the inputs cannot be fully controlled (by management) and the effect of the disturbances must be counteracted by manipulating the controllable inputs or the system itself. Controlling material availability or predicting demand fluctuations may be difficult. The national economic climate can cause shifts in the business environment that can seriously change any of these inputs. In other words, not all manufacturing system inputs are fully controllable. The manufacturing systems themselves differ in structure or physical arrangement. However, all the manufacturing systems are serviced by a production system. Because the oldest and most common manufacturing system is functionally organized, most production systems are functionally organized as well. Walls usually separate the people in these functional areas from all other areas. Breakdowns in communication links are common. Long lags in feedback loops result in manufacturing system problems.

CLASSIFICATION OF MANUFACTURING SYSTEMS DESIGNS

Five manufacturing system designs can be identified: the job shop, the flow shop, the linked-cell shop, the project shop, and the continuous process. The *continuous process* primarily deals with liquids, powders, and gases (such as an oil refinery), rather than discrete parts. Figure 2-3 shows the four traditional systems.

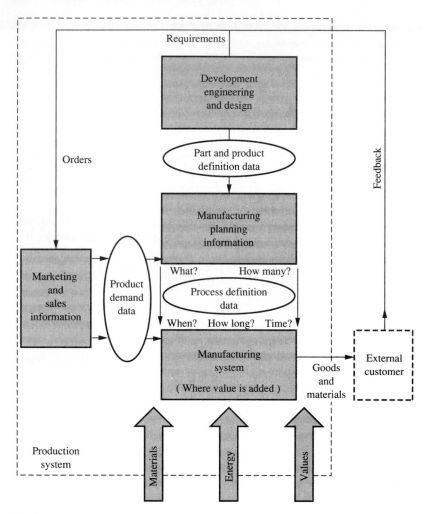

FIGURE 2-2
The manufacturing system, the heart of the company, lies within and is served by the production system.

The most common system in the United States is the *job shop*, characterized by large varieties of components, general-purpose machines, and a functional layout, (see Figure 2-4). This means that machines are collected by function (all lathes together, all milling machines together, etc.) and the parts are routed around the shop in small lots to the various machines.

Flow shops are characterized by large lots, special purpose machines, less variety, and more mechanization. Flow shop layouts are typically either continuous or interrupted. If *continuous*, they basically run one complex item in great quantity and nothing else. A transfer line producing an engine block is a typical example. If *interrupted*, the line manufactures large lots but is periodically changed over to run a similar but different component. Changing over may take hours or even days.

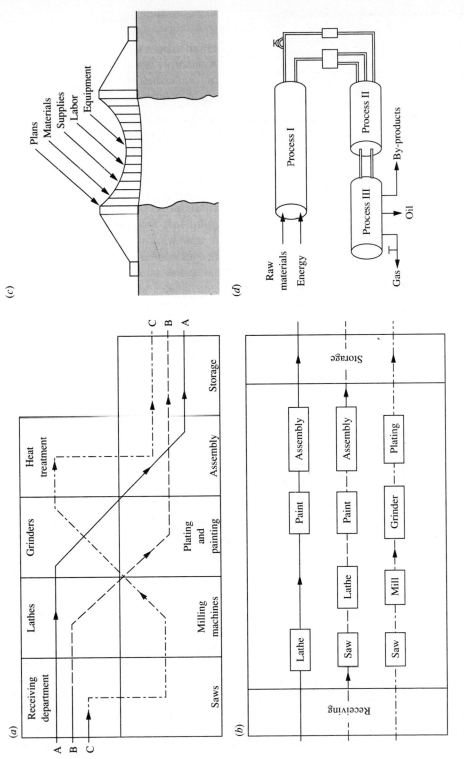

FIGURE 2-3

Schematic layouts of four classical manufacturing systems: (a) job shop (functional or process layout), (b) flow shop (line or product layout), (c) project shop (fixed position layout), and (d) continuous process.

31

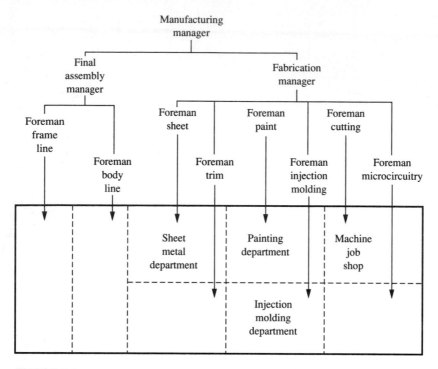

FIGURE 2-4
The layout of a plant designed as a job shop is by process, so a functionalized layout and organization result. The machine shop is shown in Figure 2-6. (*Schonberger, 1982.*)

The *project shop* is characterized by the immobility of the item being manufactured. In the project shop, workers, machines, and materials come to the site. Bridges and roads are good examples in the construction industry. In the manufacturing industry, locomotives and large airplanes are good examples. The number of end items is usually not very large, but the lot sizes of the component parts going into the end item can vary from small to very large. The job shop usually supplies parts and subassemblies to the project shop in small lots.

The *linked-cell* manufacturing system, composed of connected (linked) manufacturing cells, uses a unique form of inventory and information control (kanban) (see Figure 2-5). Smart manufacturing managers know they must examine the job shop system and redesign it to improve overall efficiency. Manufacturing companies are converting their batch-oriented job shops into linked cells. One popular way to form a cell is by using group technology.

Group technology is a philosophy in which similar parts are grouped into families. Parts of similar size and shape can often be processed by a similar set of processes. A part family based on manufacturing would have the same set or sequences of manufacturing processes. The set of processes can be arranged or grouped to form a cell. Thus, with GT, job shops can be restructured into cells, each cell specializing in a

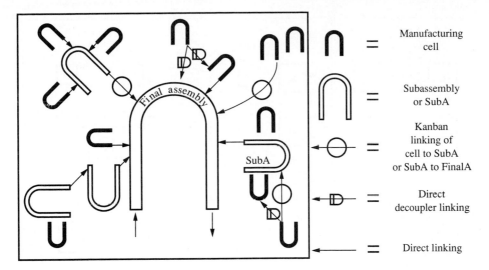

FIGURE 2-5
A plant designed as a CMS is product oriented. The cells are linked directly to the subassemblies (subprocesses put at point of use) or with kanban. Only the final assembly is scheduled.

particular family of parts. As shown in Figure 2-6, when processing sequences in the job shop were evaluated, it was found that three cells were needed to accommodate what was previously manufactured in the job shop. No new machines were needed. In fact, some machines were no longer needed. The machines will have at least the same amount of utilization as in the job shop, but the products will spend far less time getting through the processes. The parts are handled less, machine set-up time is shorter, in-process inventory is lower, throughput time is greatly reduced, and the worker is better utilized.

JOB SHOPS

The job shop's distinguishing feature is the production of a wide variety of products that results in small manufacturing lot sizes, often one of a kind. Job shop manufacturing is commonly done to specific customer orders, but in truth many job shops produce to fill finished goods inventories. Because job shops must perform a wide variety of manufacturing processes, general purpose manufacturing equipment is required. Workers must have relatively high skill levels to perform a range of different work assignments. Job shop products include space vehicles, aircraft, machine tools, special tools, and equipment. The distribution of total factory capacity for the job shop is shown in Figure 2-7. The 6 percent production fraction is equivalent to the 36 percent value shown in Figure 1-11. This calculation assumes that theoretical 100 percent capacity equals 365 days × 24 hours in a day. These are rather depressing figures, but they clearly demonstrate that the productivity problem lies in making the manufacturing system (not the unit processes) more productive.

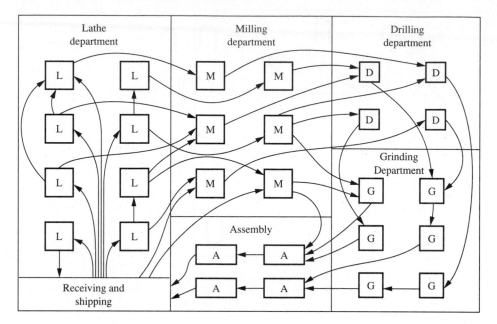

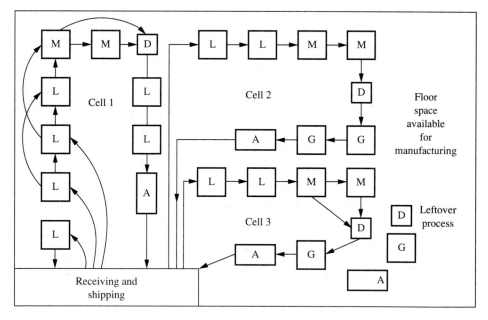

FIGURE 2-6
The classical manufacturing system in common use today—the job shop—requires a systems-level conversion to be reconfigured into manufacturing cells.

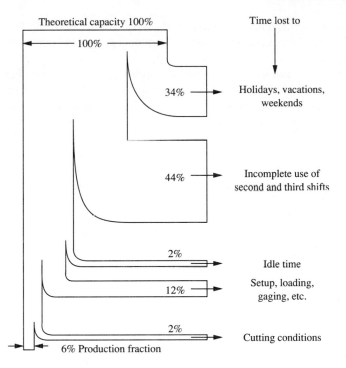

FIGURE 2-7

Distribution of total factory capacity of machine tools in the job shop. Typical values are shown. (*Carter, C.F. Mfg. Eng. Aug. 82.*)

In the job shop, machine tools are functionally grouped according to the general type of manufacturing process: lathes in one department, drill presses in another, plastic molding in still another department, and so forth. The advantage of this layout is its ability to make a wide variety of products. Each different part requiring its own unique sequence of operations can be routed through the respective departments in the proper order. *Route sheets* are used to control the movement of the material. Forklifts and handcarts are used to move materials from one machine to the next.

As the company grows, the job shop evolves into a production job shop (PJS) as was shown in Figure 1-12. The production job shop (PJS) becomes very difficult to manage as it grows, resulting in long product throughput times and very large in-process inventory levels.

The PJS manufacturing system builds large volumes of products but still builds in lots or batches, usually medium-sized lots of 50 to 200 units. The lots may be produced only once, or they may be produced at regular intervals. The purpose of batch production is often to satisfy continuous customer demand for an item. This system usually operates in the following manner. Because the production rate can exceed the customer demand rate, the shop builds an inventory of item A, then changes to product B to fill other orders. This involves tearing down the setups on many machines for A and resetting them for product B. When the stock of the first item becomes depleted, the machines are set up again for product A, and the inventory for A is rebuilt.

The manufacturing equipment can be designed for higher production rates. For example, automatic lathes capable of holding many cutting tools and automatically loading a new piece of stock are used rather than an engine lathe. Machine tools are often equipped with specially designed workholding devices, called jigs and fixtures, which increase process output rate, precision, accuracy, and repeatability.

Industrial equipment, furniture, textbooks, and components for many assembled consumer products (household appliances, lawn mowers, etc.) are made in production job shops. These systems are called machine shops, foundries, plastic molding factories, or pressworking shops.

It is estimated that as much as 75 percent of all piece part manufacturing is in lot sizes of 50 pieces or fewer, making the production job shop an important portion of total manufacturing. Along with flow shops, use of the PJS is common practice in America.

FLOW SHOPS (LINES)

The flow shop has a product-oriented layout (see Figure 2-8). When the volume gets very large, especially in an assembly line, it is called *mass production*. This system can have (very) high production rates. Specialized equipment, dedicated to the manufacture of a particular product, is required. Dissimilar machines are grouped into a flow line. One machine of each type is typical, except where duplicate machines are needed to balance the flow. The entire plant is often designed exclusively for the production of the particular product, with special purpose (rather than general purpose) equipment.

The investment costs of specialized machines and specialized tooling are high, as are the risks. Many production skills are transferred from the operator to the machines, resulting in lower manual labor skill levels than in a PJS. Items are made to 'flow' through a sequence of operations by material-handling devices (conveyors, moving belts, transfer devices, etc.). The items move through the operations one at a time.

The time the item spends at each station or location is fixed and equal (balanced). Line balancing means that the amount of work done at each station is about the same in order to reduce idle time at a station. The lines are set up to operate at the fastest possible speed regardless of the system's needs. The system is not flexible.

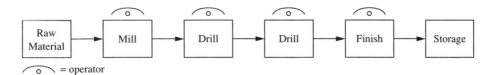

= operator

FIGURE 2-8
Schematic of dedicated flow line manufacturing system.

In the flow line manufacturing system, the facilities are arranged according to the product's sequence of operations. The line is organized by the processing sequence needed to make a single product or a regular mix of products. A hybrid form of the flow line produces a batch of products moving through clusters of work stations or processes organized by product flow. Usually, the setup times to change from one product to another are long and often complicated.

Most factories are mixtures of the job shop and flow line systems. The demand for products can precipitate a shift from batch to high-volume production, and much of the production from these plants is consumed by that steady demand. Subassembly lines and final assembly lines are further extensions of the flow line, the former usually being more labor intensive.

Ever since the birth of mass production, various approaches and techniques have been used to develop machine tools that would be highly effective in large-scale manufacturing. Their effectiveness was closely related to the degree of product design standardization and the length of time permitted between design changes. A machine that will produce a part with a minimum of skilled labor can be developed if the part or product is highly standardized and will be manufactured in large quantities. A completely tooled automatic screw machine is a good example of such a machine for the manufacture of small parts. An automated transfer machine for the production of V-8 engine blocks at the rate of 100 per hour is an example of a supermachine to mass produce large parts. See Figure 2-9 for some examples of transfer machines. These specialized machines are expensive to design and build and usually are not capable of making any other product. These machines must be operated for long periods of time to spread the cost of the initial investment over many units. Although highly efficient, they are used only to make products in very large volume. Desired changes of design in the product must be avoided or delayed because it would be too costly to scrap the machines. Such systems are clearly not flexible.

The development of the numerical control (NC) machine tool in the late 1950s and early 1960s permitted programmable control of the position of the cutting tool with respect to the workpiece. By the late 1960s automatic cutting tool changers had been added to the NC machine, and the machining center was developed. Computers were added, and now the computer NC machine tool is readily available to all manufacturers. See Figure 2-10 for an example of a CNC machine tool.

Products manufactured to meet the demands of the free economy, mass consumption markets of today need to have changes in design for improved product performance as well as style changes. Therefore, hard automation systems need to be as flexible as possible while retaining the ability to mass produce. This recognition led to a combination of the transfer line with an NC machine, and the *flexible manufacturing system (FMS)* was born. The primary components of the FMS are NC machine tools, a material-handling system, cutting tools, workholding devices (pallets), and computer control networks. Today, the machine tools are CNC, usually horizontal or vertical spindle milling machines. The FMS design shown in Figure 2-11 has eight 4-axis CNC machining centers, each equipped with a 90-cutter tool magazine and a pallet-changing system. The system claims to make more than 500 different parts. Such a system must be scheduled and can be as complex as the job shop it replaced.

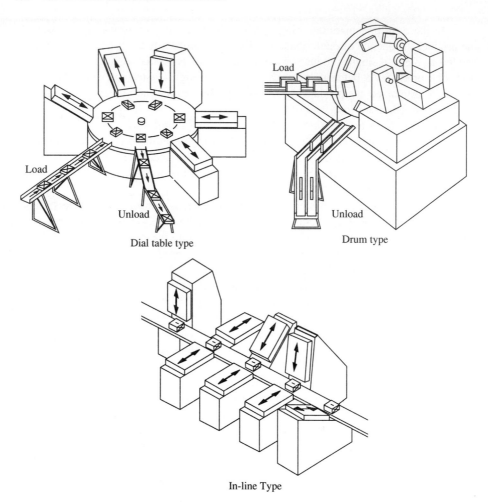

Dial table type

Drum type

In-line Type

FIGURE 2-9
Examples of transfer machines.

Modern CNC machines are capable of automatically changing tools, workpieces (pallet changer), and cutting parameters. It seemed logical to marry these NC machines to the transfer line. The FMS was originally called the variable mission manufacturing system. Most FMSs have a system manager supervising the FMS, primarily by monitoring the system and supervising all other human workers: material handlers who perform loading/unloading tasks, a roving operator who presets tools and reacts to unscheduled machine stops, and a mechanical/hydraulic technician who repairs machines and auxiliary equipment.

Much has been written about FMSs, and research into these systems continues unabated. They are very expensive to design, require years to bring on stream, and are complex and difficult to analyze and control. By the end of the 1980s, it would

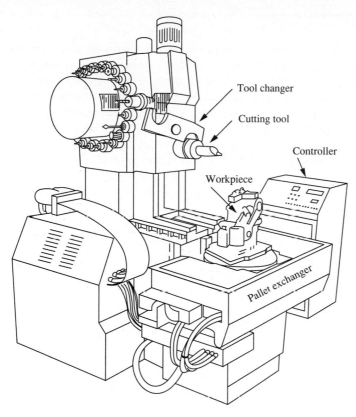

FIGURE 2-10
The CNC machining center permits many different machining operations to be performed in a single setup.

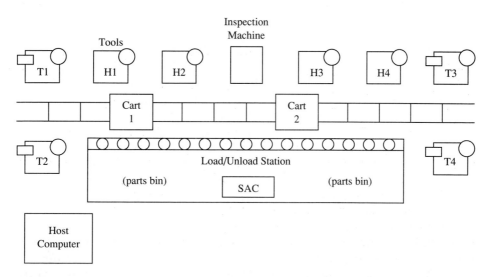

FIGURE 2-11
Design of a flexible manufacturing system used at Detroit Diesel Allison of Indianapolis, Indiana.

appear that fewer than 400 such systems exist in the world. Almost all these systems are found in very large companies that can afford large capital outlays or that have received governmental (military defense) backing for the system. The FMS represents the supermachine philosophy at its ultimate. Fundamentally, it is an attempt to blend the flexibility of the job shop with the productivity of the flow shop manufacturing systems. Parts usually require two or three passes through the FMS. The fixtures in the FMS are costly and complex. The FMS control computer must control the conveyor, maintain the NC library of programs and download these to the machines, handle the scheduling of the FMS, track the tool maintenance, track performance of the system, and print out the management reports. Not surprisingly, in the FMS, software is often the major limiting factor.

PROJECT SHOPS

In the typical project manufacturing system, a product must remain in a fixed position or location during manufacturing because of its size and/or weight. The materials, machines, and people used in fabrication are brought to the site. Locomotive manufacturing, large aircraft assembly and shipbuilding use fixed-position *layout*.

Fixed-position manufacturing is also used in construction jobs (buildings, bridges, and dams). As with the fixed-position layout, the product is large and the construction equipment and manpower must be moved to it. When the job is completed, the equipment is removed from the construction site.

The project shop invariably has a job shop/flow shop manufacturing system making all the components for the large, complex project and thus has a functionalized production system.

CONTINUOUS PROCESSES

In the continuous process, the product physically flows. Oil refineries, chemical processing plants, and food processing operations are examples. This system is sometimes called *flow production* when referring to the manufacture of either complex single parts (such as a canning operation) or assembled products (such as TVs). However, these are not continuous processes, but high-volume flow lines. In continuous processes, the products really do flow because they are liquids, gases, or powders.

The continuous process is the most efficient but least flexible manufacturing system. It usually has the leanest, simplest production system because this manufacturing system has the least work-in-process (WIP), making it the easiest to control.

LINKED-CELL MANUFACTURING
SYSTEM (L-CMS)

The linked-cell manufacturing system (L-CMS) is the newest manufacturing system. It is composed of manufacturing and assembly cells linked by a pull system for material control. In the cells, operations and processes are grouped according to the manufacturing sequence that is needed to make a group of products. This arrangement is much like that of the flow shop but is designed for flexibility. The cell is often

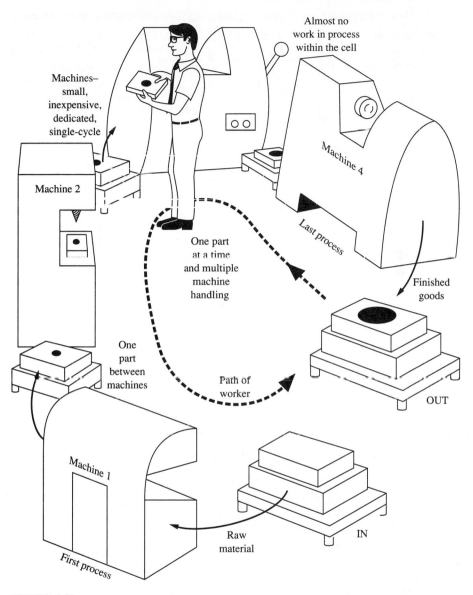

FIGURE 2-12
Small manned cell with four machines and one walking worker.

configured in a U-shape, enabling the workers to move from machine to machine, loading and unloading parts. Figure 2-12 shows an example of a simple manned manufacturing cell. The machines in the cell are usually all single cycle automatics so they can complete the machining cycle untended, turning off automatically when finished with a cycle. The cell usually includes all the processing needed for a complete part or subassembly.

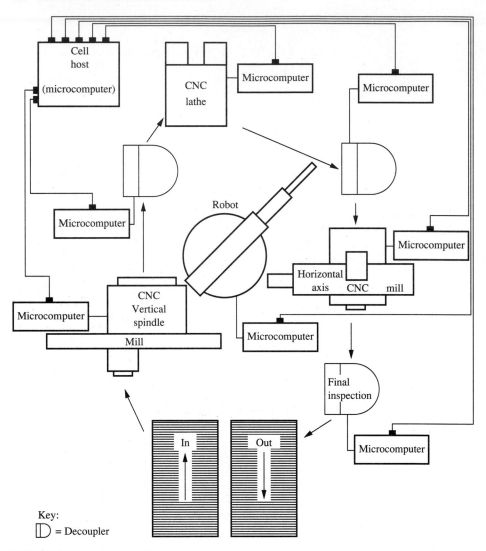

FIGURE 2-13
Unmanned robotic cell will have CNC machine tools, a robot for material handling, and decouplers for flexibility and capability.

Continuous flow manufacturing in manufacturing cells involves the production of one piece at a time following the sequence and rules of the cycle time.

The key points are

1. Machines are arranged in the process sequence.
2. The cell is designed in a U-shape.
3. One piece at a time is made within the cell.
4. The workers are trained to handle more than one process.
5. The cycle time for the system dictates the production rate for the cell.

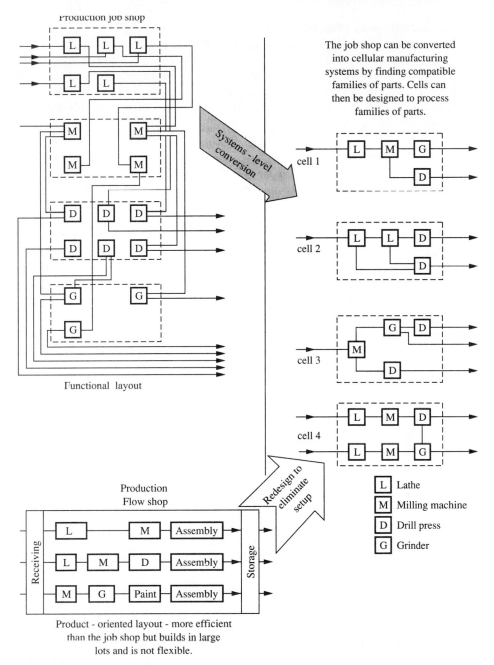

Production job shop

Functional layout

The job shop can be converted
into cellular manufacturing
systems by finding compatible
families of parts. Cells can
then be designed to process
families of parts.

Systems - level
conversion

cell 1

cell 2

cell 3

cell 4

Redesign to
eliminate
setup

Production
Flow shop

Receiving

L		M	Assembly
L	M	D	Assembly
M	G	Paint	Assembly

Storage

Product - oriented layout - more efficient
than the job shop but builds in large
lots and is not flexible.

L   Lathe
M   Milling machine
D   Drill press
G   Grinder

FIGURE 2-14
Two classical manufacturing systems in common use today—the job shop and the flow shop—require a
systems-level conversion to be reconfigured into manufacturing cells.

6. The operators work standing up and walking.

7. Slower, dedicated machines that are smaller and less expensive are used.

Cells are typically manned, but unmanned cells are beginning to emerge with a robot replacing the worker. A robotic cell design is shown in Figure 2-13 with one robot and three CNC machines. For the cell to operate autonomously, the machines must have adaptive control capability.

To form cells, the first step is to restructure portions of the job shop, converting it in stages into manned cells, see Figure 2-14. Cells are designed to manufacture specific groups or families of parts. As we will discuss later, cells are linked *directly* either to each other or to subassembly points or *indirectly* by the pull system of material control called *kanban*.

The flow shop elements within the plant are redesigned to make these systems operate like cells. To do this, the long setup times typical in flow lines must be vigorously attacked and reduced so that the flow lines can be changed over quickly from the manufacture of one product to another. The need to line balance the flow line every time it changes to another part must be eliminated. This can be accomplished with decouplers that will be covered later. The flow lines will become more flexible and compatible with the cells. Both the cells and the flow lines make piece parts for the subassembly lines and final assembly lines.

DESIGNED FOR FLEXIBILITY

Flexibility is the key design feature for CMSs. The system can react quickly to changes in customer demand or changes in the product design or the mix of products. The cells in the factory are linked directly to the subassemblies (subprocesses are put at the point of use) or with kanban. This makes the factory very product oriented. The chief design criterion is flexibility in the following areas:

- Operation of equipment — rapid tool change, no adjustments, and automatic error detection.
- Changeover — ease of setup and speed of exchange of tooling and dies.
- Process — (1) differences in the operations and processes for different parts; (2) different sequences of operations, different lengths of cut; (3) ability to handle a different mix, a different order in the mix, or a different volume in the mix (more A and less B).
- Capacity or volume — ability to increase or decrease production output, rate, and volume; room for expansion.

COMPARING CELLS TO OTHER SYSTEMS

Table 2-1 provides a brief comparison of IMPS versus the job shop philosophies. The idea in the job shop now is to find the bottlenecks (the constraints) in the system and work to eliminate them. Queues of material are viewed as a necessity that permits succeeding operations to continue when there is a problem with the feeding operation. *The IMPS approach recognizes the job shop design as the fundamental problem. Better management (management by constraints) will result in only small improvements in*

TABLE 2-1
How IMPS philosophy differs from that of a typical U.S. company

Factors	IMPS	Typical job shop
Inventory	A liability. Every effort must be extended to minimize inventory.	An asset. It protects against forecast errors, machine problems, late vendor deliveries. More inventory is "safer" and necessary.
Lot sizes	Keep reducing the lot size. The smallest quantity is desired for both manufactured and purchased parts.	Formulas. Keep revising the optimum lot size with some formula based on the trade-off between the cost of inventories and the cost of setup.
Setups	Eliminate/reduce them by extremely rapid changeover to minimize the impact. Fast changeover permits small lot sizes and allows a wide variety of parts to be made frequently.	Low priority. Maximum output is the usual goal. Rarely does similar thought and effort go into achieving quick changeover.
Vendors	Vendors are remote cells, part of the team. Daily, multiple deliveries of all active items are expected. The vendor takes care of the needs of the customer, and the customer treats the vendor as an extension of the factory.	Adversaries. Multiple sources are the rule, and it is typical to play them against each other.
Quality	Zero defects. If quality is not perfect, then improvements can be made. Continuous improvement in people and process is the goal.	Tolerate some scrap. Track what the actual scrap has been and develop formula for predicting it. Plan extra quantity to cover scrap losses.
Equipment maintenance	Constant and effective. Machine breakdown and tool failure must be eliminated.	As required. Not critical because inventory is available.
Lead times	Keep them short. This simplifies the job of marketing, purchasing, and manufacturing as it reduces the need for expediting.	The longer the better. Most foremen and purchasing agents want more lead time, not less.
Workers	The internal customer. Changes are not made until consensus is reached. Employee involvement is critcal.	Management by edict. New systems are installed in spite of the workers, not thanks to the workers. Measurements are used to determine whether or not workers are doing as directed.

productivity and quality in the job shop. It is the manufacturing system that must be restructured.

Figure 2-15 summarizes the discussion on manufacturing systems by comparing different systems based on their production rate and product flexibility — that is, the number of different parts the system can handle. The project shop and continuous processes are not shown. Cells provide the middle ground between the true job shop and dedicated flow lines. The widely publicized flexible manufacturing system (FMS) can be classified as a job shop because random order of part movement is permitted.

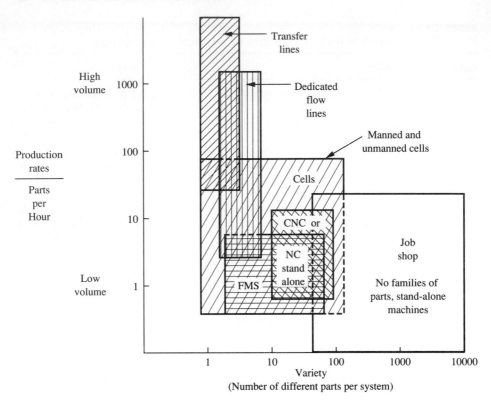

FIGURE 2-15
A comparison of different kinds of manufacturing systems with cells.

Thus it is necessary to schedule parts and machines within the FMS, just as it is in the job shop. This feature makes FMS designs difficult to link to other manufacturing sytems. The FMS often becomes an *island of automation* (the inventory piles up all around it like water around an island) within the job shop—a characteristic of supermachines.

In contrast, the cell makes parts one at a time in a flexible design. Cell capacity (the cycle time) can be quickly altered to respond to changes in customer demand. The cycle time does not depend upon the machining time.

Families of parts with similar designs, flexible workholding devices, and tool changes in programmable machines allow rapid changeover from one component to another. Rapid changeover means quick or one-touch setup, often like flipping a light switch. Significant inventory reduction between the cells is possible, and the inventory level can be directly controlled. Quality is controlled within the cell, and the equipment within the cell is routinely maintained by the worker. These features will be discussed later.

For robotic (unmanned) cells, the robot typically loads and unloads parts from one to five CNC machine tools, but this number may be increased if the robot becomes mobile. A machining center represents a cell of one machine but is not as flexible as a cell composed of multiple, simple machines because overlapping of the machining times is eliminated. Cellular layouts facilitate the integration of critical production functions while maintaining flexibility in producing superior-quality products. The cells provide job enlargement and job enrichment for the production worker.

Perhaps the most important factor in this system is that the product designer can easily see how parts are made in the cell since all the processes are together. Because quality control techniques are also integrated into the cells, the designer knows exactly the cell's process capability (i.e., the accuracy and precision of the parts made by a cell as compared to the specifications). The designer can easily configure the future designs to be made in the cell. This is truly designing for manufacturing.

CHAPTER

3

BASICS OF AXIOMATIC DESIGN AS APPLIED TO MANUFACTURING SYSTEMS

The primary functional characteristic for future factory design is flexibility.

INTRODUCTION

Chapter 3 discusses design, specifically the axiomatic design approach of manufacturing processes and manufacturing systems, and explains why design is such an important subject in manufacturing systems. Preparing this chapter, the author borrowed liberally from the papers of Nam P. Suh and his new book, *Principles of Design*, (Suh, 1990). Chapter 4 gives specifics of the design of manufacturing systems.

In Chapters 1 and 2, we learned the steps to an IMPS and the way in which value added to the product by a manufacturing system relates to the marketplace. Well-designed products that perform well (functionally) can command higher prices in the marketplace, resulting in greater profitability for the company. Well-designed processes and systems result in lower manufacturing cost and superior quality, again increasing productivity and profitability. A poorly designed product cannot be manufactured well even by the most expensive, sophisticated system. A well-designed product cannot be manufactured properly (competitively) with a poorly designed manufacturing system. How can we distinguish a good manufacturing system design from a bad design?

THE AMERICAN SUPERMARKET

Here we take an example of a system everyone is familiar with and discuss the design. The system is the American supermarket. The material handler is a shopping cart, and the shopper is the external customer. The internal customers are those who work in the supermarket—the person who restocks the shelves, the checkout clerks, and so forth. The first decision is "What are the functions that the store should fulfill?" The determination of the functional requirements will be based on the designer's understanding of the perceived needs of the customers, the store owners, and the store workers. After considering all the facts, the designer may arbitrarily decide that the functional requirements (FR) are

FR(1)   *Profitability*   The store should make a reasonable overall profit while supplying goods to the customer at reasonable prices.

FR(2)   *Accessibility*   The customer can get into/out of store and get to goods easily. The design is easy to use.

FR(3)   *Variety/selection*   The customer can get brands, kinds desired—satisfy customer needs.

Design parameters are usually measurable and represent the means by which the FRs are achieved. Three design parameters (DP) might be

DP(1)   Number of purchases per customer visit

DP(2)   Time per customer visit

DP(3)   Number of products and different kinds (brands) of a product

The designer of the store may now ask the following questions: How do I design the store and its elements to satisfy the functional requirements? How do I lay out the store—arrange it and design the shopping carts and checkout lines to make the store profitable, usable, and desirable for the external customer as well as the internal customer? The designer has no control over local product pricing or daily staffing, that is, how the "designed" system is actually used or misused (mismanaged). The same is true for products. The designer cannot control misuse of the product by the customer. In summary, the designer has no control on how the design solutions are implemented.

Suppose the designer elects to design the store so that the customer has to walk the *maximum* distance through the store in order to buy the most often purchased items (bread and milk). The design requires that these items be placed at opposite corners at the back of the store. The idea here is to try to maximize the number of items purchased by forcing the customer to walk past the maximum number of products. The entrance and exit are at the same location, in the front of the store. Trucks unload at the rear of the store. Does the design violate the FRs?

Why does the designer place produce (fruits and vegetables) in the front right corner as you enter the store? Is it because produce is the most perishable of the items in the store and the designer wants to maximize your exposure to these items to increase their turnover? At the same time, the designer installs multiple parallel checkout lines, automatic laser scanners, and shopping carts that are easily unloaded to minimize the time the customer spends checking out. How many checkout lines and carts should be put in the store? Why are they all at the same place?

Chapter 3 presents a rational basis for making design decisions about manufacturing systems based on design axioms.

Design axioms have two fundamental characteristics:

1. They cannot be proven.

2. They are general truths, so no violations or counterexamples can be observed.

These characteristics suggest that a heuristic approach is used to develop the axioms. In this approach, an initial set of axioms is established and published. The axioms are then subjected to trial and evaluation in manufacturing situations. The extent to which the hypothetical axioms satisfy the requirement for true axioms is assessed by trial and error. The axioms are further analyzed, redefined, and refined until the process converges on a set of comprehensive axioms. Here are two axioms, stated as directives rather than as observations, applied to the design of the manufacturing processes/systems (rather than the products):

Axiom 1: The Independence Axiom. Maintain the independence of the functional requirements.

Axiom 2: The Information Axiom. Minimize the information content.

Let's examine the typical supermarket design in terms of these two axioms. The first axiom says that the functional requirements must not be coupled by the proposed design. This is the case with our three FRs—they are independent. What about the design of the typical supermarket? Are the FRs suggested for supermarket designing coupled by the typical design? The placement of the milk and bread maximizes the walking distance for the customer in the store and therefore maximizes the time spent in the store. Thus, according to Axiom 1, the typical supermarket design (not one designed by our FRs) may not be a rational design since the two functional requirements are *coupled* by the action of the customer taking the longest path through the store to get the bread and milk. The designer for the typical supermarket must have chosen another set of functional requirements so that the suggested design is not a coupled design. If the two functional requirements are not coupled by the design, then we have an uncoupled design. Clearly, some of the functional requirements reflect what is desired in the layout or what the design needs to achieve.

The relationship between the functional requirements (FRs) and the measurable design parameters (DPs) is established by the design of the system. DPs represent how we propose to achieve FRs through specific system designs. For the supermarket, measurable DPs might be (throughput) time and money spent per trip. The income can be tied to profit through cost. Thus an equation can be written that ties an FR to the design parameter(s).

Throughput time, for example, is a measurable DP. It is the sum of the time needed to (1) get from car to store (WT), (2) collect groceries (ST), (3) check out (COT), (4) return to car (RT). Thus,

$$\sum_{min} (WT + ST + COT + RT) = \text{minimize total time}$$

The second axiom states that among all the designs for supermarkets that satisfy the first axiom, the simplest design is the best. My wife dislikes the new supermarket in our town because of the complicated way the store is arranged (designed) giving it poor accessibility.

How can we redesign the typical supermarket to improve the design—perhaps decoupling FRs? Suppose we put the entrance and exit at opposite ends of the store and provide a means (valet service) to bring your car from the entrance to the exit, just in time to load up your goods when you have checked out. You would still have to walk past all the goods (maximize your exposure) while minimizing your time spent shopping. The delivery trucks could come to the sides of the store, in some cases directly to the department they are servicing. This design increases the cost of doing business (valet service for the cars) but may improve (decouple) profitability and accessibility. Another alternative might be to distribute checkout counters (and exits) at other locations in the store—two or three on each side—and redesign the store to maximize customer accessibility.

DEFINITION OF DESIGN

The design process entails several steps as shown in Figure 3-1. It begins by defining the functional requirements (FRs) that satisfy the perceived needs of the customer for a product, process, system, or even an organization. The problem definition stage is one of the most important steps in the design process. This conceptual stage is followed by the creation of a *physical entity* that satisfies the stated functional requirements. This process depends on the creativity and experience of the designer. At this stage of the methodology, basic principles are needed on which to base design decisions. Then the proposed idea is analyzed and rationalized. Next a prototype of the design is built so that the initial designs can be compared with the original needs for fidelity. There is an essential difference here between designing the product and designing the manufacturing system. It is routine to build a working prototype of the product, but it is difficult to build a working model of the manufacturing system. The extensive use of graphical models and physical simulation helps gather information on the feasibility and fidelity of the design but nothing replaces the real thing in system designs utilizing people. This comparison is the ultimate check for correctness of all the decisions made at the various stages of the design process. Therefore, design can be defined as the creation of a solution in the form of products, processes, or systems that satisfy perceived needs through the relationship between functional requirements (FRs) and measurable design parameters (DPs).

For manufacturing systems, the designer specifies how materials are transformed by specifying the processes and the spatial arrangement among them. In other words,

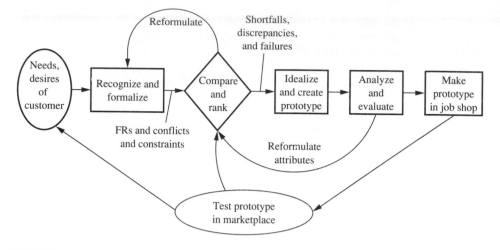

FIGURE 3-1
The traditional design loop.

the designer creates a set of *information* in the form of drawings, networks, circuits, software, and/or equations that describes the manufacturing system, the material flow, and the transformation that occurs in the materials passing through it.

Since design deals with transformation from a functional to a physical domain, a good designer must be able to operate in both areas. For example, the designer must be able to encapsulate the perceived needs for a product or a process into a set of functional requirements that can indeed satisfy the needs. In the case of the supermarket, the designer arbitrarily defined the FRs to be accessibility, profitability, and variety. The FRs could have been broken down into FRs for the external customer versus FRs for the internal customer. Depending on how well one establishes the FRs to meet the perceived needs of the customer, the solution (or the result of the designing process) can be quite different. In many ways, this ability to reduce complex (and often ill-defined) *needs* into a set of realistic and independent functional requirements is the hallmark of a creative mind. Once a set of functional requirements (FRs) has been defined, the creation of a physical system that can fulfill the FRs follows. The design axioms play the most important role at this stage by helping the designer discard unpromising ideas that do not meet the criteria of functional independence and minimal information content.

AN EXAMPLE: HONDA MOTOR COMPANY— MARYSVILLE, OHIO

The Honda Accord, the top-selling car in America, is built in Marysville, Ohio. The manufacturing system at Honda is designed with the idea that customer satisfaction should be the ultimate goal of every facet of the company, including not just product design and sales but also manufacturing engineering.

Customer satisfaction means something a little different at Honda. Honda has two customers:

1. The internal customer—the user of the Honda manufacturing system
2. The external customer—the buyer/user of the Honda product

At Honda, the ultimate goal of manufacturing engineering is to implement the necessary technologies that will enable manufacturing to produce products that satisfy the external customer while recognizing the needs of the internal customer. Honda's decision makers do not want to imitate or copy the manufacturing technology of other companies. They do not believe they can make an exceptional product using the same technology as other manufacturers. Therefore, Honda builds almost 100 percent of its manufacturing systems.

Today, Honda's manufacturing engineering group is responsible for the in-house development, including the design and manufacture, of

- 100 percent of the body welding systems, excluding parts conveyors
- 100 percent of the dies and molds used for stamping skin panels, major engine castings, instrument panels, and bumper fascia
- 90 percent of the main machining lines for engine and transmission parts such as gears, cylinder blocks and heads, and so on.

In addition to the two plants in Marysville where Accords, Civics, and motorcycles are built, Honda is building a new plant in Ohio to produce Civics and another to make engines and transmissions. Manufacturing engineering will provide 70 percent of the new paint application equipment and 50 percent of the automated assembly equipment for these new plants.

Today, the words *international* and *customer satisfaction* have almost become clichés while everyone is looking for ways to become more productive and efficient. However, at the time Honda was formulating its company principle, the industries of Japan were struggling just to survive in the ruins of World War II. Who could have dreamed that any Japanese company would become an international leader!

Concurrent Engineering at Honda

Honda strives for simultaneous continuity of manufacturing and innovation in the manufacturing systems. In reality, this approach is the key to Honda's success. Honda has been cultivating flexibility in its manufacturing system that enables them to implement innovative technology continuously. Full product model changes can be implemented into the existing manufacturing system without any loss of production time—no shutdown for model changes.

Honda manufacturing engineering is continually struggling with two questions while pursuing the ultimate goal of building/running the manufacturing systems needed to manufacture products that satisfy the customer:

1. *What is customer satisfaction for manufacturing engineering?*
   Honda has been working to establish the shortest lead time for developing new equipment for its manufacturing systems. This is the key to concurrent engineering. It shortens the time between product design and product realization in the marketplace. It also allows product engineers to concentrate longer on product designs while permitting them to be "on time" with the introduction of a new model. In addition, Honda is trying to develop flexible equipment, capable of being changed over very quickly from one part (or product) to another.

2. *How can Honda keep its manufacturing facilities competitive?*
   It is often said that the recent success of Japanese companies is due to their efforts toward constantly improving their manufacturing systems. However, Honda is not satisfied with only moderate constant improvements in its facilities. Honda tries to achieve large increments of improvement through simultaneous changes in the product design and the manufacturing system. In addition, it focuses on resolving conflicts between the internal and the external customer.

Internal versus External Customer Satisfaction

The internal customer is the user of the manufacturing system and the equipment. The external customer is the user of Honda products. As expected, some conflicts arise as manufacturing engineering deals with its internal and external customers.

There is a set of factors for which Honda manufacturing engineering must set criteria and establish priority in the development and improvement of the manufacturing system. However, the two sets of customers have different requirements that must be considered if real customer satisfaction is to be achieved.

TABLE 3-1
Factors for achieving customer satisfaction for the external customer—the Honda product user

Factor	Requirements for manufacturing engineering
Attractiveness	Fit and finish (appearance)
	New technology (new options)
	Constant improvement and innovation
	Flexibility to make model changes
Quality	High accuracy
	Durability
	Reliability
	Maintainability
Price/cost	High efficiency (good gas mileage)
	Low investment (low initial cost)
	Long warranty
Delivery	Mixed-model production (random-order)
	Quick start-up for new model

The factors given in Table 3-1 are important for external customer satisfaction.

The factors needed to satisfy internal customers, the people who use the equipment, are given in Table 3-2.

As these tables show, conflicts between the two customers' priorities will arise on any factor. If all the factors are weighted equally, the cost of manufacturing can rapidly get out of hand. Priorities must therefore be established, and some factors cannot be fully implemented into every system. Fortunately, they are not all of equal importance.

The biggest dilemmas are cost and quality. Regardless of how attractive a product may be, or how "first-class" the manufacturing system, the products must sell at a reasonable price and have superior quality. The key points in achieving external customer satisfaction are to minimize the initial cost and produce a highly efficient (low maintenance cost, good gas mileage) automobile.

In general, manufacturing systems and equipment are designed and developed with internal customer requirements as the priority. This is natural because these factors have a more visible impact on manufacturing operations than those related to the customer who uses the final product.

This is true even though the decision makers in manufacturing and manufacturing engineering both know that the factors affecting the external customer must receive manufacturing's highest priority.

TABLE 3-2
Factors for achieving customer satisfaction for the internal customer—the equipment user

Factor	Requirements for manufacturing engineering
Safety	Meet safety standards Design to prevent accidents
Reliability	Consistency Durability
Quality of job/environment	Easy to operate Fail-safe design No dirty, unpleasant, or labor-intensive work
Maintainability	Consider the technical level of production Design and layout considerations
Reflect opinions	Get feedback from customer Listen to everyone during implementation Stay in touch after start-up Avoid bureaucracy—develop a trim and flat management
Good service	Technical support system Training manuals

Honda's Requirements for Manufacturing Systems Design

Honda develops manufacturing equipment, processes, and systems by placing priority on the factors that affect the external customer and then adapting the manufacturing system design so it will meet the highest priority requirements of their internal customers. Therefore, when Honda's decision makers plan a manufacturing system, they establish, with manufacturing, the necessary criteria for each factor, set the priorities, and then work to achieve those priorities by any means possible. By following this procedure, they try to achieve the best control of quality, inventory, manufacturing, and cost while solving the discrepancies between the requirements of the two customers.

This approach requires new methods and processes that are free from conventional thinking. Therefore, as Honda engineers and production workers struggle to develop manufacturing systems that meet all the criteria, they follow the functional and design requirements given in Tables 3-3 and 3-4. The goal here is to develop the shortest, most compact and efficient continuous flow manufacturing system possible. As the system matures and inventory is continuously removed from the links, the system becomes more compact. A comment on the highest speed at each step: As the processes are improved and quality goes from good to superior, the speed (production rate) at each step can be increased. This reduces the number of different machines producing the same item, and ultimately the necessary daily quantity can be manufactured within a single serial system. Duplicate machines are eventually eliminated, which reduces product variability.

For example, Honda has developed a welding machine that holds and simultaneously (tack) welds all the sheet metal for a style of car body (Accord). Every Accord manufactured in America is welded on this one machine. This ensures that every Honda body will be identical to the next. The machine can be changed over from two-door to four-door bodies in less than ten minutes. Minimizing the number of steps and the size of the equipment reduces the cost and space required. Quality problems are also reduced with less handling of the parts.

In another case, Honda has developed a machine that integrates the processes of boring and honing, which usually occur sequentially. By combining these processes into one tool, they eliminate variables caused by handling the parts between the two

TABLE 3-3
Honda's functional requirements for manufacturing systems

Uniqueness

Creativity

Efficiency in cost

Efficiency in utilization (minimize waste)

TABLE 3-4
Honda's design requirements for manufacturing systems

The highest speed

The minimum number of steps in each process

One step, one machine

Multiple functions at one step (if no interaction)

Minimum size of equipment

---

processes as well as the wasted transfer time. Honda has also developed an NC gear grinding machine that incorporates CBN grinding wheels and induction heat treatment. This one-step serial gear grinding machine is five times faster than conventional methods.

HIERARCHY OF THE DESIGN PROCESS

Our discussion of supermarket design was restricted to the most important, first-order requirements of the system. The designer did not worry, for example, about the specific ways in which the customer traversed the store or where other items were stored on the shelves. This is always the case in design endeavors. That is, the functional requirements and the corresponding physical solutions can be *decomposed* and prioritized. It is fortunate indeed that there is a hierarchy in design, in both the functional and the physical domains, and that the FRs can be decomposed. Because of this hierarchy, only a limited set of FRs needs to be considered together at a time, reducing the complexity of the design task immensely.

The complexity of the design process increases rapidly as the number of requirements to be considered increases. Therefore, after establishing a set of FRs at a given level of the hierarchy, the designer has to switch over to the physical domain and establish a physical model or system that satisfies the specified FRs. Then, the designer goes back to the functional domain and establishes the next level of FRs. For example, in the case of the supermarket, one of the physical solutions for satisfying FR(2) concerned the location of bread and milk. At the next level, the designer must decide how big to make the store and the respective storage locations. The bigger the store, the greater the selection, but the customer spends more time getting his or her selection (less convenient) and the initial cost of the store is greater.

The designer must recognize and take advantage of the functional and physical hierarchies. A good designer can identify the most important FRs at each level of the hierarchical tree by eliminating the secondary factors from consideration. Less able designers often consider all the FRs of all levels simultaneously rather than making use of their hierarchical nature. With this approach, every design problem will appear to be too complex and formidable to solve.

FUNCTIONAL REQUIREMENTS OF DESIGN

As noted previously, the perceived needs for a product or a process must be reduced to a set of independent functional requirements (FRs). The terms *functional requirement* and *independence* have specific meanings in the context of the design axioms. Functional requirements are *the minimum set of independent requirements for a specific need that completely characterize the design objective*. By definition, functional requirements are independent; that is, each functional requirement is independent of other functional requirements and thus can be stated without consideration of any other functional requirement.

FRs state *what* we wish to achieve through a design, whereas DPs state *how* we hope to achieve them. Therefore, the best and most impartial way of defining FRs is in a *solution neutral environment*. That is, FRs are defined without any preconceived physical solution in mind. Otherwise, the FRs may simply reflect the designer's bias or the attributes of an existing design.

An acceptable set of functional requirements is not necessarily unique. For example, the FRs for the supermarket are not unique to the supermarket. Also, another designer might have chosen a different set of FRs, depending upon his or her judgment of the perceived needs (for the supermarket, the need to eat). The designer is free to choose any arbitrary set of functional requirements consistent with the perceived needs. The physical solution will be different with a different set of FRs. However, the set of FRs must be self-consistent and minimal, in the sense that none are redundant; that is, all functional requirements must be independent from one another.

In summary,

1. There is a hierarchy, in both the functional and physical domains.
2. There is a correspondence between each level of the functional and the physical hierarchies.
3. In order to decompose the functional requirements, one must conceive a physical solution for each element at each level of the hierarchy. That is, the complete FR hierarchical tree cannot be established without conceiving physical solutions at every corresponding level of the physical hierarchy. Nam Suh (1990) provides examples of functional and physical hierarchies.

CONSTRAINTS IN DESIGN

Constraints in the context of axiomatic design are defined as the required limitations on acceptable solutions. Constraints may be classified as either *input constraints*, which limit design specifications, and/or *system constraints*, which limit the manufacturing system. Input constraints are usually expressed as limitations on size, weight, materials, and cost, whereas the system constraints are based on the capacity of machines, the available skill for manufacturing, and even the laws of nature. A typical design constraint for the supermarket would be the size (square footage) of the store or the number of checkout lines. An input constraint might be the number of carts or the maximum speed of the carts in the store.

By definition, a constraint is different from a functional requirement. The constraint does *not* have to be independent of functional requirements and other constraints of design, whereas all FRs are independent of one another. In the supermarket example profitability, accessibility, and variability (selection) are independent FRs. Therefore, the requirement that FR(1) be satisfied should not in any way compromise or affect FR(2) or FR(3), whereas the time (i.e., a constraint) may be affected by any change in the FRs.

ROLE OF INFORMATION IN MANUFACTURING AND DESIGN

The world of design and manufacturing consists of the generation, transmission, conversion, and maintenance of *information*. The design methodology generates information in the form of drawings, layouts, equations, material specifications, schedules, operational instructions, and so forth. Information is also required to run machines, to set the processing conditions, to control the flow of materials through the factory, and to orchestrate the functioning of the entire manufacturing system. The smaller the amount of information required to manufacture a product, the simpler is the manufacturing system.

Two appropriate questions to ask at this stage would be: "Why do we need information?" and "What happens if we do not have a sufficient amount of information?" The obvious answer is that if we do not have the necessary information, the probability of achieving the desired output from the system would be less than one. That means that the products manufactured without sufficient information may not arrive at the right place at the right time with the right quality characteristics. Without the requisite information, the required knowledge for the execution of the task is not available.

The concept of information cannot exist in the absence of the concept of *dimensional tolerance*. Suppose you are considering the manufacture of a rod 0.5 m long. This is the nominal size, but it cannot be made to exactly that size, so a tolerance is applied (by the designer) to the part drawing to reflect that fact. The designer can specify anything from 0.5 ± 0.1 m to 0.5 ± 0.000001 m. Depending on whether the rod has to be cut to within 10^{-1} m or 10^{-6} m, the process selected, the setup time, the operation of the machine, the temperature control, and so forth, can be significantly different. For example, if the rod has to be cut within ± 0.000006 m (6 microns), an ordinary hacksaw cannot be used because it is unable to cut to the specified tolerance. To achieve the specified tolerance, the rod may have to be measured carefully and additional grinding performed, which requires more information. In general, the amount of information required is much smaller when the tolerance is larger, since the probability of success is larger.

DESIGN AXIOMS AND COROLLARIES

As stated in a previous section, the purpose of designing a product or process is to create a physical entity that satisfies the specified functional requirements (FRs) with the least expenditure of resources in the form of materials (including energy), labor, and capital. To accomplish this goal, design decisions must be made rationally at every step of the decision-making process. This can be done most effectively by using the axioms that govern good designs. In addition to these axioms, corollaries and theorems can be developed, which can, in some cases, be used in making design decisions more readily.

By definition, axioms are fundamental truths that are always observed to be valid and for which there are no counterexamples or exceptions. They are reduced from a large number of observations by noting the common truth that holds in all cases. Corollaries are a direct consequence of one or more of these axioms. From these corollaries and axioms, theorems can be derived that can be used in making design decisions. Design rules, which apply to specific design/manufacturing situations, can be derived from these basic principles.

Axioms[1]

Two design axioms govern good design practice, as briefly described in the introduction to this chapter. Axiom 1 deals with the relationship between functions (i.e., "what we want") and physical variables (i.e., "how we hope to achieve the functions"); whereas Axiom 2 deals with complexity. These axioms may be stated more fully as follows:

> **Axiom l: The Independence Axiom.** Maintain the independence of functional requirements.
>
> *Alternative statement 1:* An optimal design always maintains the independence of functional requirements.
>
> *Alternative statement 2:* In an acceptable design, the design parameters and the functional requirements are related so that each functional requirement is satisfied independently without affecting other functional requirements.
>
> **Axiom 2:   The Information Axiom.** Minimize the information content.
>
> *Alternative statement:* The best design is a functionally uncoupled design that has the minimum information content.

Axiom 1 states that the functional independence specified in the problem statement in the form of FRs must be maintained in the design of a solution, whereas Axiom 2 states that, of the designs that satisfy Axiom 1, the design with the minimum information content is the best.

A design that satisfies Axiom 1 by maintaining functional independence is called an *uncoupled design*. A design that renders functions interdependent is a *functionally*

---

[1] From *Principles of Design*, by Nam P. Suh (1990), adapted to manufacturing systems by J T. Black.

coupled design and violates Axiom 1. A coupled design may often be decoupled by adding appropriate additional components, but such a decoupled design is inferior to an uncoupled system generated by a complete redesign.

Corollaries

Many corollaries can be derived as a direct consequence of the two axioms of design. These corollaries may be more useful in making specific design decisions, and since they can be applied to actual situations more readily than the original axioms, they may even be called design rules:

Corollary 1:   Decoupling of Coupled Design. Decouple or separate parts or aspects of a solution if FRs are coupled or become interdependent in the proposed designs.

Corollary 2:   Minimization of FRs. Minimize the number of functional requirements and constraints. Strive for maximum simplicity in overall design or the utmost simplicity in physical and functional characteristics. For example, use the minimum number of steps in each process. Production problems and costs have a direct correlation with the complexity of the manufacturing system, and any efforts made to simplify the system will result in significant savings. One of the best ways to simplify the system is to simplify the design of the products themselves.

Corollary 3:   Integration of Physical Parts. Integrate design features into a single physical process, device, or system when FRs can be independently satisfied in the proposed solution. The design should move toward the idea of one step (in the process) on one machine with multiple operations at each step.

Corollary 4:   Use of Standardization. Use standardized or interchangeable processes and operations if the use of these elements is consistent with functional requirements and constraints.

Corollary 5:   Use of Symmetry. Use symmetrical shapes and/or arrangements if they are consistent with functional requirements and constraints. For example, make right-hand and left-hand parts together and then separate them.

Corollary 6:   Largest Tolerance. In stating FRs specify the largest allowable tolerance for products and their component parts. Using the largest possible tolerances and finishes on parts reduces costs. Tolerances on surface roughness and dimensions play an important role in the final achievement of a simple manufacturing system.

Corollary 7:   Uncoupled Design with Less Information. Seek an uncoupled design that requires less information than coupled designs in satisfying a set of FRs. In IMPS most of the inspection is carried out manually by the operators when the parts are produced in the cells. In such a situation the number of critical dimensions should be minimized (minimize information).

Corollary 1 states that functional independence must be ensured by decoupling if a proposed design couples the functional requirements. This will be demonstrated by the cell design that uncouples the worker from the machines and the machining times from the cycle times. Decoupling does not necessarily imply that the system has to be broken into two or more separate physical parts or that a new element has to be added to the existing manufacturing system design. Functional decoupling may be achieved without physical separation. However, in many cases, such physical decomposition may be the best way of solving the problem, as when decouplers were added to manufacturing and assembly cells. Cells and decouplers will be discussed in more detail in Chapters 4 and 11.

Corollary 2 states that as the number of functional requirements and constraints increases, the system becomes more complex and thus the information content is increased. The conventional belief that one system is better than another because it makes more than is necessary is not correct. A design should fulfill the precise needs defined by the functional requirements—no more, no less! In a JIT system the right amount is available at the right place at the necessary time. Overproduction is not an advantage. Similarly, a process or system that fulfills more functions than specified will be more difficult to operate and maintain than one that meets only the stated functional requirements. Reliability may also decrease when a machine or system fulfills more functional requirements than required because of the increased complexity.

Corollary 3 states that the number of physical processes should be reduced through integration of parts without coupling functional requirements. However, mere physical integration is not desirable if it increases information content or couples functional requirements. Good examples of physical integration that are consistent with Corollary 3 are found in the Honda plant that developed the boring-honing machine or shortened its engine transfer line from 16 to 8 steps.

Corollary 4 states a well-known design rule: Use standard parts, methods, operations, and routes to reduce inventory and minimize the information required for material routing, manufacture, and assembly. Special parts should be minimized to decrease inventory costs and simplify inventory management, as per Corollary 3. Interchangeable parts allow for the reduction of inventory as well as the simplification of manufacturing and service operations; that is, they reduce the information content. They reduce it even more if the design permits generous tolerances.

Corollary 5 is self-evident. Symmetrical parts require less information. They are easier to manufacture and to orient in assembly. Not only should the shape be symmetrical wherever possible, but hole location and other features should be placed symmetrically to minimize the information required during manufacture and use. Symmetrical parts promote symmetry in the manufacturing process.

Corollary 6 deals with tolerances. Reducing tolerances increases the cost and the difficulty of manufacturing a product. More information is required to produce parts with tight tolerances. On the other hand, if the tolerance is too large, the errors in assembly will accumulate, and other functional requirements cannot be satisfied. Therefore, the specification of tolerances should be made as large as possible but should remain consistent with the likelihood of producing functionally acceptable parts. The correct tolerance band minimizes the overall information content. When the tolerance band is too narrow, information content increases since the subsequent manufacturing processes require more information. Excess tolerances reduce reliability and thus increase the need for maintenance, which also increases information content.

Corollary 7 states that an uncoupled design always involves less information than a coupled design. This corollary is a consequence of Axioms 1 and 2. Its implication is that if a designer proposes an uncoupled design that has more information content than a coupled design, the designer should return to the drawing board to develop another uncoupled or decoupled design with less information content. The L-CMS system described in this book represents a system that can operate with the minimum amount of paperwork and information. It is the model for the paperless FWAF.

In addition to these corollaries, many other corollaries and theorems have also been derived (from the axioms and corollaries) that may be considered design rules. Theorems are propositions that follow from axioms or other propositions that have been proven. There can be a large number of theorems, depending on the specific design problem under consideration. One theorem related to manufacturing processes and manufacturing systems design is as follows:

> **Theorem: Design/Manufacturing Interface.** When the manufacturing system compromises the independence of the FRs of the product, either the design of the product must be modified or a new manufacturing system must be designed and/or used to maintain the independence of the FRs of the products.

The L-CMS is a new manufacturing system—It is the design for the FWAF.

4

THE DESIGN OF MANNED MANUFACTURING AND ASSEMBLY CELLS

The first step is always the hardest.

INTRODUCTION

In this world of international competition, the success of a manufacturing company depends on the design of its manufacturing system. The manufacturing system must satisfy the needs of its *users*, the internal customers of the company. To do this, the system should have the following factors in its design:

Safety	consistent with safety standards designed to prevent accidents—a fail-safe design
	no dirty jobs, no heavy manual work
Flexibility	easy for the user to change
Reliability	consistent, repeatable, maintainable, robust
Involvement of employees	suggestions adhered to, employees respected
	everyone has an input
	small, trim management team

Good service   good support from engineering and technical staff
            good training manuals
            good operating manuals

Understandable   Easy for user to understand, control, and operate

  The products made by the manufacturing system go to the external customer. To attain customer satisfaction the manufacturing system must have the functional requirements of superior quality, competitive prices (lowest unit cost), and on-time delivery with attractive products. Most important, the manufacturing system must be flexible—able to adapt rapidly to changes in customer demand and desires (tastes).

  The basic, traditional kinds of manufacturing systems described earlier were job shop, flow shop, continuous process, and project shop. The newest system is the linked-cell manufacturing system, L-CMS, composed of manufacturing and assembly cells linked together with a pull system of inventory control. Design strategies for manufacturing systems will be described in this chapter, but space does not permit detailed explanations of all methods by which cells can be formed. The main point to remember is that this is an evolutionary project that restructures the factory floor.

LINKED-CELL MANUFACTURING SYSTEMS (L-CMS)

A linked-cell manufacturing system is the newest type of manufacturing system. Figure 4-1 shows an L-CMS, composed of manufacturing cells, subassembly cells, and final assembly lines. The basic building block is the manufacturing cell, in which processes are grouped according to the sequence of processes and operations needed to make a group or family of parts or products (see Figure 4-2). This arrangement functions much like that of the flow shop in that parts move through the cell one at a time; however the cell is designed for flexibility. It is typically arranged in a U-shape so that the workers can move from machine to machine, loading and unloading parts. The machines in the cell are all at least single-cycle automatics so that they can complete the machining cycle untended, turning themselves off when finished with a machining cycle. The cell usually includes all the processing needed for a complete part or subassembly. Between each machine in the cell, a decoupler holds one part, processed and inspected, ready to be pulled into the next machine. (Decouplers for unmanned cells will be discussed in Chapter 11 in more detail.) Decouplers in the manned cell permit the worker to move in the opposite direction to the part flow. Figures 4-3 and 4-4 show the same cell operated by two workers. The material flow in the cell is sustained by the decouplers. The shaded decouplers in each cell are used to connect the work areas of the operators. Notice that the operators in Figure 4-4 are moving in the direction opposite to the part flow through the cell. The decoupler elements permit this to happen. Notice that in Figure 4-3 worker 1 is handling different machines from those in Figure 4-4, so a different balance is achieved. The workers can decide how to divide up the work in the cell.

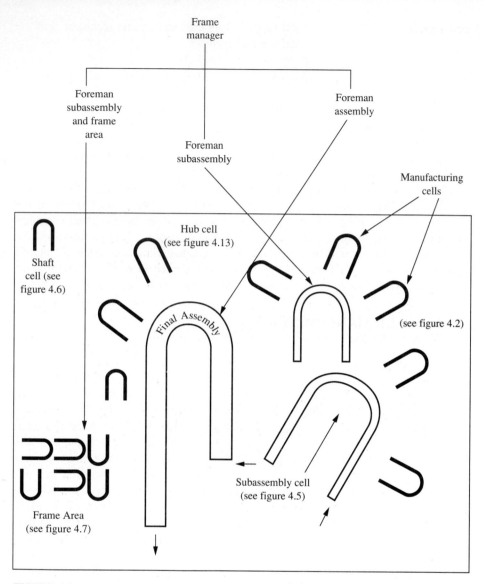

FIGURE 4-1
The L-CMS is product oriented. The cells are linked directly to the subassemblies (subprocesses put at point of use) or with kanban.

    The first step in forming cells is to restructure portions of the job shop, converting it in stages into manned cells. Cells can be linked *directly* to one another (or to subassembly points), or more commonly they can be linked *indirectly* by the pull system of inventory control called *kanban*. Linking will be discussed in Chapter 9.

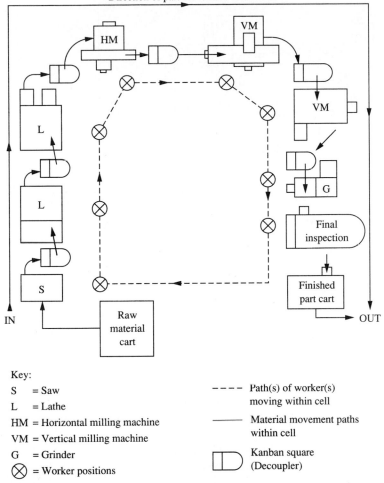

Direction of part movement within cell

Key:

S   = Saw
L   = Lathe
HM = Horizontal milling machine
VM = Vertical milling machine
G   = Grinder
⊗   = Worker positions

– – – –   Path(s) of worker(s) moving within cell

————   Material movement paths within cell

Kanban square (Decoupler)

FIGURE 4-2
Manned manufacturing cell for a family of parts with seven machines operated by one worker.

The flow and assembly lines within the plant are also redesigned to make these systems operate like cells. To do this, long setup times typical in flow lines must be vigorously attacked and reduced so that the flow lines can be changed quickly from the manufacture of one product to the manufacture of another (see Chapter 5). Line balancing of the flow line every time it changes to another part can be simplified by the proper design and the use of decouplers. The flow lines will become more flexible and compatible with the cells. Both the cells and the flow lines make piece parts for the subassembly cells and final assembly lines. The resources within the system that do not depreciate—direct labor and direct material—are fully utilized and minimized.

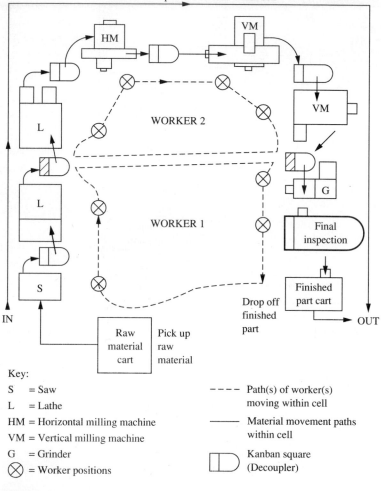

FIGURE 4-3
Manned cell, two workers.

DECOUPLERS IN MANUFACTURING AND ASSEMBLY CELLS

Decouplers are placed between the processes, operations, or machines to provide cell flexibility, quality control, production control, and process delay. The term *decoupler* was coined by Black (Black & Schroer, 1988) based on the first axiom of manufacturing design.

Two axioms govern good design. Axiom 1 deals with the relationship between functions and physical variables, and Axiom 2 deals with the complexity of design.

Axiom 1: Maintain the independence of functional requirements.

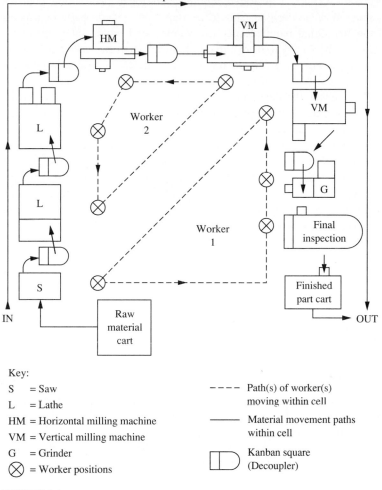

FIGURE 4-4
Manned cell, two workers, different balance.

Axiom 2: Minimize the information content of the design.

The key functional requirement for the cell is flexibility. Functionally, the parts are processed one at a time and pulled through the cell. The worker can walk in either direction (with the part flow or against the part flow) without backtracking. When the worker walks in the direction opposite to the flow of parts, there is a problem. How do we get parts and information to move in the opposite direction to the movement of the worker? This is an example of a coupled design. A coupled design can be decoupled by adding extra components. A decoupled design is inferior to an uncoupled design (a design that satisfies Axiom 1) in that it requires additional information content. The first axiom states that the designer should decouple or separate parts or aspects of a solution if the functional requirements are coupled or become interdependent. Therefore, in a cell, it is necessary to have one part between each successive process — the device that holds the one part is the decoupler — specifically, a production control type of decoupler.

The decoupler reduces the dependency of one process or work station on the next. In robotic cells, the decoupler replaces the functional capability of the worker. The decouplers in manned cells (Figure 4-2) permit the worker to travel in the opposite direction to the part movement. Parts are pulled from the final inspection decoupler one at a time, as needed. The decoupler also permits different parts to pass one another within the cell. Decouplers can also provide functional quality control (with inspection) and process delay. A process delay decoupler would delay the part movement to allow the part to cool, heat, cure, and so forth, for longer than the required cycle time. Except for process delay, the decoupler does not act as a buffer. It holds only one part, completely processed to that point in the cell. The material in the cell is called the *stock-on-hand*.

WIP VERSUS SOH

Notice that the parts have arrived at the input side of the cell in a cart. A different set of carts connects the output side of the cell to the place where the parts are to be used. The carts between the cells are part of the withdrawal kanban links.

Downstream cells and final assembly lines are protected against problems in the upstream cells by the inventory in the withdrawal kanban (WLK) links between the cells. The material in the cells is stock-on-hand (SOH). The material between the cells is the work-in-process (WIP) inventory.

Decouplers and fixtures that can accommodate a variety of parts make the flow lines more flexible and compatible with the cells. Both the cells and the flow lines make piece parts for the subassembly and final assembly lines. Decouplers will be covered more extensively in Chapter 11.

HOW AN ASSEMBLY CELL WORKS

The primary difference between the manufacturing cell and the assembly cell is that the operations in the assembly cell are usually entirely manual. That is, the operator must stay at the station for the duration of the task. The operator cannot simply load a part into the machine, start the machine, and have it complete the operation(s). Here we will examine a typical assembly cell. The assembly cell shown in Figure 4-5 has eight stations and can be operated by one to eight workers, depending on the required output for the cell. The squares in the system are used to pull material through the cell, so the kanban squares are production control decouplers.

Suppose there is a worker at every station, so the cell is operating at maximum capacity (this is not the usual case). The removal of material from the kanban square

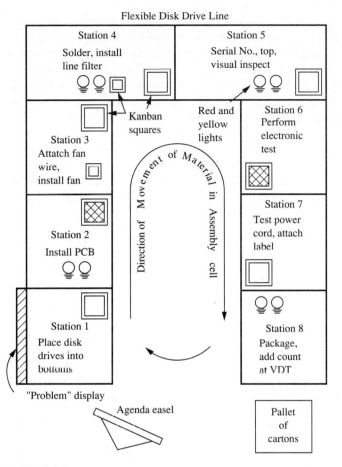

FIGURE 4-5
An assembly cell for disk drives, designed by workers at Hewlett-Packard,
Greeley Division, with kanban squares.

at station 3 by the worker at station 4 is a signal for the worker at station 3 to attach
the fan wire and install the fan. At this time the worker at station 3 removes material
from the kanban square at 2, signaling station 2 to install the PCB (printed circuit
board). If the kanban square at the station has material in it, the operator must wait
until it is removed before beginning the next assembly. In this situation the operation
times at each station must be balanced, and the station with the longest time will
control the output of the cell.

The kanban squares are examples of a visual production control system that is
very fast and accurate. Workers can easily see the signal and (when a part has been
removed) quickly react to the signal to "make one" to replace the one that has been
removed.

If the cell is required to operate at peak capacity all the time (eight operators), the operations at each station must be configured to require the same amount of time (on the average), and any variance will cause disruptions in the throughput times and production rates. Extensive redesign of the station, its hardware, and methods may be required to achieve a good balance. This greatly reduces the flexibility of the cell. Now let us see how this design can be used to eliminate line balancing in the normal sense. Suppose the cell has only two workers. One worker performs the first, second, seventh, and eighth operations by walking from one station to the next. The other worker does the third, fourth, fifth, and sixth. The two shaded decouplers then link the two workers. Only the total time it takes for the workers to make the half loops must be balanced. Obviously any two squares could be used to achieve this objective. Thus one worker could do three tasks and the other five tasks to make the times balance. The foreman and workers can do this rebalancing quickly.

Alternatively, the two workers could simply follow each other around the cell and both perform each assembly step in sequence. This practice is called the *rabbit chase* and it also eliminates the need to do precise line balancing for the entire cell or the partial loops. Thus, the design of a cell with walking worker(s) eliminates the need for precise line balancing within the cell.

Little work has been done on the ergonomics and human factors of the walking worker versus the seated or standing worker. Having the worker mobile as well as multiprocess is a key element in the design of manned cells. The walking worker is a critical element in making the cell flexible.

The workers use the red and yellow lights mounted above the work stations to signal when they are in trouble (yellow) and may be delayed. When a problem is severe enough to halt the flow, the worker turns on the red light. This stops the line and all the workers. When the problem is solved and the light is turned off, they all begin together. Problems in the cell are documented and posted on the display board at station 1. At the end of the day, these problems are discussed and improvements are suggested.

The assembly cell can be operated by one worker when demand is very slow or as many as eight workers when demand is at the maximum level. This is flexibility in output. The big difference between manufacturing and assembly cells is that the machines in manufacturing cells are usually single-cycle automatics, able to complete the process cycle untended, unless it is a simple manual operation or a process like seam welding. In the assembly cells, the operations are usually manual (less automated) so the operator cannot let the process run untended.

AN EXAMPLE OF HOW A MANUFACTURING CELL WORKS

One of the cells shown in Figure 4-1 was designed for the manufacture of a family of shafts. The cell has product flexibility due to a unique feature in its design. The machine times (MT) are decoupled from the cycle time (CT) while products are built one at a time. The raw material for the shafts arrives in carts (see detail in Figure 4-6). Five machining processes and one final inspection operation are needed to produce a

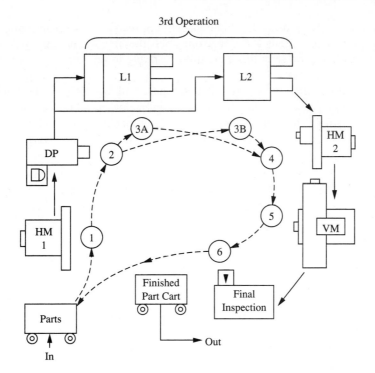

Key

DP	= Drill press	→ - - -	= Path of worker moving within cell
L	= Lathe		
HM	= Horizontal milling machine	→———	= Material movement paths
VM	= Vertical milling machine	①	= Worker positions

Work Sequence	Operation Name	Time Manual	Time Walking	MT Machine
1	Mill ends on work on HM 1	12"	5"	30"
2	Drill hole on DP	15"	5"	20"
3	Turn-bore on L1 or L2	13"	5" 8"	180"
4	Mill flat on HM 2	12"	8" 5"	20"
5	Mill steps on VM	13"	7"	30"
6	Final inspection	10"	5"	—
	CT = 75" + 35" = 110"	75"	35"	280"

FIGURE 4-6
Detail of the shaft cell in Figure 4-1.

shaft. The cycle time for the shaft cell in Figure 4-6 is 110 seconds. This is the sum of the manual time the worker spends at the machines plus the time spent walking from machine to machine. The worker in this example is walking in the same direction as the part flow.

The total machining time for a part is 280 seconds, with the longest MT being 180 seconds for the third operation. The MTs for any individual machines are (on the average) less than the CT. Therefore, except for the third machine, no machine will delay the worker in walking around the cell. Because the third operation, turn-bore, has a long MT—180 seconds—compared to the needed CT of 110 seconds for the cell, the third operation is duplicated in the cell. Thus, its MT is $\frac{180}{2}$ or 90 seconds on the average, again less than 110 seconds. The general rule is

$$MT_i < CT \qquad (4.1)$$

where

$i = 1$ to 6 machines.

The machining times for the other parts in the family will vary from part to part because the length of cut (L) will be different for different sizes of shafts. MTs in the table in Figure 4-6 are calculated from Eq. 4.2 for machine 2. Similar equations are used for other processes.

$$MT = \frac{L + \text{allowance}}{\text{feed} \times \text{rpm}} \qquad (4.2)$$

As the length of cut or feeds and speeds are varied between parts in the family of parts, the machining times are also varied. However, the design of cells has determined that

$$MT_{ij} < CT \qquad (4.3)$$

where

$i = 1$ to number of machines in cell

$j = 1$ to number of parts in family

Thus, the shaft cell can change from one part to another without rescheduling—CT was not affected by the change in parts—so this cell represents an uncoupled design.

All machines in the cell can run untended while the operator walks from machine to machine. The decouplers for this cell were not shown. At each machine, the operator performs various manual tasks (unloads, inspects, deburrs, or loads parts into a machine). The time to change tools and perform setups is not shown. This design relaxes the line-balancing problem (common to flow lines and transfer lines) while greatly enhancing flexibility. The CT is controlled by the time it takes the worker or workers to complete a walking loop through the cell or cells and to perform the manual operations at each machine. Therefore, the CT can be altered by adding or deleting (parts of) workers. This will be discussed later in this chapter.

There is no need to balance the MTs for the machines. It is only necessary that no MT be greater than the required CT. Since the MT to turn-bore is greater than the CT ($180 > 110$), the process is duplicated and the worker alternates machines on his or her trips through the cell. The duplicated machines must do identical work.

CYCLE TIME FOR THE CELL

The requirements of the manufacturing system dictate the CT for this cell. Like all other cells in the plant, the shaft cell is designed to produce parts as needed, when needed, by the downstream processes and assembly lines.

The demand rate for the parts determines the CT according to the following calculations:

$$CT = \frac{\text{hours in a shift} \times \text{number of shifts}}{\text{daily demand for parts}} \qquad (4.4)$$

where

$$\text{Daily demand for parts} = \frac{\text{monthly demand (forecast plus customers' orders)}}{\text{number of days in a month}}$$

In the linked-cell factory, cells fabricate components for the subassembly and final assembly lines. The cell is designed to produce parts at exactly the rate the subassembly cell needs the parts and no faster. Piece parts are fabricated at the rate needed by the cells.

An example from Honda, in Marysville, Ohio, will be helpful. Suppose the factory is producing 300 cars per day. The body for each car needs 24 pieces of sheet metal. All 24 pieces of sheet metal are produced on one stand of presses. The presses stamp out 300 hoods, and then the dies are changed and 300 roofs are stamped out. The dies are changed again, and 300 right-side body panels are produced. It takes about 10 minutes to change the dies. The presses produce a part every 6 seconds or 10 parts per minute or 300 parts in 30 minutes. Thus, the stand can produce the necessary daily quantity of sheet metal parts every day (two 8-hour shifts). The daily demand was based on the monthly demand. The required CT for the presses was based on the daily demand.

Overproduction will result in the need to store parts, transport parts to storage, retrieve the parts when needed, keep track of the parts (paperwork), and so on. Overproduction requires people and costs money but *adds no value*. Underproduction causes shortages of parts and stops the system.

HOW SUPERIOR QUALITY IS ACHIEVED

As long as the MT for a particular machine does not exceed the CT for the cell, the machining speeds and feeds can be relaxed to extend cutting tool life and reduce the wear and tear on the machines. The common relationship between cutting speed and tool life is

$$VT^n = C \qquad (4.5)$$

where

$$V = \text{cutting speed}$$
$$T = \text{tool life}$$
$$n \text{ and } C = \text{empirical constants}$$

Typical values for the exponent *n* are 0.14 to 0.4, so the equation shows that a modest reduction in speed results in large increases in tool life. The relaxation in cutting speed *increases the reliability of the process, reducing the probability of a breakdown or of producing a defect.*

If the cutting process can be run a full eight-hour shift without changing tools, quality will be more controllable and consistent. No computer analysis is needed to find which process within the cell is the bottleneck (machine with the longest MT). Everyone in the manufacturing system can see and understand how the cell functions, which process will most likely delay the cell CT, and where to put the critical resources to get the greatest productivity gains. The overall system design is simple.

FLEXIBILITY IN CELL DESIGN

The key functional design criterion or requirement for a manufacturing or assembly cell is flexibility. (Cells should not be confused with flexible manufacturing systems [FMSs]. Cells are operationally very different from FMSs.) Cells have several types of flexibility.

To be flexible, the process must be able to handle changes in the product design (i.e., engineering design changes are routine facts of life) as well as the design of new products. The latter is called *concurrent design* and reflects the ability of the company to bring new products to the market quickly.

Thus, to be flexible, the manufacturing system must be able to be reconfigured (redesigned) easily. The design of the manufacturing system should not be viewed as fixed and unchangeable as is often the case in the job shop or the flow shop. The design of the manufacturing system dictates the material flow, which must be done efficiently.

To be flexible, the existing manufacturing system should also be able to adapt to changes in the mix of products in the existing volume as well as changes in the existing volume—changes in the customer's demand for the product. That is, the production rate for the cell can be readily changed simply by adding or subtracting (parts of) workers. This idea is in use at Wendy's, a fast-food manufacturing cell for hamburgers. At lunchtime, many workers are in the cell, so the production rate is high. In mid-afternoon, when business is slow, fewer workers are in the cell.

Manufacturing and assembly cells need to adapt to changes in demand on a monthly or perhaps biweekly basis rather than a daily basis, but the concept is the same. Let's examine another L-CMS design to see how flexibility is incorporated.

Figure 4-7 shows the frame area of Figure 4-1 in more detail. This area contains six manufacturing cells and one subassembly cell, which directly feeds the mixed model final assembly line. These seven manned cells are linked by kanban or linked directly to a nearby cell. The subassembly line is directly linked to a "point of use" in

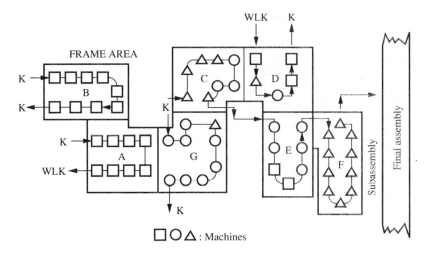

FIGURE 4-7
The frame area has seven manned cells. Cells C, E, and F are directly linked. The rest are linked by kanban.

the final assembly line. Cell E is directly linked to cell F. Cell H (not shown in this figure) withdraws parts from cell D as needed, using kanban links. In the linked-cell system, the WIP between the cells is controlled by the withdrawal kanban. The inventory within the cells is called the *stock-on-hand*. When the cell can make a very high percentage of perfect parts, has no machine breakdowns and virtually no setups, the kanban link can be replaced with a direct link. This will be discussed in more detail later in Chapter 9.

Figure 4-8 shows the frame area with two different allocations of workers. In the upper diagram, eight workers are tending the machines in seven cells. The cycle time was 120 seconds per unit. The next month a longer cycle time was needed because the demand decreased. Six workers were allocated to the seven cells, resulting in a decrease in the production rate and an increase in the cycle time to 165 seconds. Notice that all the cells in this area have the same cycle time. For a cycle time of 120 seconds, each worker is tending 9 or 10 machines. The workers in these cells spend from 10 to 15 seconds at a machine and 5 seconds walking to the next machine.

The frame foreman tries to allocate the minimum number of workers needed to keep the area running without problems. Notice that some cells are completely run by one worker. Other cells have two workers sharing the tasks and machines so a part of a worker is used to run a cell. If the demand increased, more workers would be added and two workers might be operating one cell. Decouplers between the machines (not shown) tie the workpiece movements together within the cell.

Manufacturing and assembly cells use unseated (walking) workers, like Wendy's, with its manufacturing cell for hamburgers that has multifunctional workers who perform many tasks and duties as well as run different processes.

Changes in consumer desires can alter the mix of parts. Cells make families of parts. Let us say the part family has four different parts. All four parts have the same

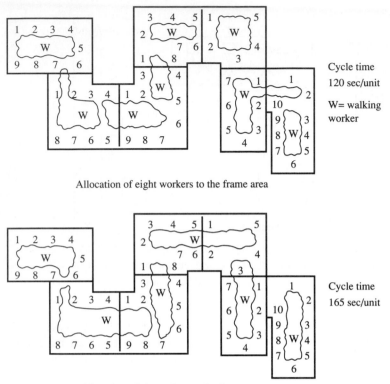

Cycle time
120 sec/unit

W= walking
worker

Allocation of eight workers to the frame area

Cycle time
165 sec/unit

Allocation of six workers to the frame area

FIGURE 4-8
The number of workers can be reduced as the demand decreases, thereby increasing the cycle time.

sequence of processes. When the parts differ in size, their MT will differ because the machining times (MT) depend on the length of the cut as noted previously.

However, altering the MT will not disturb the cell's production rate *because the cell CT is dictated by the time it takes the worker to walk around the cell.* Thus, the mix of parts in the family can be changed without disturbing the production rate, as long as the CT is greater than the MT.

If the same set of parts was made in a CNC machining center, the CT for each part would depend very heavily on the MTs, and parts of different sizes would have very different CTs. Also the CT in the CNC machining center would be longer because the MTs are performed serially by one spindle rather than overlapped by many spindles. In the cell, if the MT for one process is greater than the required CT for the cell, the following alternatives are available:

1. The process is duplicated as shown in Figure 4-6 to effectively halve the MT.
2. The process is speeded up to reduce the MT. There are many ways to accomplish this (increase depth of cut, feed rates, cutting speeds), but they can all result in

complications. For example, increasing the cutting speed (increasing RPM in Eq. 4.2) will result in decreasing the tool life, degrading the quality, having to make more cutting tool changes, and so forth.

3. The cell is run overtime for a period at the same MT, and the difference is absorbed in the kanban loops. This is obviously only a temporary solution.

4. Some operations done on the machine with the longest MT are shifted to another machine that has time available.

5. The product is redesigned.

Finally, if product demand is too high for the cell to meet the system's needs, the cell is cloned (replicated) to double the capacity. *Proven manufacturing capacity is, therefore, quickly doubled, and so is flexibility.* When the cell is replicated, capacity is actually more than doubled. Suppose you have a cell making two parts, A and B. Demand reaches the point where the cell must be replicated. Now one cell can make all As and the other cell can make all Bs. Setup between A and B is eliminated as each cell becomes dedicated. However, if demand should decrease, then one of the cells could go back to making both A and B. Excess capacity is available to add new parts to the cells, leading to a condition called *less-than-full-capacity (LTFC) scheduling*.

The cell can also adapt to changes in product design for new or existing products. Cells can be designed for product design change flexibility. Twenty years ago, the job of designing the manufacturing system was called *plant layout*. It was done by the industrial engineers when a new plant was being built, or it simply developed as the plant grew. Once the plant was laid out (designed), the job was considered to be done. Now we recognize that the manufacturing system must be constantly redesigned (reconfigured) to maintain flexibility, improve quality, reduce costs, decrease throughput time, and lower in-process inventory. That is, to be flexible in the factory with a future, the manufacturing system and the manufacturing/assembly cells must be easy to redesign. The equipment on the plant floor must be easily relocated in order to restructure the cells or relocate the cells within the plant. Machines must be simple, programmable, and able to be mounted on air pallets or wheels. Power, water, and air connections must be overhead on tracks for easy access. Equipment should not be bolted to the floor unless absolutely necessary.

The product designer can now know the process capability for a family of parts (i.e., for an entire cell). Parts can then be designed accordingly. This is truly designing for manufacturing.

HOW (AND WHY) CELLS ARE LINKED

At the outset, the cells are linked by a pull system of material control, called kanban. *Within the cells*, the parts move one at a time from machine to machine. This one-piece part movement eliminates queues (storage banks) between the processes, reduces material handling, and saves floor space. To manufacture with cells, setup time must be reduced, so the rapid exchange of tooling and dies (RETAD) is very important. This is step 2 in the IMPS strategy. The machines must also be improved to inform operators when something is going wrong so they can solve the problem quickly. Therefore,

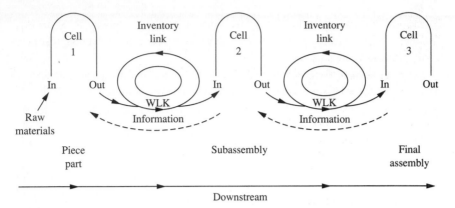

FIGURE 4-9
The cells are linked with controllable inventory buffers called kanban links or loops.

methods must be implemented to prevent defects and machine breakdowns. These are steps 3 and 4 of the IMPS strategy. Nevertheless, problems will occur within the cells, and buffers must be used to protect the downstream elements from delays in upstream cells. Therefore, the inventory buffer is *between the cells* within the kanban links (see Figure 4-9).

Parts move between the cells in small lots of uniform size, using kanban links. The size of the inventory buffer between the cells equals the number of parts in a container times the number of containers. The size of this inventory buffer is *controlled* and *minimized* by controlling the number of containers in the inventory links. The inventory buffers protect the downstream portion of the system against machine tool breakdowns, defects, and delays within the cell. Material is pulled as needed by the downstream processes. The critical functions of production and inventory control are infused into the manufacturing system. The cells are linked to the subassembly and final assembly lines as well. This aspect of the L-CMS is discussed in Chapter 9.

SEQUENTIAL SETUPS

A manufacturing cell that is producing a family of parts must have the machines changed over between parts. Changeover is handled sequentially within the cell. Here is example of how this works for a cell of four machines. In the manufacturing and assembly cells as well as the assembly lines, setup work begins at the head (or start) of the cell (or line) and moves through the cell (or line) just ahead of the first unit for the part (or model). Setup becomes an integral part of the operation of the cell. The setups in manufacturing cells are synchronized with those of final assembly as the lot sizes are reduced along with setup times. As shown in Figure 4-10, when numerous processes are involved in the manufacturing cell of a family of parts, sequential setup changes are utilized. Here, a changeover from part A to part B is being described for a cell with four processes. The worker is moving in the same direction as the part

Process/machine	1	2	3	4
	A19	A18	A17	A16
	A20	A19	A18	A17
Setup change 1	Setup change	A20	A19	A18
Setup change 2	B1	Setup change	A20	A19
Setup change 3	B2	B1	Setup change	A20
Setup change 4	B3	B2	B1	Setup change
	B4	B3	B2	B1
	B5	B4	B3	B2

FIGURE 4-10
Example of changeover from part A to part B for four-process cell.

flow and changes each machine over from A to B sequentially. After the worker has made four trips around the cell, the cell is making B parts. At the outset, the setup times may be long compared to the machining time (the run times) but eventually the setup times are reduced to less than the average time the worker spends at each machine.

The setup operation flows through the cell just like another workpiece. Eventually the setup should become one-touch—very quick with one handling of the workholder (like flipping a light switch). The setup change should permit defect-free products to be made from the start. The first part will be good. Ultimately, the ideal condition of no setup between different parts can be achieved, although dropping the setup time to very short intervals may be difficult in lathe operations. That is, turning machines usually require a change in workholder and a change in tooling when parts are changed.

THE CELL (MANNED) FOR LOT SIZE = 1

The cell in Figure 4-11 is designed to fabricate a family of four parts with five machines. The cell makes parts one at a time and produces in lot sizes of one as well. That is, any of the machines can quickly switch from one part to another. Between each machine is a decoupler that holds one part of each family member (i.e., four parts) processed through that stage of the cell. The four parts are all different in size and shape. The triangular part is not machined in machine 4 at all, so it has a machining time of zero. The worker is walking opposite to the movement of the parts. The parts are pulled through the cell by the decouplers.

Parts removed from the final inspection decoupler dictate what the cell needs to make and when the cell needs to make it. If a square part is pulled out of the final decoupler, the worker unloads machine 5, removes a square part from decoupler 4, and loads it into machine 5. This creates a need to replace the part in decoupler 4. The worker walks to machine 4, unloads a part, places the part in decoupler 4, removes a square part from decoupler 3, then loads it into machine 4. This creates

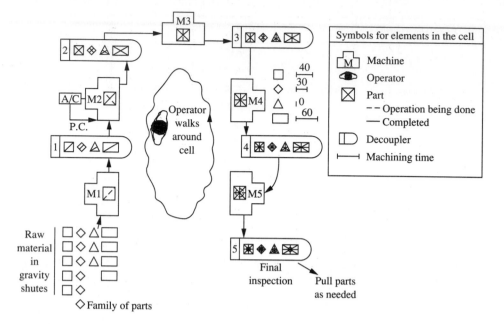

FIGURE 4-11

Example of manned cell for machining a family of parts, showing the path of the worker moving opposite to the part flow.

the demand in decoupler 3 for a part. Thus, the parts are pulled through the system. Obviously the cell must be fully loaded with parts, processed in stages and waiting in the decouplers.

The cycle time for the manufacture of any of the four parts is the same. Remember, CT is determined by the time it takes for the worker to make one complete walking loop around the cell. This kind of cell requires that setup is virtually eliminated, the processes make no defective parts, and the machines rarely, if ever, break down.

Machine 2 has been equipped with an adaptive control (A/C) feedback loop to control the behavior of the process, optimizing some aspect of it. A/C feedback is not the same as a pokayoke device, which tries to prevent defects from occurring.

STANDARD OPERATIONS ROUTINE SHEET

The standard operations routine sheet shown in Figure 4-12, is used to plan the manufacture of one of the parts in the family within the cell. The plan shows the relationship between the manual operations performed by the worker, the machining operations performed by the machine, and the time spent by the worker walking from machine to machine. The manual operations include *loading and unloading* the machine, *checking quality*, *deburring*, *taking chips out* of fixtures, *marking parts* with identifying numbers, and so forth.

Standard operations routine sheet

Item no. name of items	Standard operations routine sheet	Date of Manufacture	Required daily quantity	Manual operation U L I
Process		Worker's group	480 minutes/ required quantity (cycle time)	Machine processing — — — Walking

Work sequence	Name of operation	Time Manual	Machine	Operations time (seconds) 6 12 18 24 30 36 42 48 54 60 66 72 78 84 90 96 102 108 114 120
1				
2				
3				
4				
5				
6				
7				
8				
9				
10				
11				

0 6 12 18 24 30 36 42 48 54 60 66 72 78 84 90 96 102 108 114 120

Operations time (seconds)

FIGURE 4-12
Example of standard operations routine sheet used to plan the work for a manufacturing cell.

83

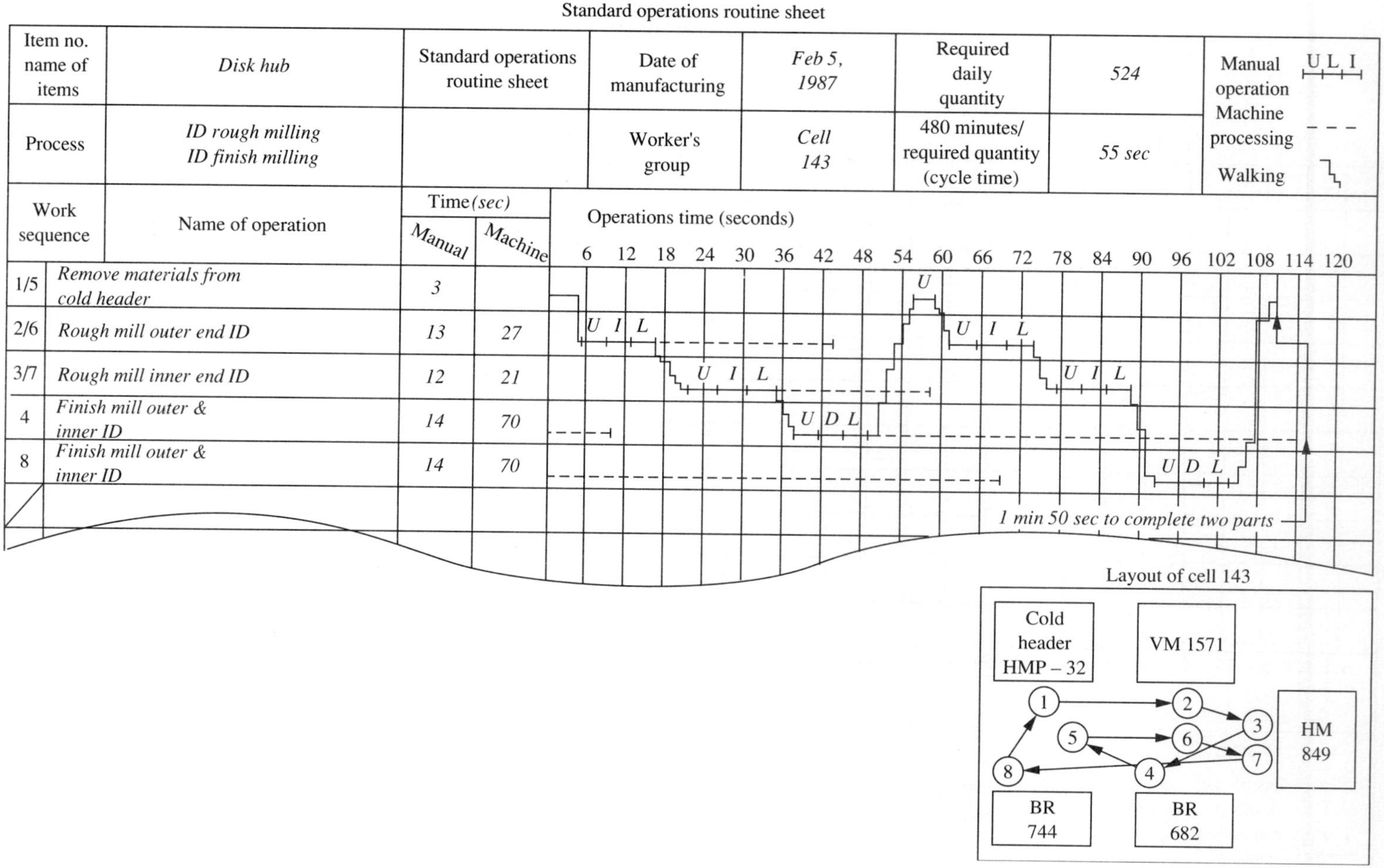

Standard operations routine sheet

Item no. name of items	Disk hub	Standard operations routine sheet	Date of manufacturing	Feb 5, 1987	Required daily quantity	524	Manual operation — / Machine processing – – – / Walking ⌐
Process	ID rough milling / ID finish milling		Worker's group	Cell 143	480 minutes/ required quantity (cycle time)	55 sec	U L I

Work sequence	Name of operation	Time (sec) Manual	Machine
1/5	Remove materials from cold header	3	
2/6	Rough mill outer end ID	13	27
3/7	Rough mill inner end ID	12	21
4	Finish mill outer & inner ID	14	70
8	Finish mill outer & inner ID	14	70

Operations time (seconds): 6 12 18 24 30 36 42 48 54 60 66 72 78 84 90 96 102 108 114 120

1 min 50 sec to complete two parts

Layout of cell 143

Cold header HMP – 32 · VM 1571 · HM 849 · BR 682 · BR 744

FIGURE 4-13

Example of a standard operations routine sheet for a manned cell. The hub manufacturing machine is a four-station cold header, which makes preformed blanks for the first milling machine—VM-1571. Manual operations are U = unload, L = load, D = deburr, I = inspect, MT = machining time. The cycle time is 55 seconds. Daily production is 524.

The cycle time for the cell is determined by the needs of the system for the parts made by the cell. Figure 4-13 shows the SORS for a small manned cell.

Parts in the cell move from machine to machine one at a time. For material processing, the machines are typically capable of completing a machining cycle initiated by a worker. The U shape puts the start and finish points of the cell next to each other. Every time the operator completes a walking trip around the cell, a part is completed. As shown in Figure 4-13 machining processes are overlapping and need not be equal (balanced) as long as no MT is greater than the CT. For this cell, the cycle time is 55 seconds. The total machining time was $27 + 21 + 70 = 118$ seconds. An NC machining center capable of performing the three machining operations could replace the cell. However, the cycle time for a part would jump from 55 seconds to over 118 seconds because combining the processes into one machine prevents overlapping of the machining times. The CT for the cell can be readily altered by adding (a portion of) additional worker(s) to the cell.

DESIGN OF L-CMSs FOR THE CUSTOMERS

The cell has multiprocess workers: they can operate more than one kind of process (or multiple versions of the same process). They also perform inspection and machine maintenance duties and thus are multifunctional. The workers devise ways to eliminate setup time. Notice that cells eliminate the job shop concept of one person/one machine and thereby greatly increase worker productivity and utilization.

The people who run the processes are the company's most valuable asset. They, the users of the manufacturing system, are its internal customers. In reality, these customers are often the company's most poorly used asset. For the most part, they have been denied their working rights. Redesigning the manufacturing systems into cells greatly helps restore their rights. These people must be given respect and the opportunities to improve themselves and to contribute. The PJS manufacturing system must be restructured because it isolates people, restricts their communication, and greatly increases feedback time on product quality problems.

There will be conflicts between the user of the manufacturing system and the customer of the products. The biggest dilemma is cost. However attractive a product or however perfect the manufacturing system, the product must sell at a reasonable price, be economical for the buyer to use (have high efficiency). Generally speaking, the needs of the internal customer dictate the design and development of the manufacturing system, even though the factors affecting the final (external) customer who buys the final product are of the highest priority. Thus, the approach is to develop a system that places top priority on the factors affecting the final customer and then adapt the system to meet the highest requirements of the internal customer (the production workers). Resolving the conflicts between these two customers requires an environment where new ideas are free from conventional thinking.

OTHER TOOLS FOR MANUFACTURING SYSTEMS DESIGN

Most companies "design" their first cell by trial-and-error techniques. With the advent of newer, easier-to-use languages, *digital simulation* is gaining wider usage in the design and analysis of manufacturing systems. Another technique being extensively researched is called *physical simulation*. This approach uses small robots and scaled-down models of machine tools (minimachines) to emulate real world systems. The minimachines employ essentially the same minicomputers and software as the full-scale systems. In this way, the development of the software needed to integrate the hardware in the cell and design of the cell control logic (software) can be done prior to the installation of the full-scale system on the shop floor. In addition, physical simulation is an ideal way for providing low-cost hands-on education in manufacturing systems. Unmanned cells (and FMSs) can be simulated at quite reasonable costs.

GROUP TECHNOLOGY

Group technology (GT) offers a systems solution to the reorganization of the functional system, restructuring the job shop into cellular manufacturing systems.

In a manufacturing facility, GT groups component parts of similar design or manufacturing sequences into families. Machines can then be collected into groups or cells (manufacturing cells) to process the family. The arrangement of machines in the cell defines the manufacturing sequence.

The entire shop may not be able to convert into cells immediately. Thus, the manufacturing system will be a mix, evolving toward a perfect linked-cell system over time. Scheduling problems are created when in-process times for components made by cells are vastly different from those made under traditional job shop conditions. However, as the volume of parts in the functional area is decreased, the total system will become more efficient and simpler.

Finding families of parts is one of the first steps in converting the functional system to a cell. There are a number of ways to accomplish this. Judgment methods using axiomatic design principles are, of course, the easiest and least expensive, but also the least comprehensive. Eyeball techniques work for restaurants, but not in large job shops where the number of components may approach 10,000 and the number of machines 300 to 500.

However, consider the problem of a manufacturing engineer trying to justify the cost of an NC machining center. What does he do? He uses his experience and judgment, to select as many high-cost, complex parts as can be machined on the NC center, and performs an economic analysis to cost-justify the new machine. In fact, he has found a family of component parts (or at least a partial family), and the NC machining center represents a type of cell (one machine). The same approach is valid for forming a manned cell of conventional machines.

Production flow analysis (PFA) uses the information available on route cards. The idea is to sort through all the components and group them by a matrix analysis, using product routing information (see Figure 4-14). This method is simple, cheap, and fast, but more analytical than tacit judgment. PFA is a valuable tool in the systems reorganization problem. For example, it can be used as an "up-front" analysis, a sort of "before-the-fact" analysis that will yield some cost/benefit information. This would give decision makers some information on what percentage of their product would be made by cellular methods, what would be a good first cell to undertake, what

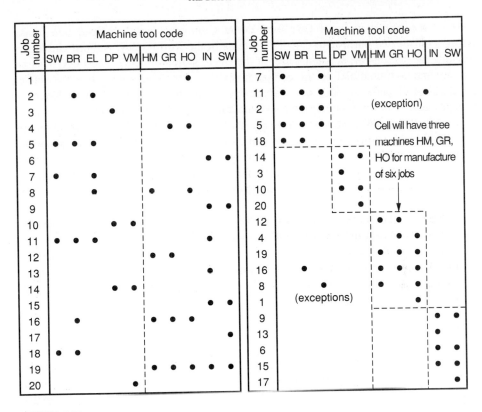

FIGURE 4-14
PFA uses the information in the route sheets to suggest new product grouping.

other analysis method would work best for them, how much money they might have to invest in new equipment, and so forth.

In short, PFA can greatly reduce the uncertainty in making the decision on reorganization. As part of this technique, an analysis of the flow of material in the entire factory is performed, laying the groundwork for the new linked cell layout of the entire plant.

The use of PFA to identify the elements of the first cell permits the company to implement that first cell without waiting until all the parts in the plant have been coded.

Many companies converting to a cellular system have used a *coding/classification (C/C)* method, which is more comprehensive than PFA. There are design codes, manufacturing codes, and codes that cover both design and manufacture.

Classification sorts items into classes or families based on their similarities. It uses a *code* to accomplish this goal. *Coding* is the assignment of symbols (letters, numbers, or both) to specific component elements based on differences in shape, function, material, size, and manufacturing processes.

No attempt to review coding/classification methods will be made here. C/C systems exist in bountiful number in published literature and from consulting firms.

One of the largest users of GT, John Deere Company, has developed one of the most sophisticated but usable C/C GT systems in the world today. Auburn University became the first on-line academic user of the Deere system in 1987. Most C/C systems are computer-compatible, so the computer sorting of the codes generates the classes of families of parts. It does not find groups of machines. If the code is based on design data, errors in forming good manufacturing families will occur.

Whichever C/C system is selected, it should be tailored to the particular company and should be as simple as possible so that everyone understands it. It is not necessary that old part numbers be discarded, but every component will have to be coded prior to the next step in the program, finding families of parts. This coding procedure is costly and time-consuming, but most companies opting for this conversion understand the need to perform this analysis.

The families of parts will not all have the same material flow and therefore will require different designs (layouts). In some families, every part will go to every machine in exactly the same sequence, no machine will be skipped, and no backflow will be allowed. This, of course, is the purest form of cellular system. Other families may require some components to skip some machines and some machines to be duplicated. However, backflow is still not allowed.

PILOT CELLS

The formation of families of parts leads to the design of cells, but this step is by no means automatic. It is the critical step in reorganization and must be carefully planned. Many companies begin with a pilot cell so that everyone can learn and understand how cells function. The company should proceed with the development of manned cells and not wait until all the parts have been coded. I am aware of many companies that started coding and have not yet formed a cell. Perhaps the simplest approach is to select a logical group of products and form a cell to manufacture them. Only in this way will everyone learn how cells operate and how to reduce setup time on each machine. Machines will not be utilized 100 percent. For some machines, the utilization rate may not be what it was in the functional system. The system will be highly utilized. *The objective in manned cellular manufacturing is fully to utilize the people*, enlarging and enriching their jobs. In fact, one of the inherent results of the conversion to a L-CMS is that the workers become multifunctional. That is, they learn to operate many machines and/or perform many duties or tasks.

In the manned cellular system, the worker is decoupled from the machine so that the utility of the worker is no longer tied to the utility of the machine. This means there may be fewer workers in the cell than machines.

In unmanned cells, utilization of the equipment is more important because the most flexible element in the cells (the worker) has been removed and "replaced" by a robot and decouplers (see Chapter 11).

The manned cellular system provides the worker with a natural environment for job enlargement. Greater job involvement enhances job enrichment possibilities and clearly provides an ideal arrangement for improving quality. Part quality can be checked between each step in the process.

Other methods for designing cells including eyeball or tacit judgments, involve

1. Finding the key machine, often a machining center, declaring all parts going to this machine a family, and moving machines needed to complete all parts in family around the key machine. Often it will be prudent to off-load operations from the key machine to other machines in the cell.
2. Building a cell around a common set of components like gears, splines, spindles, rotors, hubs, shafts, and so on. There are "natural" families of parts that will have the same or similar sequences of processes.
3. Building a cell around a common set of processes. For example, drilling, boring, reaming, keysetting, and chamfering holes makes up a common sequence used in manufacturing holes on parts going onto shafts.
4. Building a cell around a set of parts to eliminate the longest (most time-consuming) element in setups between parts being made in the cell. This was the approach used by Harley-Davidson.
5. Picking a product or products, then designing a linked-cell manufacturing system beginning downstream with the final assembly line (convert final assembly to mixed model) and moving upstream toward subassembly and finally to component parts and suppliers.

Another method of designing the L-CMS is what I call progressive kanban. This method takes a long time and is essentially the approach used by Taiichi Ohno. Here are the essential steps:

1. Link individual processes with a pull inventory control system (kanban). See Chapter 9 for details.
2. Continuously withdraw inventory, exposing problems in each process.
3. Solve problems and continue to reduce both the number of carts between processes and the capacity of the carts.
4. Move machines closer together as lot sizes approach five or ten and the number of carts approaches three.
5. When quality is high, machine maintenance excellent, setup times short or one-touch, put machines side by side, forming a cell.
6. Reduce lot size to one and eliminate carts.

BENEFITS OF CONVERSION

The IMPS strategy of simplifying the manufacturing system before applying automation avoids risks and makes automation easier. The conversion to cellular manufacturing systems results in significant cost savings over a two- to three-year period. Specifically, manufacturing companies report significant reductions in raw materials and in-process inventories, setup costs, throughput times, direct labor, indirect labor, staff, overdue orders, tooling costs, quality costs, and the costs of bringing new designs on line. However, this reorganization has a greater, immeasurable benefit. It prepares the way for automation. The progression from the functional shop to the factory with linked cells and ultimately to robotic cells with computer control for the entire system must be accomplished in logical, economically justified steps, each building from the previous stage. If you have been wondering how to accomplish CIM, now you know. *Integrate first, then automate and computerize*: IM,C.

Cellular manufacturing offers these advantages:

- Quality feedback between manufacturing and assembly operations is much faster.
- Material handling is markedly reduced.
- Setup time is reduced or even eliminated.
- In-process monitoring, feedback and control of inventory, and quality are greatly improved.
- A smoother, faster flow of products through the manufacturing operations is achieved.
- Cycle time variability and line-balancing constraints are reduced.
- Implementation of automation of manufacturing operations is easier.
- Process capability and reliability are improved.

CONSTRAINTS TO CONVERSION

Aside from the failure to recognize cells as a new form of manufacturing system, a major effort on the part of a business is required to undertake a conversion to L-CMS. The constraints to implementation are as follows:

1. *Systems changes are inherently difficult to implement*. Changing the *entire* manufacturing and production system is a huge job. This change requires an attitude change because it empowers workers to find the problems and solve them.

2. *Companies spend freely for product innovation but not for process innovation*. It is easier to justify new hardware for the old manufacturing system than to rearrange the old hardware into a new manufacturing system (linked cells). However, anyone with capital can buy the newest equipment, often creating another island of automation.

3. *Decision makers fear the unknown*. Decision making is choosing among the alternatives in the face of uncertainty. The greater the uncertainty, the more likely it is that the "do-nothing" alternative will be selected. While converting to linked cells will free up additional capacity (setup time saved) and capital (funds not tied up in inventory), such conversions will require expenditure of funds for equipment modification, employee training (in quality, maintenance, and setup reduction), and so forth. The long-term payback equals a high-risk situation in the minds of the decision makers.

4. *Decision makers use faulty criteria*. Decisions should be based on the ability of the company to compete (attractiveness, cost, quality, reliability, delivery time) rather than output or cost alone.

5. *The conversion to cellular manufacturing systems represents a real threat to middle managers.* Within the production system, the functional areas that they have been responsible for are shifted and integrated into the manufacturing system. Also the short-term perspective of (financially oriented) middle managers versus long-term nature of the program results in resistance to change in addition to the erosion of their functional empires.

6. *There is a lack of blue-collar involvement in the decision-making process of the company.* Getting the production workers involved in the decision-making process is itself a significant change. The managers of the manufacturing system have problems adjusting to this situation as well. The workers must be rewarded for their ideas and suggestions. Bulletin boards can be used to post notes containing suggestions from the hourly associates. Suggestions must be recognized and a high percentage of the good ideas implemented.

Clearly, education is needed to overcome these constraints. The attitudes of management and workers must change. Changing to L-CMSs requires an evolutionary, dynamic philosophy, but such conversions offer great potential for markedly improving quality and productivity.

SUMMARY

The cell makes parts one at a time in a flexible design. Cell capacity (the cycle time) can be quickly altered to respond to changes in customer demand. The cycle time does not depend upon the machining time.

Families of parts with similar designs, flexible workholding devices, and tool changes in programmable machines allow rapid changeover from one component to another. Rapid changeover means quick or one-touch setup, often like flipping a light switch. Quality is controlled within the cell, and the equipment within the cell is routinely maintained by the workers. The paths that materials take within the factory are defined by the control links, so the production control function is integrated—the blood flows within the veins and arteries. As quality improves, significant inventory reduction between the cells is possible, and the inventory level can be directly controlled.

Most important, manufacturing systems must be designed to be flexible. They must adapt to changes in customer demand and in product design. Also, the manufacturing system must deliver quality products at the lowest possible cost with the shortest possible delivery time. Using cellular manufacturing systems, composed of manned manufacturing and assembly cells, linked with a pull system of production control has proven to be the way to accomplish these objectives.

5

RETAD: THE RAPID EXCHANGE OF TOOLING AND DIES

For the want of a bolt, the die shoe was lost.

INTRODUCTION

In an IMPS, discrete parts are mass-produced in small lots, resulting in sharp reductions in inventory. For small-lot production, equipment must be designed and arranged so that material moves easily and quickly from one process or operation to another. Small-lot production requires that setup time be reduced or eliminated, completely altering the economics of lot (or batch) manufacturing. All the workers need to be involved and trained in the methodology of setup reduction (i.e., single-minute exchange of dies—SMED). A team whose job is to implement the rapid exchange of tooling and dies (RETAD) is developed. Such efforts can achieve a significant reduction in setup time (waste).

The objective of RETAD is to reduce and simplify setup time, eliminate scrap and rework, and reduce inspection times. Indirectly, as setup time decreases, so does operator frustration. The real question is, "Why haven't we done this before?" Probably because we never saw the need. Setup was viewed as a given, something that had to be accepted. Setup time was measured or estimated and converted into a cost using economic order quantity (EOQ) calculations. The most economical way to handle that cost was computed. This was a suboptimal solution inconsistent with the needs of the entire manufacturing system. EOQ calculations ignored the cost of quality, long delivery times, material handling, and other wastes.

THE ECONOMICS OF RAPID EXCHANGE OF TOOLING AND DIES

Almost without exception, every textbook in production, operations, or inventory planning and control presents the calculations for computing the EOQ: the quantity that balances the cost of holding the inventory caused by large quantities against the cost of performing the setup. The equation is usually given as

$$EOQ = \sqrt{\frac{2SD}{ic}} \tag{5.1}$$

where the S in the numerator is setup cost (or order cost). The analysis assumes that S is a constant, but it has been shown that setup time can be markedly reduced and likewise the EOQ.

Another way to approach this problem is by looking at the manufacturing cost. This calculation is based on the following equation in its most basic form:

$$TC = FC + (VC \times Q) \tag{5.2}$$

where

TC = the total cost to make the part
FC = the fixed cost
VC = the variable cost per unit
Q = the quantity to be built

Fixed costs include costs that are not sensitive to changes in the build quantity. Setup cost is the primary fixed cost. It is calculated by multiplying the time to do the setup by the cost per unit time. Cost per unit time equals the labor cost plus cost of lost production time, including the cost of stopping production during a change-over.

The variable cost is a unit cost composed of the direct labor cost per unit and the material cost per unit. Figure 5-1 shows those costs in their classical fashion,

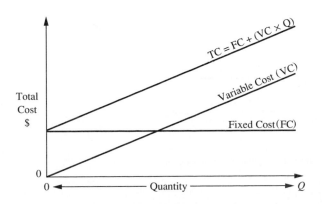

FIGURE 5-1
Classical representation of total cost versus quantity.

with linear relationships assumed for this discussion. This plot shows that as the total quantity built increases, so does the total cost.

If the total cost is divided by quantity, Eq. 5.2 becomes

$$\frac{TC}{Q} = \frac{FC}{Q} + VC \qquad (5.3)$$

and is now expressed in terms of the cost per unit. The information plotted in Figure 5-1 is now recast in Figure 5-2. This classical function is in many textbooks and journals but does not accurately present how cost per unit varies with quantity for a given process. Note that the variable cost is now the constant or horizontal line in Figure 5-2 so that at large quantities, the total cost per unit approaches the variable cost. This simple plot has been the driving force behind the American manufacturing production system philosophy to mass produce in large lots and spread the setup costs over many units. Figure 5-2 also reflects the basic idea called *economies of scale*, but this plot does not extend to the right indefinitely. At some point Q will become so large that the capacity of the process will be exceeded and another process must be considered.

However, Figure 5-2 is a misrepresentation because invariably the data are graphed on log-log paper for easy viewing and graphical analysis. The data, thus transformed, give the reader a distorted impression that cost per unit changes very gradually with quantity. The cost per unit does decrease with quantity because the fixed costs are spread over many units, but let us take another look.

Figure 5-3 shows Figure 5-2 as an undistorted, nontransformed relationship between cost per unit and quantity being built. When graphed on Cartesian coordinates rather than log-log coordinates, the total cost per unit plunges rapidly toward the

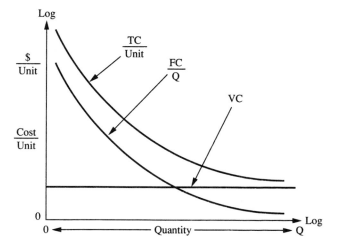

FIGURE 5-2
Typical textbook model of cost per unit versus quantity—a log-log or semilog plot is used.

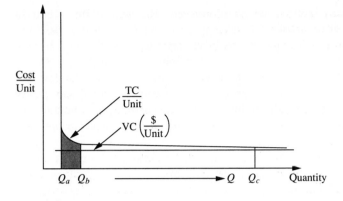

FIGURE 5-3
The true picture of total cost/unit versus quantity—plotted on Cartesian
coordinates.

variable cost per unit time, turns sharply, and then runs nearly parallel to VC/Q
over much of the span of the build quantity. The cost per unit always decreases
while approaching the variable cost per unit at its minimum. The change from rapidly
changing cost per unit to very slowly changing cost per unit occurs over a very narrow
range of quantities (Q_a to Q_b—the shaded area in Figure 5-3). From Q_b to Q_c the
rate of change in cost per unit is very small compared to Q_a to Q_b.

To see what happens to this economic picture when setup time (and cost) is
greatly reduced or eliminated, examine Figure 5-4. The total cost function very
quickly becomes equal to the variable cost function. The dashed line in the plot

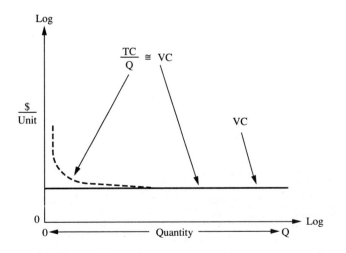

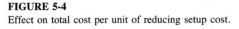

FIGURE 5-4
Effect on total cost per unit of reducing setup cost.

depicts setup cost as greatly reduced but not eliminated. The point is this: The cost per unit is constant for all quantities when setup costs are eliminated. Therefore, manufacturers using the IMPS strategy can build in very small lots for basically the same unit cost as the company not using IMPS and building in large lots. *This is a competitive edge in flexibility.* In fact, building in small lots costs far less per unit. The reasons are that less inventory needs to be managed and stored and quality improves. Layers of inventory are stripped away to reveal problems, and the throughput time is greatly improved. Thus, the economics of eliminating setup are very persuasive.

Now take a look at Figure 5-5, which shows the total cost per unit versus quantity (log-log plots for clarity) for three different processes, any of which could be used to make the same item.

The cost-per-unit data determine the process to use for a given quantity. The three competing processes are examined on the basis of their cost per unit to determine which processes to select to make a given part. There is no minimum cost here, only processes representing lower unit costs at different production quantities. Separating the alternatives are break-even points, or the so-called break-even quantities (BEQ). These are the quantities at which the cost per unit to build the item is equal for either of two processes. Thus, for cost per unit versus quantities, the classical approach determines the quantities over which certain processes are more economical than others. The selection of the lowest cost alternative is based on the quantity that must be built to fill the demand. If one accepts setup cost as a given, this is a valid but suboptimal approach.

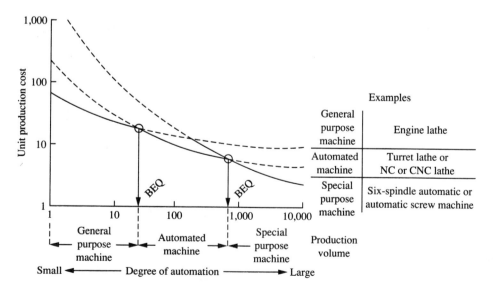

FIGURE 5-5

Three different processes, any of which can be used to make the same item, are compared on the basis of cost per unit versus quantity. BEQ = break-even quantity. Solid line represents minimum cost/unit.

In IMPS, a very different approach is taken to this problem. Setup time is reduced and products are built in the smallest low sizes possible. As the unit cost approaches the variable cost, material cost tend to dominate the variable cost per unit.

The delightful news is that eliminating setup is not some complex, sophisticated undertaking. It requires knowing some simple rules and applying good operations and methods analysis and common sense. Clearly, it could have been done long ago, but most companies failed to see the need.

GETTING ORGANIZED TO ELIMINATE SETUP TIME

Most setup problems are related to materials, manufacturing processes and systems, and management. Contrary to popular opinion, labor is usually a minor factor. Many companies have used a team approach rather than individual efforts. The recommended approach combines a RETAD team and individuals trained in SMED fundamentals. The SMED methodology is outlined in Chapter 1 and is completely described by Shigeo Shingo in a book on this subject (Shingo, 1985). The RETAD team tackles long, difficult setup problems; develops RETAD standard procedures; and trains operators in SMED. The following sequence of steps is recommended:

1. Select a full-time project leader who believes in the IMPS philosophy and setup reduction.
2. Select a project team to do the work. The setup improvement team typically includes some or all of the following people: a setup operator, an industrial engineer, a design engineer, a toolmaker, a machine operator, a consultant (who has experience in setup reduction), a foreman or supervisor, a manager from the project area, and a union leader.
3. Hold a series of informational meetings with management and staff supervisors and foremen, and all workers including the union committee. These meetings must emphasize that the RETAD program will result in *faster but more frequent setups* and that the workers will be responsible for much of the effort. These meetings must explain *what* is do be done, *why* it is to be done, *who* is to do it, and *how* it is to be done. Suggestions will be welcomed. Keep the union advised and involved. Invite the union president to your team meetings. This program has nothing to hide. The sole motivation is that by reducing setup time, manufacturing runs can be shortened, inventory and costs can be reduced, and productivity can be improved.
4. Select specific areas of the plant for the pilot projects. This may be a collection of machines, processes, and operations that you plan to organize into a work cell or line. As soon as machines have been moved into cells, the setup problems will have to be addressed. Harley-Davidson formed cells specifically to reduce setup so it was able to obtain immediate increases in capacity and eliminate many long setups. The initial pilot project may have long setups, scheduling problems, large

inventories (lots of work-in-process), a high inventory value, or severe quality problems.

5. Once the team is trained in SMED and setup operations, begin specific training of operators and current setup people in SMED. The methodology is so simple and direct that everyone can do it. Besides, the company does not have time to wait until the RETAD team gets around to all the machines in the plant. The attack on setups must be company-wide.

ORGANIZING THE PROJECT TEAM

Regardless of the team size or makeup, every member must be well trained in setup reduction and have a positive attitude. The feeling that the job can be done better and less expensively is vital for the success of this initial team and the project itself. Do not neglect the operators. Include them on the team on a rotational basis. They will know more about how to eliminate setup time on their jobs than anyone else.

The proper atmosphere is important here. This should be a grassroots program, coming from the shop floor. This is not another engineering project. The project team may even consist of shop floor experts assisted by technical people. A key element is that the people who developed the existing setup should not be on the team to try to improve it because they have vested interests. Problems with pride of authorship are best avoided. A fresh perspective is sometimes the best approach, particularly since we are all good critics but few are creators.

An alternative to the team approach is to do most of the work through existing channels. The people in engineering and tool design only review setups and try to invent solutions. This serves two purposes: (1) it generates some high-quality ideas, and (2) it introduces support areas to the idea of quick setups that can apply to other work areas. However, this approach often fails to unearth many easy, low-cost, readily implemented solutions. Harley Davidson discovered that with the team approach, it was able to reduce the setup time from three hours to under twelve minutes on the first machining line the team studied.

As you can imagine, the temptation here is to do other improvement tasks with the project team, including process improvement, changing the process sequence, quality standards, and so forth. This approach may be the easiest to take but is not the most effective. The major objectives of the setup team should be to develop and implement solutions to reduce setup time and to train all the operators and foremen in setup reduction. Therefore, by spending time establishing objectives and obtainable goals, the project team avoids trying to solve all the problems they will encounter in areas other than setup and also avoids trying to solve all the setup problems themselves.

To summarize, the role of the project team is to

- Train and involve all operators, supervisors, and support personnel
- Gain experience from the worst setup projects
- Prepare plans and set priorities
- Determine installation timing
- Coordinate group efforts
- Create and maintain the enthusiasm of everyone involved

SMED, OTED, AND NOTED

SMED which stands for *single-minute exchange of die*, means that the setup time is a single-digit number of minutes, within 9 minutes and 59 seconds. This concept was developed by Shigeo Shingo (1981,1985), an industrial engineer, who used the scientific methods of motion and time study analysis. When setup time can be reduced to less than a minute, SMED is called *OTED—one-touch exchange of die method*. Finally, the idea of nontouch exchange of dies, called *NOTED*, was developed. In NOTED, the exchange of tooling and dies is automatic as in a machining center with an automatic tool changer and automatic pallet changer.

SETTING VERSUS ADJUSTMENT

Total setup time is the time from the last good part of the previous setup to the first acceptable part in the new setup. Anything affecting that time frame is in the scope of a setup reduction program (see Figure 5-6). The typical manufacturing sequence is to setup the equipment or machine tool, run some parts, inspect the parts, adjust the machine, run another sample, measure, adjust, and so on until an acceptable part

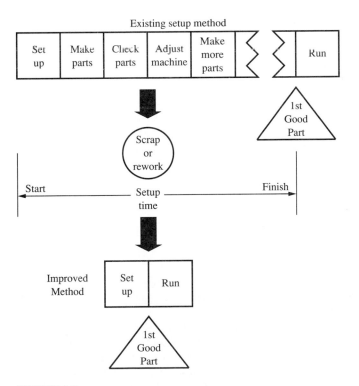

FIGURE 5-6
The improved method of setup reduces setup time through the elimination of unnecessary elements like adjustment.

is made. This method generates scrap and rework and creates many opportunities for nonproductive time.

A key to reducing that time is eliminating adjustment. A significant difference exists between *setting* and *adjusting*. The channel selector on your TV *sets* the TV to a channel. The thermostat in your house *sets* the temperature. If you can tinker with the *settings*, that tinkering or fine-tuning is *adjustment*. Eliminate *adjustment* whenever you can.

The rapid exchange of dies and tooling can reduce setup time from hours to minutes. This can be of remarkable benefit to the manufacturing industry. Available machinery capacity will be increased by reducing setup time. However, don't use the additional capacity to overproduce as overproduction leads to higher inventory costs.

ADOPTION OF RETAD PROGRAMS

RETAD is a revolutionary idea. Many manufacturing people will not believe that setup time can be greatly reduced, due to their natural resistance to change and their belief that the existing system cannot be altered. Another misconception is that a lot of capital funds would have to be spent because highly sophisticated equipment will be needed to accomplish a large reduction in setup time. RETAD is really motion and time study analysis, a scientific method, and common sense, applied to setups. The reduction of setup time permits more frequent tool and die exchanges, smaller lot sizes, lower inventory carrying costs, and shorter production lead times.

THE BASIC STEPS FOR REDUCING SETUP TIME

The basic steps of a program for the reduction of setup time are

1. Determine the existing method.
2. Separate the internal elements from the external elements.
3. Convert internal elements to external elements.
4. Reduce or eliminate internal elements.
5. Apply methods analysis and practice doing setups.
6. Eliminate adjustments.
7. Abolish the setup itself.

DETERMINING THE EXISTING METHOD

Operations analysis, using motion study and time study, can be used to determine what is currently being done for the setup. The usual objective is to improve work methods, eliminate all unnecessary motions, and arrange the necessary motions into the best sequence. The operation is broken down into short elements and activities that consume the most time. Problem-solving techniques can be applied separately to each particular activity to achieve the lowest possible time. Figure 5-7 shows an example of an operation analysis done by Shigeo Shingo at the Toyo Kogyo Co., Ltd., in Hiroshima, Japan, on three press-molding machines. Production operations were broken down into several short elements, and the time consumed for each element was recorded. The important points were classified for reconsideration for improvement. Notice the amount of time spent doing adjustment.

Because the existing setups are often quite long, videotaping of two or three setups is very helpful for later review and analysis. Having the operator (working with the team) review the videotape will reveal much waste in the existing setup, even without doing an operations analysis. Expect to find problems like these:

- All the dies are of different sizes and heights.
- Every die needs a different shut height on the press, so adjusting is always necessary.
- Dies are held in with long threaded bolts often having stripped threads and badly worn or burred heads.
- Tools, nuts, and bolts needed for the exchange are missing.
- The operator is unable to locate the tool or die to be inserted.
- Taking the old die out and/or putting the new die in the machine is at least a two-person job.
- In general, there is a lot of wasted motion and time.
- In general, nothing is standardized.
- Typically, about 20 percent of the time is spent in adjusting (making a part, checking it, adjusting settings, repeating) and 10 percent of the time in securing the dies.

Content of Operation / Machine	(A) Preparation and Subsequent Arrangement after Operation	(B) Main Operation		(C) Allowances			
		Essential Operation	Auxiliary Operation	Physical	Fatigue	Job	Workshop
800 Ton Press — Main Operation	47.0%	3.0%	24.0%	1.0%	5.0%	6.0%	14.0%

Break down of elements in (A)	sec.	%
die transportation	869	3.5
securing die	2940	11.7
adjusting	5475	21.7
removing die	1789	7.2
miscellaneous	610	2.4
		47.0

FIGURE 5-7
Operations analysis on an 800-ton press. (*Shingo, 1981.*)

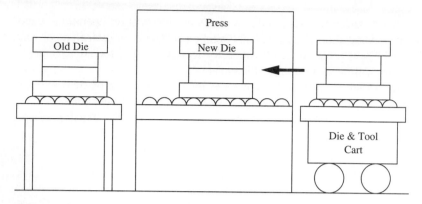

FIGURE 5-8
Roller conveyors can be used for staging and exchanging dies to reduce the internal setup time.

SEPARATING INTERNAL FROM EXTERNAL ELEMENTS

Internal or mainline elements refer to setup actions that require the machine to be stopped. *External* or off-line elements refer to actions that can be taken while the machine is running.

These two kinds of elements must be rigorously separated. Once the machine is stopped, the worker should never leave it to handle any part of the external setup. As part of the external setup, the die, tools, and materials should be ready for insertion

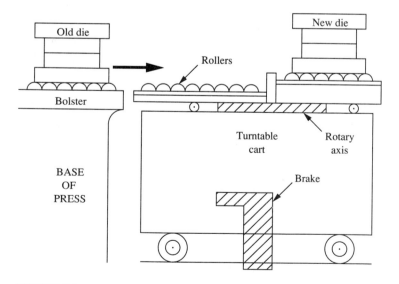

FIGURE 5-9
A die-exchange cart that holds both the old and new die on a rotary table, adding flexibility to the die exchange process.

into the machine. Any modification or repairs to tooling or dies should have been made in advance. In the internal setup, only removal and insertion operations should occur.

The exchange of the old die for the new die can be facilitated by having dies lined up ready for insertion when the press is stopped. To enhance the exchange, roller conveyors can be used for staging and changing the dies, as shown in Figure 5-8.

A turntable cart, based on the same principle as a lazy Susan, shown in Figure 5-9, adds to the versatility of the exchange. Alternatively, the table may hold four to

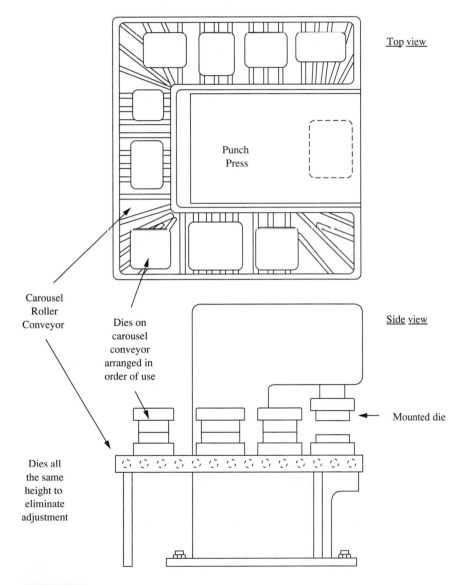

FIGURE 5-10
Punch press equipped with carousel conveyor for quick change of dies.

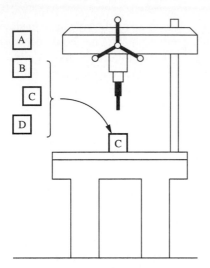

FIGURE 5-11
Typically, a machine that has four jobs with four different fixtures or jigs would need four different setups, each consisting of changing fixtures and aligning the cutting tool with the workpiece.

six small dies in designated locations, and the dies can slide in and out. The entire table is on wheels so that it can be rolled out of the way during a run.

The typical procedure is as follows (actual method to be standardized and practiced):

- Detach the old die from the die-holder plates of the machine.
- Push the table cart over to the press and secure the table next to the press with the brake or stopper.
- Push the old die onto the table.
- Rotate the table and unload the new die onto the bolster.
- Pull the table away from the press and attach the new die to the machine, using the same set of bolts.

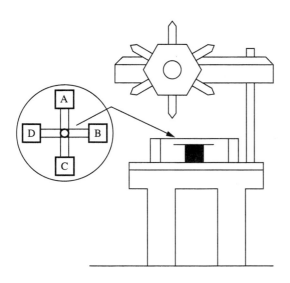

FIGURE 5-12
With redesign, the four fixtures are mounted on a turntable and quickly aligned and locked into position. A turret replaces the spindle and an automatic downfeeding device replaces the handwheel.

Figure 5-10 shows yet another approach to the rapid exchange of dies—a carousel conveyor. This solution is less expensive and has greater capacity (more dies) than the turntable cart but is a little less flexible. A cart services a group of presses and allows dies to be inserted in any order, as needed. A carousel conveyor is constructed around the press, and the dies are arranged on the carousel in the order of use. The operator will generally be responsible for getting the right dies in the right order for the day's production as the first order of business in the morning.

The same idea can be applied to metal-cutting machines, as shown in Figure 5-11. Suppose you have a vertical spindle machine that is doing four jobs with four different fixtures. Each setup consists of removing the old fixture, then installing and aligning the new fixture to the spindle of the machine. Through redesign, the four fixtures are mounted on a turntable, and each is automatically aligned to the spindle when rotated into position (see Figure 5-12). This is an example of OTED.

A higher-level solution might involve a turret mill with an oversized table. Remember that machines in cells process families of parts. Reducing the variety of parts coming to the machines permits you to modify the machine so that setup times can be eliminated altogether. Figure 5-13 shows how setup was eliminated for four milling parts by permanently locating four fixtures (for four different parts) on one table. This is an example of NOTED.

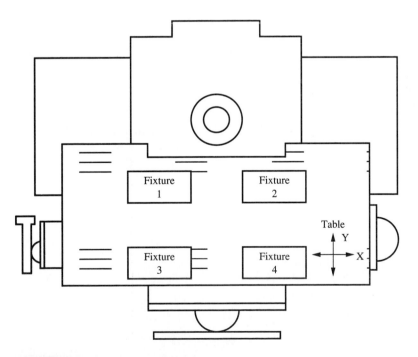

FIGURE 5-13
Top view of the table of a vertical-spindle milling machine with oversized table holding four fixtures.

CONVERTING INTERNAL SETUP
TO EXTERNAL SETUP

One of the most important concepts in reducing setup time is converting internal setup operations to external operations. Chief among the elements that can be readily shifted from internal to external are

Searching time	trying to find the correct die
	looking for the right tools, carts, fixtures, nuts, bolts, and so on
Waiting time	waiting for cranes, carts, skids, or instructions
Setting time	setting dies, tooling, fixtures, and so forth

If an activity can be safely performed when the machine is running, then it can be shifted to the external setup. An example might be preheating the metal molds in a die-casting machine (using the waste heat of the furnace from this machine) before inserting them into the machine. This means that trial shots, often needed to heat the dies to the right operational temperature, can be eliminated and the production run started sooner. Temperature sensors on the dies show the operator when they are at the right temperature for good molding.

The external operations for preparing the dies, tools, and materials should be made into routines and standardized. The internal die exchange process should also be standardized. Such standardized operations should be documented and posted on the wall for the workers to see. Have the workers practice the setups during slack times to master and improve the routine method. Make sure the best times are posted for all to see. Do not lose sight of safety. A defect-free exchange is the primary goal.

REDUCING OR ELIMINATING
INTERNAL ELEMENTS

Eliminating or reducing the internal elements in the setup time cycle will directly affect the setup time. In the exchange of dies, for example, the process of changing (adjusting) the shut height of the punch press often takes 50 percent to 70 percent

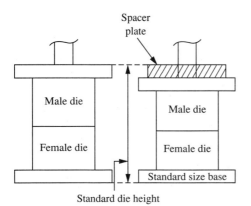

FIGURE 5-14

A spacer plate can be used to standardize die height, which eliminates the need to change the shut height of the press. (*Monden, 1983.*)

of the total internal setup time. This activity is considered essential to the proper setup of the machine and often requires highly skilled personnel. However, the entire activity can be eliminated by standardizing the shut height of the press. Liners and permanent spacers are added to the die set so that altering the stroke of the machine is never necessary (see Figure 5-14). If the sizes (and shapes) of all the dies are completely standardized during the tool design phase, setup times will be shortened tremendously. This, however, is an expensive long-range solution. Therefore, only a portion of the functions necessary for setups is standardized at the outset. The liner or spacer approach shown in Figure 5-14 for equalizing the die height is an economical approach to this problem.

INTERMEDIATE WORKHOLDER CONCEPT

If the base plate is made the same size regardless of the size of the die, then every die set can be located on the bolster plate in exactly the same position. This is an example of the intermediate workholder concept. To wit, workholding devices are designed so that they all appear the same to the machine tool. This usually requires the construction of intermediate jigs or fixture plates to which the jig or fixture is attached. The dies, jigs, or fixtures are all different sizes, but the plates are identical.

The cassette tape holder for your VCR is an example of an intermediate workholder. To the VCR, every cassette appears to be the same and can be quickly loaded and unloaded with one handling—one touch. From the outside, every tape appears to be the same, but on the inside every tape is different. If you think about the workholding devices in terms of the intermediate workholder concept, one-touch setups can be quickly achieved.

If the height of the base plates is standardized, the same fastening bolts, nuts, and tools can be used for all the dies (see Figure 5-15). Bolts are the most popular fastening devices in tool and die mounting. A bolt fastens at the final turning of the nut and loosens at the first turn. Therefore, only a single turning of the nut is really

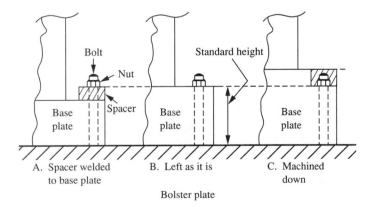

FIGURE 5-15
Standardizing the height of the base plate reduces the need for different length bolts and fastening tools. (*Monden, 1983.*)

needed. Quick-acting fasteners have been designed to take advantage of this fact (see Figure 5-16 for examples.)

To shorten the time required to remove a bolster plate or die base plate, the outside diameter of the nut was made a size smaller than the inside diameter of the hole, and the U-shaped washer was used. The plate could then be detached very quickly by loosening the nut with only one turn, pulling out the U-shaped washer, and then lifting out the plate without removing the nut.

The bolt holes of the plate can be altered to a pear shape and the U-shaped washer used again. As a result, when the nut is loosened by only one turn and the U-shaped washer pulled out, the plate can be rotated or slid and then lifted off. The

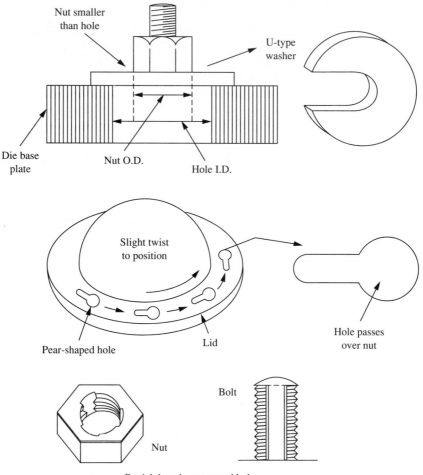

FIGURE 5-16
Three quick-acting fasteners that reduce internal setup time: (1) U-shaped washer, (2) pear-shaped bolt holes, (3) nut and bolt with corresponding portions of each machined off so that both elements have partial threads. (*Shingo, 1981.*)

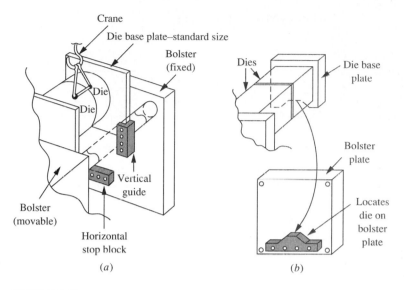

(a)   (b)

FIGURE 5-17
(a) Cassette system can be used to quickly locate the die sets, using guide blocks and stop block; (b) Die location device with truncated location guide. (*Shingo, 1981.*)

nut can pass through the bigger part of the pear-shaped hole without being detached from the bolt.

Three portions of the outside of the bolt can be machined off along with corresponding portions of the screw thread of the nut. Then, when the nut is pushed down by matching the screw portions of the nut to that of the bolt, the nut can be tightened with a partial turn. This method is not recommended for heavy loads or in vibration environments.

The intermediate workholder concept can be extended to a cassette system that will allow very rapid setups by providing automatic die location. An example is shown in Figure 5-17. The size of the die base plates must be standardized to fit into the guide blocks. Figure 5-17 also illustrates a location device for die installation using a partial V-shaped element. This device locates the die-holder plate in two directions without the need to standardize the size of the base plate. Such devices can be used in presses to locate dies on the bolster plate.

POWER CLAMPS

Although hydraulically operated clamps have been in use for many years, new devices and improved designs have increased their usefulness and capabilities (see Figure 5-18). While manual clamping methods may still provide a low-cost alternative, pneumatic and hydraulic power-clamping devices increase the potential of reducing internal time. New models offer improved seals and cylinder bore finishes, extended guide plungers with positive stroke steps, leak-free fittings, and compact sizes that facilitate rapid clamping in setups. These developments allow fluid operating pressures to be increased from about 2,000 psi (13,800 kPa) to over 7,500 psi (51,700 kPa). This pressure increase permits smaller and more powerful clamps to be used.

SPRING/ HYDRAULIC CLAMPS

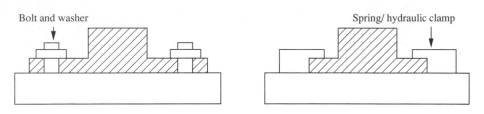

FIGURE 5-18
Spring-loaded, hydraulic, or pneumatic clamps for holding dies or fixtures in position can further reduce internal setup time.

ADVANTAGES OF POWER CLAMPING

Power clamping has four basic advantages over manual clamping:

1. Reduction of internal setup time. Dies can be loaded and unloaded in a fraction of the time needed with manual clamping. Obviously, the more clamping points there are, the greater the advantage. A single switch or lever can activate a number of clamps either simultaneously or automatically in some definite sequence.

2. Repeatability (quality). The clamping force is constant from operator to operator, shift to shift, and setup to setup. Operators may be bright and alert in the morning, but tend to tire in the afternoon. This feature is important as the number of die exchanges increases (i.e., as the lot size decreases).

3. Maintainability. Constant hydraulic/pneumatic pressure on the clamping device helps maintain secure gripping of the device despite vibrations and impact.

4. Safety. Operator safety is enhanced because (a) fatigue is significantly reduced and (b) clamps that must fit into limited-clearance zones can be remotely activated.

Hydraulic systems have several advantages. They are small and compact; leaks are visible; pressures are conveniently adjustable, as with air; and they are self-lubricating. But they also have some limitations. They require more expensive pressurization and plumbing as well as rigid metal tubing or relatively expensive high-pressure hoses; when leaks occur, they are messy; the relative high pressures make some people uneasy.

Pneumatic (air) clamps are also available for rapid clamping. They are simpler to apply than hydraulics; supply and adjustment are convenient; they are clean; and leaks are innocuous, other than hissing noise. On the other hand, shop air systems are typically in the 60–120 psi range versus 2,000–3,000 psi for hydraulic systems. Consequently, for a given clamping force, pneumatic cylinders must be larger, with the size ratio inversely proportional to the square root of the relative pressures. For example, with air at 100 psi and oil at 2,000 psi, the minimum size ratio would be $\sqrt{100}$ to $\sqrt{2,000}$ or 1 to 4.47 using standard diameter cylinders.

As far as safety is concerned, using oil at 3,000 psi (compared to air, at say 100 psi) is really not as risky as it might first appear. Air used at 3,000 psi is compressed by a factor of 200 (3,000 ÷ psi atmospheric pressure). An accidental line rupture would produce an explosion as the air reverts to atmospheric pressure. By contrast, oil is relatively incompressible. At 3,000 psi, the volumetric compression is only 1.5 percent. For a hydraulic clamping system of 15 cubic inches, that 1.5 percent would come to only $\frac{1}{4}$ cubic inch volume change. A line rupture would produce an oil shower—but that would be the worst of it.

APPLYING METHODS ANALYSIS, STANDARDIZING, AND PRACTICING SETUPS

One of the least expensive ways to improve setup times is by applying methods analysis to examine in detail the methods of the internal setup. Methods analysis techniques are the subject of many basic texts and handbooks. The secret is to teach these basic methods to all the operators so that everyone is looking for ways to reduce setup time and improve the process. This is part of making the operator multifunctional—able to do many things other than "just run the machine and make parts."

A large punch press or large molding machine will have many attachment positions on its left and right sides as well as on its front and back. The setup actions for such a machine can take one worker a long time. However, methods analysis can lead to the development of parallel operations for two persons, eliminating wasteful movement and reducing internal setup time. Even though the total labor hours for the setup do not change, the effective operating hours of the machine increase. If a setup time of one hour were reduced to ten minutes, the second worker would be needed for only ten minutes during the internal exchange. Setup specialists perform many of the external setup operations and assist the machine operators in setup actions.

The dies, tooling, fixtures, part design, part specification, and methods are standardized. Once a standardized setup method has been achieved, it must be documented by the workers. This means that workers are asked to write down, step by step, the setup procedure for each machine (within a cell). This write-up is compared to the standard to see if the worker is doing what should be done. Extra and missing steps will become apparent. Here's a revolutionary idea: have the setup teams practice setups during slack periods of the working day to further reduce the internal setup time. The methods analysis will eliminate unnecessary movements and reduce manual effort, extraneous walking, and so forth.

ELIMINATING ADJUSTMENTS

Eliminating adjustments from the setup operation is a critical step in reducing internal time. The use of spacers on die sets in a die setup eliminates the need for adjusting the shut height on a press. The shut height is never changed for this family of dies. However, situations always occur that require the machine to be *reset*. Even then, the number of actual setting positions needed on most machines or operations is usually quite limited, especially in cells. *Setting is an activity that should be considered independently of adjustment.* This can be accomplished by instrumenting the machine as necessary to permit the re-establishment of initial (or previous) setup conditions

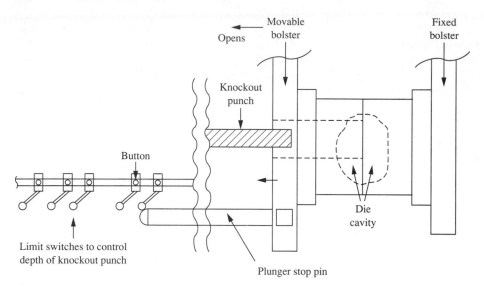

FIGURE 5-19
Installing limit switches at all required positions eliminates knockout-stroke adjustments. (*Shingo, 1981.*)

without any trial and error. The use of digital readouts or limit switches, for example, expedite resetting the machine without adjustment or fine tuning. The setup conditions should be determined, recorded, and marked so they can be readily reproduced time after time. A record of speed, feed, and depth of cut should be posted along with data on temperature, pressure, and the like. Step-function settings, like the push buttons on a car radio, can eliminate adjustment.

Molding machines typically require a different stroke for the knockout punch, depending on the size of the die being used. The stroke of the machine is halted with a limit switch. To find exactly the right stroke position, an adjustment (movement of the limit switch) is always necessary. A molding machine put into a cell environment requires only five positions for the limit switch. Instead of the one limit switch, five limit switches can be installed, one in each of the five required positions. A simple electric circuit is rigged to send electric current only to the limit switch that needs to be activated. As a result, the need to adjust limit switch position is eliminated (see Figure 5-19). The mechanism is left alone, and only a function switch is changed to accomplish the change in setting. No adjustment of the limit switches is ever needed because they are not moved.

In the machining cell for shafts, suppose four different lengths of shaft are made on the same lathe. Each shaft must have a hole drilled in it for a locking screw. A stopper is used to automatically control the depth of the hole being drilled. Previously, the position of the stopper on the machine had to be changed and adjusted for each different shaft. To eliminate this adjustment, a rotary stopper is used that has four different thicknesses of stoppers. The stopper is properly rotated to correspond to the length of shaft during changeover. (See Figure 5-20 for a schematic of the rotary stopper.)

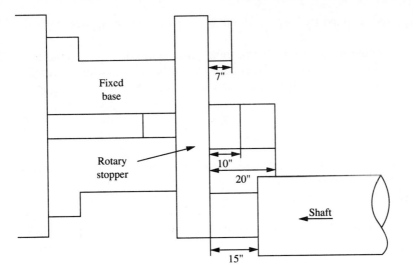

FIGURE 5-20
A rotary stopper can be used in lathe operations to provide four stopping positions without the need for adjustment.

Machine tool manufacturers do not know the applications of their products in a particular company, so they provide machines with continuously variable positional settings. Machines placed in cells, however, have limited applications, and the setting process can be converted to steps, often through the use of templates or digital read-outs, to accomplish setting without adjustment (see Figure 5-21). Boring machines are often equipped with stops to produce the correct depth of cuts on parts. A template can be devised to quickly position the stops for part A and relocate the stops for part B.

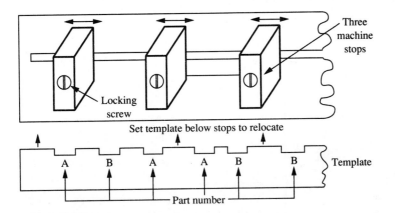

FIGURE 5-21
A template can be used on a boring machine to speed up the relocation of the machine stops. The template is notched out to insure proper location by part number.

This eliminates the "cut and try" aspect of the first B part after changeover from the A parts.

When the setting must be done with higher precision, eliminating adjustment may be difficult unless a gage is used. This gage should be built in with a magnified scale for quick, easy reading. Digital readout scales that show the exact value are very helpful.

ABOLISHING THE SETUP ITSELF

The final approach to RETAD is to abolish setup entirely or have it done automatically, but this is usually an expensive solution. Some ways to abolish setup have already been suggested, but here are two additional approaches that can eliminate setup:

1. Redesign the product so it is uniform and uses the same part in various products.
2. Produce the various parts at the same time. This can be achieved by two methods:
   a. In the first method, the parts are processed in parallel using less expensive, slower machines. For example, an arbor press instead of a large punch press is placed in a welding cell to provide a simple bending function. Each worker handles a small arbor press as well as other welding jobs in the cell. This press has a small motor and can perform the same function as a heavy punch press. If several presses of this kind are available, they can be used in parallel and dedicated to producing one type of part at low cost. Multiple versions can be made available to produce a limited variety of parts.
   b. The second method uses the "set-of-parts" system. For example, in the single die of the punch press, two different shapes of parts A and B are produced as a set, punched at the same time, then separated. No changeover is ever done. This requires that parts A and B be needed in the same quantities. Honda does this with doors, producing the front left and right doors simultaneously. Another example of this idea is shown for plastic forming in Figure 5-22.

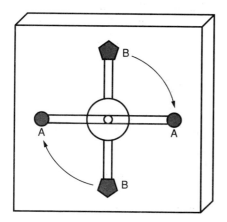

FIGURE 5-22
A mold with cavities for two types of knobs, A and B, which need two different kinds of resin and are needed in different quantities. Passageway now set to make A knobs. (*Shingo, 1981.*)

On a plastic-forming machine, different kinds of plastic resin (for type A and type B knobs for different types of television sets) are needed. As shown in Figure 5-22, the mold inlets for type A and B molds are at right angles to each other. When the mold is rotated 90 degrees, the different plastic resins are delivered to the required cavities. Thus, type A or type B knobs can be produced without attaching or detaching the mold. This system does not require both parts to be made in the same quantities.

For additional discussion and examples on eliminating setup times, refer to the books on group technology that show the elimination of setup as a natural outgrowth of the formation of part families.

SUMMARY

The reduction or elimination of setup time is a critical step in converting any system to an IMPS. This effort is usually one of the first that a company will be able to undertake. The results are immediate and obvious, but this does not mean that the setup reduction program is a short-term project.

Table 5-1 shows the results of a setup reduction program at the JKC company, where it took four years to reduce setup time to under 100 seconds for 62 percent of the setups. Getting to this level of setup time reduction will typically come in phases. The first phase will require little capital expenditure, and solutions can be achieved in a relatively short time. Reductions of 20 percent to 30 percent are typical. No analysis other than videotaping is required.

The second phase involves operations analysis; minor modification to dies, tools, fixtures, machines, and procedures; and some modest expenditures. Again, benefits of 30 percent to 50 percent can be achieved in a relatively short time.

The third phase can involve methods analysis, design changes, standardization of all dies, tools, parts, machines, operations, and procedures. Large capital expenditures may be required, and the complete conversion to rapid setups may take years to achieve. Benefits of 10 percent to 40 percent may be expected.

TABLE 5-1
Setup reduction results at JKC

Setup time	1976	1977	1980
60 minutes	30%	0	0
30–60 minutes	19%	0	0
20–30 minutes	26%	10%	3%
10–20 minutes	20%	12%	7%
5–10 minutes	5%	20%	12%
100 seconds–5 minutes	0	17%	16%
100 seconds	0	41%	62%

Source: (Wantuck, 1983)

CHAPTER

6

INTEGRATED QUALITY CONTROL

The cost of quality is the expense of doing things wrong.

INTRODUCTION

The real secret is to *inspect* (i.e., measure something about a product or process) to prevent a defect from occurring in the first place. The cost of controlling quality is the expense of finding and reworking defective products. Also, to achieve a high quality level economically, a product must be designed to be manufactured without defects. Then manufacturing systems must be designed to achieve superior quality at the least cost in a flexible way. The latter usually means that the company has designed and built its own manufacturing equipment and understands that linked-cell manufacturing systems are a key to technological competitiveness.

The United States is currently in serious trouble with respect to product quality. Before World War II, the quality of Japanese products was poor—they were difficult to sell, even at extremely low prices. After World War II, the United States, one of the few countries with manufacturing facilities undamaged by the war, prospered, fueled by postwar economy. It was secure in the position of world leader in productivity and quality. As part of the Marshall plan, a National Productivity Center was developed in Japan. Experts in statistical quality control, like Deming and Juran, went to Japan and aided Japanese industry by teaching statistical quality control (SQC) methods.

The Japanese took the advice of these men seriously. Believing that everyone in the United States practiced SQC, they not only acted on the advice, but elaborated and improved it. They taught SQC methods to their engineers and quality control departments. They expanded the quality training program to include managers and supervisors at all organizational levels and in all company departments. The seeds for total quality management programs were being sown. They also did something that American companies never thought of doing. They educated the production workers in process quality control fundamentals and techniques. The people who ran the processes learned how to control the quality of the processes! Japanese managers, production workers, and engineers became the best-trained people in the world in quality control. But the training encompassed all departments, not just manufacturing. Improvements were made in all functions, including product design and field service. Because the training was carried on at all levels, Japanese managers were able to utilize the experience of the entire company, including the work force.

While SQC methods are used by the majority of U.S. companies, the Japanese have developed many new methods of quality improvement and control. These methods depend less on sampling, statistics, and probabilistic approaches and are therefore more reliable.

This chapter will briefly discuss the traditional methods of statistical process control and then introduce some of the more popular modern thinking.

The integration of the control of quality into the manufacturing system begins with giving workers the responsibility and authority to make good products. This is the key to attacking the source of the defects in components. The fundamental idea is worth repeating: *Inspect to prevent the defect from occurring rather than to find the defect after it has been made.* Putting this simple idea into practice, however, is not so simple. It requires that the manufacturing system be changed to accommodate the techniques and methodology of integrated quality control, IQC.

STATISTICAL QUALITY CONTROL

Statistical quality control began at the Bell Telephone Laboratories in the 1920s. Since that time, it has become very popular throughout the world, being used by a multitude of industries. There is a variety of statistical quality control tools. The two most popular techniques are acceptance sampling and control charts. Both these methods use inductive statistics, which means that a small amount of data (a sample) is used to draw conclusions about a much larger, if not infinite, amount of data. This large amount of data is often called the *parent population*. The decisions based on the sample cannot be stated with absolute certainty. Therefore, uncertainties are encountered, calling for the mathematics of uncertainty—probability and statistics.

ACCEPTANCE SAMPLING

The purpose of sampling is to draw a conclusion about a process by examining only a fraction of it. Sampling inspection (looking at some) is needed when it is difficult, costly, or impossible to measure an entire population. For example, the expense involved in observing all the data may be prohibitive, the required inspection process may destroy the product, or all the product may have yet to be manufactured.

Sampling inspection requires the determination of the maximum percentage defective that can be considered satisfactory. That is, by definition, some level of defectives must be accepted. This percentage defective is called the *acceptable quality level (AQL)*. After determining how many samples need to be taken to achieve this level of acceptance (or rejection), sampling inspection is carried out. Samples should offer a true, unbiased representation of the parent population, but this depends on many factors, such as the size of the sample and the way it was collected. However, is difficult to obtain a truly unbiased sample of a population. For example, if the inspectors always draw parts from the top of each box of parts, the operators quickly learn to put the best parts on top so that their best work is inspected and the entire lot is accepted. But it is the AQL concept of satisfactory defects that creates the most problems with sampling inspection. By the definition of the AQL, a certain level of defectives can be found acceptable. Today, in our world of high-quality competitiveness, defectives are not acceptable in any number.

CONTROL CHARTS

Control charts are used to track the mean and variability of a process by plotting selected sample statistics. When a process produces a product, no two products are exactly alike because of variations in the manufacturing processes, in the materials, and in operator performance. Variability, whether large or small, is always present, and many sources can contribute to it. In 1924, W. A. Shewhart of Bell Telephone Laboratories developed statistical charts for process control. A good process will be repeatable: that is, it will make parts within the specifications or tolerances prescribed by the design engineer, who specifies the nominal size. Recognizing that no two products are identical, the designer applies a tolerance to the desired size. The process(es) selected should produce all the parts within the desired tolerance range.

By traditional SQC thinking, the factors that contribute to product variation can be classified as either inherent (random or chance) causes or assignable causes. *Chance causes* are considered a natural, consistent part of the process, difficult to isolate or eliminate or too small to worry about. Some examples are variations in material chemistry or properties, measurement errors, machine vibrations, and variations in human performance. *Assignable causes* are events that produce detectable changes in the accuracy or the precision of the process. These changes are usually large in magnitude and controllable. Examples of assignable causes are tool wear, cutting tool chatter, temperature fluctuations, and pressure variations. When only chance causes are present, the process is considered to be under control. However, when assignable causes occur, the process must be analyzed to determine the source of the assignable error, the problem eliminated, and the process controlled.

Shewhart realized that it should be possible to determine when variations in product quality are the result of random chance causes or due to a major process change, an assignable cause. He developed control charts for this purpose. There are several different types of control charts, but only the charts for variable data will be discussed here. The $\overline{X}$ chart monitors the process mean, and the R chart (or σ chart) monitors the process variability. Control limits for both charts are usually set at three standard deviations above and below the process average. An example of $\overline{X}$ and R charts (the most common types of control charts) is shown in Figure 6-1. In these charts, sam-

Variables control chart $\bar{X}$ and R
Averages and ranges

Part/asm. name	Retainer		Operation	Bend clip		Specification	.50 - .90 mm		Chart no.	1
Part no.	1234567		Department	105		Gage	Depth gage micrometer		Unit of measure	mm
Parameter	Gap, Dim. "A"		Machine	030		Sample size frequency	5/2 Hours		Zero equals	N/A

Date	6/8				6/9				6/10				6/11				6/12				6/15				6/16
Time of day	8	10	12	2	8	10	12	2	8	10	12	2	8	10	12	2	8	10	12	2	8	10	12	2	8
Operator																									
Sample Measurement / Value of X — 1	.65	.75	.75	.60	.70	.60	.75	.60	.65	.60	.75	.80	.80	.70	.80	.65	.80	.60	.75	.65	.60	.60	.80	.60	.65
2	.70	.85	.80	.70	.75	.70	.80	.70	.80	.70	.75	.75	.75	.75	.85	.70	.80	.75	.65	.65	.55	.65	.65	.60	.65
3	.65	.75	.80	.70	.85	.75	.65	.80	.85	.60	.85	.90	.65	.70	.80	.80	.80	.60	.85	.60	.65	.65	.65	.65	.60
4	.65	.85	.70	.75	.80	.85	.75	.75	.75	.65	.65	.50	.65	.70	.75	.80	.75	.70	.70	.60	.85	.75	.65	.70	.70
5	.85	.65	.75	.65	.65	.75	.70	.75	.85	.80	.75	.85	.75	.70	.90	.80	.65	.70	.55	.60	.65	.80	.75	.65	.70
Sum	3.50	3.85	3.80	3.40	3.75	3.65	3.65	3.60	3.90	3.35	3.75	3.80	3.60	3.55	4.10	3.75	3.80	3.35	3.50	3.10	3.30	3.45	3.50	3.20	3.30
Average $\bar{X}$	.70	.77	.76	.68	.75	.73	.73	.72	.78	.67	.75	.76	.72	.71	.82	.75	.76	.67	.70	.62	.66	.69	.70	.64	.66
Range R	.20	.20	.10	.15	.20	.25	.15	.20	.20	.20	.20	.40	.20	.05	.15	.15	.15	.15	.20	.05	.30	.20	.15	.10	.10

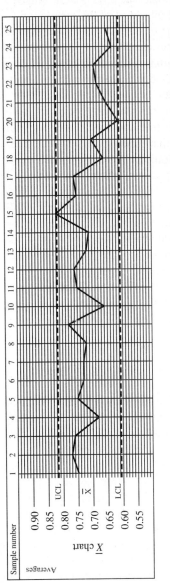

$\bar{X}$ chart — Averages

Sample number: 1 – 25
Vertical scale: 0.90, 0.85 (UCL), 0.80 ($\bar{\bar{X}}$), 0.75, 0.70, 0.65 (LCL), 0.60, 0.55

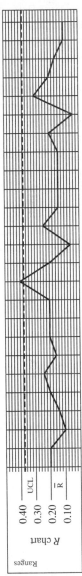

R chart — Ranges

Vertical scale: 0.40 (UCL), 0.30, 0.20 ($\bar{R}$), 0.10

FIGURE 6-1
Example of $\bar{X}$ and R charts.

119

ple statistics ($\overline{X}$ and R values) are plotted. Most values will fall within the control limits, indicating that a normal condition prevails. Shewhart based his charts on the knowledge that sample statistics (data) will be normally distributed about their own mean regardless of the shape of the population from which the samples were drawn. If a point (the average of the sample measurements) does fall outside the control limits, it is probably due to an assignable cause. Another indication of an assignable cause is, for example, a run of seven points up or down. A run of eight points all above or below the central line is also an unlikely event, indicating that something about the process has changed.

The historical function of control charts has been to control the accuracy (the aim), the precision (the variation), and the stability (the drift) of a process after all variability except that produced by chance causes has been removed. However, the charts have not traditionally been operated by the people who run the processes (the users of the manufacturing system). Rather, the charts have been kept by people in the quality control departments. Inspectors were sent to the factory floor to gather sample data. The inspector's job became that of the quality enforcer or process controller. The production worker viewed the job as meeting production rate standards, regardless of quality. If the product was bad, so what? It could be reworked or scrapped. Over the years, an adversarial relationship developed between manufacturing and quality control.

Let's examine the decision-making situation a bit further. As shown in Figure 6-2, deciding about all (the parent population), based on looking at some, can result in two kinds of errors (as well as two correct decisions):

Type I or α error   Viewing the process as bad, when it is not making defects.

Type II or β error   Viewing the process as good, when it is making defects.

The standard control chart sets its control limits at 3σ (three standard deviations). This means that the probability of making a Type I error is very remote while the probability of making a Type II error is usually quite large. Why is this so? Psychologically speaking, when the person who makes decisions about the quality of a process is not the same as the person who runs the process, the decision maker will set the probabilities of the errors (which represent mistakes in decision making) so as not to be embarrassed. If the sample indicates that the process is bad, the decision maker (DM) has to take action, maybe even recommend stopping the process. If no problems are found, the DM looks bad in the eyes of those who work in the manufacturing system. On the other hand, a Type II error requires no action by the DM and therefore no blame is usually assigned. The *do nothing* decision shifts the blame for making the defects to the production worker. The external customer suffers because defects are permitted to leave the process.

Within manufacturing cells, the workers are given the tools to control the quality of the processes. SPC can be used to regulate the process. However, while some methods of inductive statistics do integrate the worker into the quality control system, they do not guarantee zero defects or even extremely low defect rates.

The sample suggested to
the DM that

	The process had not changed	The process had changed
The truth was that the process had not changed.	DM takes no actions as nothing is wrong.	DM Takes action, but nothing can be found to be wrong with the process; Type I– α error, DM embarrassed.
The truth was that the process had changed.	DM takes no action, but process making more defects Type II– β error.	DM takes action, finds problem with process. DM Looks good!

FIGURE 6-2
Sampling results in two kinds of errors in decision making. Decision maker = DM.

A common misconception about control charts is that they indicate what went wrong in a process. Control charts should be used as detection devices, to indicate *when* something went wrong, but not what went wrong. If control charts are not used correctly, they are nothing but a waste of time. For example, some companies actually take all the data and then wait until the end of the shift to plot the points! By this time, it is too late to react to trends and out-of-control points.

INTEGRATED QUALITY CONTROL (IQC)

The integrated approach to quality is sometimes called *total quality control (TQC)*. Some companies have coined the term *company-wide quality control (CWQC)* because all departments in the company participate in QC, as do all types of employees. The idea is that if a company takes care of the quality, profit will take care of itself. A total quality commitment in all production resources, at all levels of management, is the requirement for IQC. Every person must have a complete understanding of quality control, the methods used to obtain it, and the benefits. Large central quality control departments are not the answer. Actual control must be integrated into the manufacturing-system. IQC is not a series of specialized techniques, but part of a manufacturing-based strategy that incorporates quality control at all levels of an organization. Line personnel must be given the necessary training to carry out quality control functions. Eventually, IQC is extended to include all the vendors, suppliers, and subcontractors in order to improve the quality of supplies and materials (see Chapter 10).

QUALITY REDEFINED[1]

It has to be cheaper to do the job right the first time. As Phil Crosby (1979) would say, quality is free, but it is not a gift. The cost of quality is the expense of doing things wrong or doing the wrong thing, like allowing defects to occur. These defects must be found and corrected, and this costs money.

Quality is the conformance to specifications or requirements. This means that the standards of conformance must be precisely stated. Failure to meet these standards of conformance costs a company money. The fastest and surest path to low-cost operations is to make the product right the first time, thereby eliminating rework and scrap. The figures on the amount of rework done in a typical factory are scary and often range as high as 40 percent, meaning that 40 percent of what the company makes requires some rework. Some authors refer to this as the "hidden factory," meaning the "rework" factory within the factory.

IQC IN MANUFACTURING CELLS

IQC goes hand-in-hand with the cellular manufacturing systems concepts. The worker(s) control the quality in the cell. The rule is *make one—check one—pass (or move) one on*. Between the processes in the cell, devices can be added to assist the worker in checking the part, thus ensuring that defective products do not get passed on. The checking can be manual or automatic. Automatic checking forms the basis for *autonomation*. This is a very important concept, though the word is often confused with *automation*. Autonomation refers to the *autonomous control of both defects and quantities*. For manned (and unmanned) cellular systems, this means that the individual processes or devices between the processes are equipped with sensors to detect

1. When sufficient product has been made (don't overproduce)
2. When something has gone wrong with the process
3. When something is changing that will eventually lead to failure in meeting product specifications (defect prevention)

Figure 6-3 shows the relationship between autonomation and IMPS. Physically, sensors and devices are incorporated into the machines and decouplers to automatically check the critical aspects of the parts at each stage of the process. Causes of defects are investigated immediately, and corrective action is implemented.

IQC CONCEPTS

Within the organization of the company, quality must be the responsibility of manufacturing. Employee involvement is absolutely necessary. This means that the primary responsibility for quality is assigned to the people who make the product. These work-

---

[1]G. Taguchi (1986) has provided yet another definition of quality—the deviation from target.

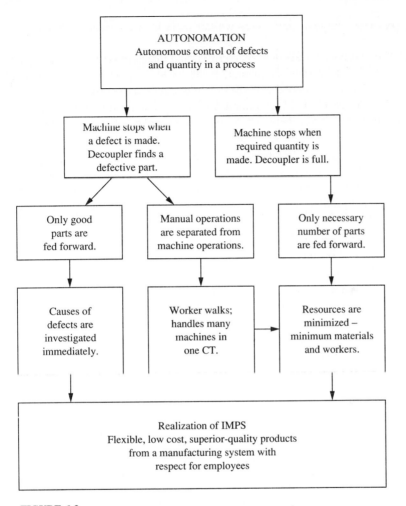

FIGURE 6-3
How IMPS is realized by autonomation.

ers must develop the habits of improvement and the desire for perfection. (They must strive for zero defects.) This requires that the desire to strive continually for perfection in quality be instilled in the workers. Remember, quality depends on the efforts of everyone, from sales through design and purchasing, manufacturing, shipping, and so forth. Changing the design of the manufacturing system is critical to changing the attitude of the workers. The effects of defective products on the L-CMS cannot be ignored. Quality comes ahead of output rates.

BASIC PRINCIPLES OF IQC

1. Control the process to prevent defects rather than inspect after the fact to find defects. The Japanese term for defect prevention is *pokayoke*. At every stage, the product must be checked; thus every worker must be an inspector. Quality is controlled at the source.

Production workers correct their own errors, and there are no separate rework lines. This requires small lots and immediate feedback to the place where the problem occurred. This does not necessarily mean that workers inspect their own work. The next worker can check the work pulled from the previous worker, or an automatic inspection device placed between the workers can check the quality characteristics. (This is one form of autonomation using decouplers—see Chapter 11).

2. Make the quality easy to see. Display boards and highly visible charts are placed on the plant floor. The boards detail the quality factors being measured, the state of recent performance, current quality improvement projects, recent award winners for quality improvement, and so forth. Quality and its characteristics must be clearly and simply defined.

3. Insist on compliance to the quality standard. Conformance to the quality standards must come first, ahead of output.

4. Give workers the authority to stop the process when something goes wrong. Mechanized processes can have devices to do this automatically (in-process inspection). More refined systems may have the ability to adjust or modify the process to correct for the problem. The machine must be programmable. (Equipping the machine or process to prevent the defect from occurring is called *pokayoke*.)

5. For the inspection of finished goods, make it a rule to check 100 percent of the attributes.

6. Make your modus operandi a constant succession of projects for quality improvement in every work area. Continuous improvement should be the routine way of life. This can be the work of quality circle groups.

7. Eliminate incoming inspection. The objective is to move toward no inspection of incoming goods. This requires the buyer to work closely with one vendor, to the exclusion of all other vendors. Ultimately, the vendor should have an IMPS and be an extension of your IMPS, becoming tightly associated with the primary company. Vendor programs are discussed more fully in Chapter 10.

8. Eliminate setup time. The drive toward small lots requires the elimination of setup time, which in turn makes it economical to reduce lot size. The concepts of EOQ and EPQ are limiting. The optimum lot size is one. This is readily achievable within cells. Obviously, the smaller the lot, the faster the feedback on quality. In addition, it is easier to spot problems. The control of the inventory level is discussed in more detail in Chapter 9.

9. Keep the workplace clean. Good housekeeping is fundamental and absolutely necessary in order for a plant to improve quality and foster better work habits. Housekeeping is the responsibility of everyone, from plant manager to foremen and workers. Housekeeping is needed to improve and maintain safety in a dangerous environment and to maintain pride and company morale. Nobody really wants to work in a dirty place. A dirty workplace is obviously a deterrent to superior-quality performance in electronics fabrication, painting, and finishing areas, but other areas of the plant must also be well maintained (see Chapter 7).

TECHNIQUES FOR IQC

The following are some common techniques for IQC. In a pull system quality problems can be exposed through the deliberate removal of workers and inventory. Inventory is used as a quality control device. That is, inventory is an independent control variable rather than a dependent variable.

Quality circles are used to find (and sometimes to solve) the problems. Widely implemented in the United States, quality circles are a technique for involving people and directing their attention to the problems in the workplace.

Fishbone diagrams, also called Ishikawa charts after their developer, are used with control charts to determine what caused the quality problem.

The machines are equipped with devices that automatically check for defects, excess production, or machine breakdowns. This is called autonomation. More sophisticated systems can have sensory devices that check features or parameters that cause or relate to defects. Ultimately, every part is checked before it is finished.

Inspecting the first and last item of a lot is called $N = 2$ sampling. If these items are good, then everything between is assumed to be good. The process is assumed to have remained stable. In reality, the process has been proven to be stable through a process capability study. Off-line Taguchi methods can be used for this. Some additional comments on these techniques is warranted.

MAKING QUALITY EVIDENT

Visual displays on quality should be placed throughout manufacturing facilities to make quality evident. These displays tell workers, managers, customers, and outside visitors what quality factors are being measured, what the current quality improvement projects are, and who has won awards for quality. Examples of visible quality are signs showing quality improvements, framed quality awards presented to or by the company, and displays of high-precision measuring equipment.

These displays have several benefits. In IMPS, customers often visit your plant to inspect your processes. They want to see measurable standards of quality. Highly visible indicators of quality such as control charts and displays should be posted in every department. Everyone is informed on current quality goals and the progress being made. Displays and quality awards are also an effective way to show the work force that the company is serious about quality.

QUALITY CIRCLES

A number of popular programs are built upon the concept of participative management, such as quality circles, improvement teams, and task groups. These programs have been very successful in many companies, but have failed miserably in others. The difference is often due to the way management implemented the program. Programs must be integrated and managed within the context of an IMPS strategy. For example, asking an employee for a suggestion that management does not use or cannot explain why it does not use, defeats a suggestion system. Management must learn to trust the employees' ideas and decisions and move the decision making to the factory floor.

TABLE 6-1
Typical problems
tackled by quality circles

Product quality
Paperwork
Hardware
Communications
Service
Processes and methods
Scrap reduction
Productivity
Cost reduction
Production delays

The quality circle movement started in Japan in 1962 and grew rapidly. Quality circles are a popular form of participative management. However, other countries often have problems duplicating the QC circle movement. Perhaps it is because quality circles are the last brick in the IQC wall, and other countries have not taken the necessary preparatory steps.

A quality circle is usually a group of employees within the same department. Meetings are held to work on problems (see Table 6-1). Figure 6-4 shows the organizational structure of a typical quality circle, composed of members, a leader, a facilitator, and a steering committee.

Quality circles usually have the following main objectives. They provide all workers with a chance to demonstrate their ideas; raise employee morale; and encourage and develop their knowledge of quality control techniques, problems, and problem-solving methods. They also unify company-wide QC activities, clarify managerial policies, and develop leadership and supervisory capabilities (see Table 6-2).

Quality circles have been implemented in U.S. companies with limited success when they are not part of an IMPS strategy. It is possible for quality circles to work in the United States, but they must be encouraged and supported by management. Everyone must be taught the importance and benefits of integrated quality control.

TABLE 6-2
Quality circle objectives

1. Develop workers' skills and knowledge.
2. Introduce a team effort among workers, supervisors, and managers.
3. Unlock the creativity inherent in workers.
4. Improve quality consciousness.
5. Create a more harmonious work force leading to higher morale.
6. Encourage commitment and contribution to corporate goals of better quality and higher productivity.
7. Encourage leadership qualities in circle leaders.
8. Improve communications and extend recognition.

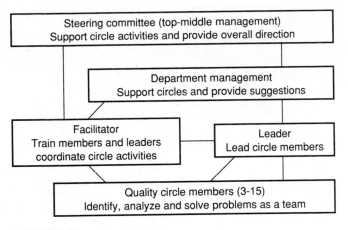

FIGURE 6-4
Structure of a quality circle organization.

CAUSE-AND-EFFECT DIAGRAMS

One of the most effective methods for improving quality is the cause-and-effect diagram, also known as a fishbone diagram because of its structure. On the main line is a quality characteristic that is to be improved or the quality problem being investigated. Fishbone lines are drawn from the main line. These lines organize the main factors that could have caused the problem (see Figure 6-5). Branching from each of these factors are even more detailed factors. Everyone taking part in making a diagram gains new knowledge of the process. When a diagram serves as a focus for the discussion, everyone knows the topic, and the conversation does not stray. The diagram is often structured around four branches: the machine tools (or processes), the operators (workers), the method, and the material being processed. Another version of the diagram is called the CEDAC, the cause-and-effect diagram with the addition of cards. The effect is often tracked with a control chart (see Figure 6-6). The possible causes of the defect or problem are written on 3" x 5" cards and inserted in slots in the charts.

POKAYOKE

Many companies have developed an extensive QC program based on having many inspections. However, all inspections can do is find defects, not prevent them. Adding more inspectors and inspections merely uncovers more defects, but does not prevent them. Clearly, the least costly system is one that produces no defects. But is this possible? Yes, it can be accomplished through two methods—pokayoke and source inspection.

Many people do not believe that the goal of zero defects is possible to reach, but many companies have achieved zero defects for a length of time or have reduced their defect level to virtually zero using pokayokes and source inspection.

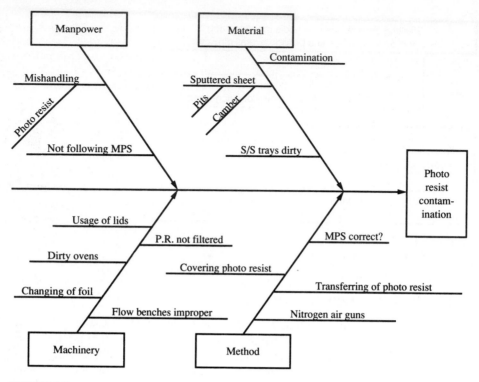

FIGURE 6-5
Example of a fishbone diagram.

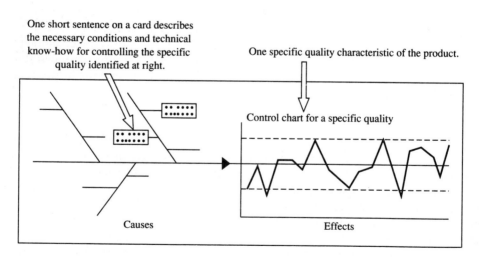

FIGURE 6-6
Basic structure of CEDAC.

Pokayoke is a Japanese word for defect prevention. Pokayoke devices and procedures are often devised mainly for preserving the safety of operations. The idea is to develop a method, mechanism, or device that will prevent the defect from occurring rather than to find the defect after it has occurred. Pokayokes can be attached to machines to automatically check the products or parts in a process. Pokayokes differ from source inspections in that they are usually attributes inspections. The production of a bad part is prevented by the device. Some devices may automatically shut down a machine if a defect is produced, preventing the production of an additional defective part. The pokayoke system uses 100 percent inspection to guard against unavoidable human error. Figure 6-7 illustrates a pokayoke device. This device ensures that the workers remember to apply labels to the products, thus preventing defective products.

Such devices work very well when physical detection is needed, but many items can be checked only by sensory detection methods, such as the surface finish on a bearing race or the flatness of a glass plate. For such problems a system of self-checks and successive checks can be used. (More on this later.)

Source inspection looks for errors before they become defects, and either stops the system and makes corrections or automatically compensates or corrects for the error condition to prevent a defective item from being made. The common term for source inspection in manufacturing processes is adaptive control (A/C).

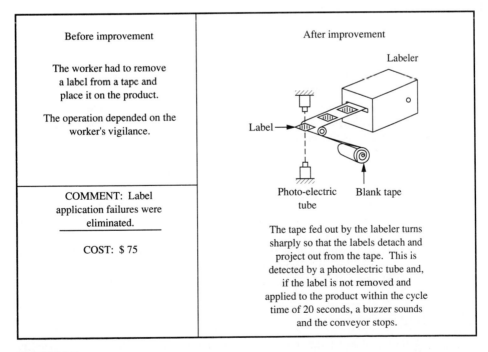

FIGURE 6-7
Example of pokayoke. (*Shingo, 1986.*)

There are two ways to look at source inspections: vertically and horizontally. Vertical source inspections try to control upstream processes that can be the source or the cause of defects downstream. It is always necessary to examine source processes as they may have a much greater impact on quality than do the processes being examined. Here is an example. Some steel bars were being cylindrically ground. After grinding, about 10 percent of the bars warped (bent longitudinally) and were rejected. The grinding process was studied extensively and no cure was found. The problem was with the heat-treating process that preceded cylindrical grinding. About 10 percent of the bars were not getting a complete, uniform heating prior to quench. These bars lay close to the door of the oven, which was not properly sealed, resulting in a temperature gradient inside. Quenching of the bars induced a residual stress that was released by the grinding and caused the warping. Horizontal source inspections detect defect sources within the processes and then introduce corrections to keep from turning errors into defects. This is commonly called adaptive control for preventing defects.

SELF-CHECKS AND SUCCESSIVE CHECKS

If the worker inspects each part immediately after producing it, this is *self-checking*. There is an immediate feedback to the worker on quality. However, it would be difficult for many workers not to allow a certain degree of bias to creep into their inspections, whether they were aware of it or not, since they are inspecting their own work. Within cells operated by multiple workers, the operator of the downstream station or process can inspect the parts produced by the upstream operator. If there is a problem with the parts, the defective item is immediately passed back to the worker at the previous station. There the defect is verified and the problem corrected. Action is immediately taken to prevent any more defective parts. While this is going on, the line is shut down.

In order for *successive checks* to be successful, several rules should be followed. All the possible variables and attributes should not be measured. This would eventually lead to errors and confusion in the inspection process. The part should be analyzed so that only one or two points are inspected. Only the most important elements are inspected or perhaps the features most prone to error. Another important rule is that the immediate feedback of a defect leads to immediate action. Since the parts are produced in an integrated manufacturing production system, this will be very effective in preventing the production of more defective parts. Suppose the cell has only one or two workers and they are not in a position to directly check each other's work after each step. Here is where the decouplers can play a role by providing automatic successive checking of the parts' critical features before proceeding to the next step. Only perfect parts are pulled from one process to the next through the decoupler.

LINE STOP

A pair of yellow and red lights hanging above the workers in the cell or assembly line can be used to alert everyone in the area to the status of the processes. A worker can turn on a yellow light when assistance is needed, and nearby workers will move to assist. A red light is turned on if the problem cannot be solved quickly and the line needs to be stopped. When the problem is solved and everyone is ready to go again, the red light goes off and everyone starts back to work.

Every worker should be given the authority to stop the production line to correct quality problems. In systems using pokayoke and autonomation, devices may stop the line automatically. The assembly line or manufacturing cell should be stopped immediately and started again only when the necessary corrections have been made. Although stopping the line takes time and money, it is advantageous in the long run. Problems can be found immediately, and the workers have more incentive to be attentive because they do not want to be responsible for stopping the line.

IMPLEMENTING IQC

The basic idea of integration is to shift functions that were formerly done in the staff organization (called the production system) into the manufacturing system. What happens to the quality control department? The department serves as the facilitator and therefore acts to promote quality concepts throughout the plant. In addition, its staff educates and trains the workers in statistical and process control techniques and provides engineering assistance on visual and automatic inspection installations. Its most important function will be training the entire work force in quality control.

Another important function of the QC department will be to work with and audit the vendors. As described in Chapter 10, the vendor's quality must be raised to the level at which the buyer does not need to inspect incoming material, parts, or subassemblies. The vendor simply becomes an extension of the buyer's plant. Ultimately, each vendor will deliver to the plant perfect materials that need no incoming inspection. Note that this means the acceptable quality level (AQL) of incoming material is 0 percent. Perfection is the goal. For many years this country has lived with the unwritten rule that 2 or 3 percent defective was about as good as you could get: Better quality just costs too much. For our systems, this was true. In order to achieve the kinds of quality that Toyota, Honda, Sanyo, and many others have demonstrated, one has to eliminate the job shop (a functional manufacturing system) and the functional production system, integrating the quality function directly into the linked-cell manufacturing system.

The quality control department also performs complex or technical inspections, total performance checks (often called end item inspection), chemical analysis, X-ray analysis, destructive tests, or tests of long duration.

INTRODUCTION TO TAGUCHI METHODS

Foreign competition has forced American manufacturers to take a second look at quality, as evidenced by the major emphasis (re-emphasis) on statistical process control (SPC) in American industry. This drive toward superior quality has led to the introduction of Taguchi methods for improvement in products, product design, and processes. Basically, SPC looks at processes and control, the latter loosely implying "improvement." Taguchi methods, however, span a much wider scope of functions and include the design aspects of products and processes, areas that were seldom if ever formally treated from the quality standpoint. Another threshold has been reached in quality control, witnessed by an expanding role of quality in the production of goods and services. The consumer is the central focus of attention on quality, and the methods of quality design and control have been incorporated into all phases of production.

The Taguchi methods incorporate the following general features:

1. Quality is defined in relation to the total loss to the consumer (or society) from less-than-perfect quality of the product. The methods include placing a monetary value on quality loss. Anything less than perfect is waste.
2. In a competitive society, continuous quality improvement and cost reduction are necessary for staying in business.
3. Continuous quality improvement requires continuous reduction in the variability of product performance characteristics with respect to their target values.
4. The quality and cost of a manufactured product are determined by the engineering designs of the product and its manufacturing system.
5. The variability in product and process performance characteristics can be reduced by exploiting the nonlinear (interactive) effects of the process or product parameters on the performance characteristics.
6. Statistically planned (Taguchi) experiments can be used to determine settings for processes and parameters that reduce the performance variation.
7. Design and improvement of products and processes can make them "robust" or insensitive to uncontrollable or difficult-to-control variations, called *noise* by Taguchi.

The methods are, however, more than just mechanical procedures. They infuse an overriding new philosophy into manufacturing management that basically makes quality the primary issue in manufacturing. The manufacturing world is rapidly becoming aware that the consumer is the ultimate judge of quality. Continuous quality improvement toward perfect quality is the ultimate goal. Finally, it is recognized that the ultimate quality and lowest cost of a manufactured product are determined to a large extent by the engineered designs of

1. The product
2. The manufacturing processes
3. The manufacturing system (integration of the product and the process)

So a new understanding of quality has emerged. Process variability is not fixed. The noise level of a process can be reduced by exploring the nonlinear effects of the products (or process) parameters on the performance characteristics.

It is predicted that future manufacturing management will include the following changes:

- Continual training and massive implementation of statistical process control (getting started in quality control)
- Use of SPC as an interim quality control measure until total quality control is fully integrated into American manufacturing (see Table 6-3)
- Training and implementation of statistical experimental design and Taguchi methods for process design and improvement of products and processes
- Concurrent (or simultaneous) engineering of products and processes to reduce the time needed to bring new designs to the marketplace
- Attitude adjustment making quality the primary consideration and the process of improvement (of processes or products) continuous
- Gradual transition from use of statistical methods to worker/machine-oriented 100 percent inspection for quality
- Massive training and implementation of total quality management (TQM) in America—extending quality to all areas of the business

TABLE 6-3
Quality control: concepts and categories

IQC category	IQC concept
1. Organization	Production responsibility
2. Goals	Habit of improvement for everyone Perfection—zero defects—not a program, a goal
3. Basic principles	Process control—defect prevention, not detection Easy-to-see quality—quality on display so buyers can see and inspect—easy to understand Insist on compliance Line stop when something goes wrong Correct your own errors 100 percent check Project-by-project improvements

4. Facilitating concepts	QC department as facilitator
	     Audit suppliers
	     Help in quality improvement projects
	     Training workers, supervisors, suppliers
	 Small lot sizes
	 Housekeeping
	 Less-than-full-capacity scheduling
	 Check machines daily, use check lists like airplane pilot
	 Total preventive maintenance
	 8-4-8-4 two-shift scheduling

5. Techniques and aids	Expose problems, solve problems Foolproof devices, pokayokes for checking 100 percent of parts $N = 2$, for checking first and last item in a lot Analysis tools Quality circles for continuous improvement

Source: Schonberger, 1982.

The next decade should bring a gradual transition from statistical process control (as a primary means of quality management) to the more extensive implementation of statistical experimental design methods to design and constantly improve product and process quality. This is a natural evolution that is essential to continual improvement in processes, products, and services. Anything less is tantamount to stagnation and potential demise. J. Stuart Hunter has paid Taguchi a great compliment:

> The philosophy proposed by Taguchi, and modern statistical practices, go hand in hand. As students and practitioners, our objective must be to apply the best of both. The last words have not been written, and likely never will be, on the choice of experimental design, the role of interactions, and the effects of data transformation for discovering how to design and produce higher-quality products. We are all involved in a learning process on behalf of product quality, and we have Professor Taguchi to thank for accelerating our education. (Hunter, 1985)

Although Taguchi methods have only very recently been introduced in the United States, they have been employed for many years in Japan (see Taguchi and Wu, 1979). As a result of Japan's emphasis on quality, limited resources, and urgent need to develop products rapidly, the Taguchi methods were developed. In elemental form, the methods allowed for design and production of products that are robust, insensitive to environmental disturbances (noise factors). Further, they are relatively easy to use and quickly produce positive results. For Japan, they were the next logical step.

The essence of superior quality is intense rivalry. Competition speeds the rate of innovation. Due to this competition in the free markets here in the United States, there is every reason to expect that proper use of Taguchi methods will force major improvements in products and processes. The methods are relatively easy to use. They do not require extensive training and education in probability, statistics, or experimental design, so they can be quickly grasped and employed. While it is true that most engineering graduates in the United States have little if any formal exposure to probability, statistics, and experimental design concepts and methods, the Taguchi methods should still prove to be extremely attractive. Product designers must seek the least costly methods to insure the quality of the desired functional characteristics.

7

INTEGRATED
PREVENTIVE
MAINTENANCE

If you are coasting, you are going downhill.

INTRODUCTION

Time must be allotted in the manufacturing schedule for checking and maintaining the equipment and the people. Unless all the elements in the manufacturing system are properly maintained, breakdowns will occur and disrupt the flow of products. Some manufacturing processes need to run continuously, but such processes already have many of the elements of IMPSs. Usually, the problem with continuous processes is long setup times (long changeover times when the system changes materials), and all the maintenance except for emergency service is performed during these shutdown periods. The people and equipment in the IMPS should be ready to produce what is needed when needed. This may not be possible if the system is running on a maximum output schedule. Equipment and people operating on a tightly balanced system can never catch up if slack time is not provided for catching up or for maintenance. The key is to develop a less-than-full-capacity schedule for the cells that includes time for maintenance. Repairs made under pressure may not be done well, leading to further downtime for re-repair, tinkering, and adjusting.

With *integrated preventive maintenance (IPM)*, operators are required to become more aware of the behavior of their equipment and its routine problems. Chief among these problems is process drift (loss of stability or loss of aim or accuracy), so IPM is closely linked to IQC. Maintaining the aim or accuracy of the process is different from maintaining the process spread (variability or precision). Finally, keep this thought in mind—if you are not maintaining or improving a manufacturing process or system, then it is degrading (layman's restatement of the second law of thermodynamics).

A 4-8-4-8 SCHEDULE

Integrated preventive maintenance covers the maintenance of machine tools, workholding devices, cutting tools, and personnel. This function is integrated into the daily regimen of the plant floor. Preventive maintenance responsibility is shifted from the maintenance department to the operators. The operators daily prepare and use machine tool checklists, much like the checklists pilots use to check out the aircraft before takeoff. We do not want any machines to crash in the plant during the eight-hour shift. Workers are also responsible for most of the routine machine tool maintenance. The maintenance department still does major machine overhauls and takes the lead role in the event of major breakdowns.

For this kind of program to operate effectively, the entire plant is run on a 4-8-4-8 schedule. The four-hour time blocks between the two eight-hour shifts allow for maintenance or unavoidably long setups. In addition, the eight-hour shift can begin early or run over when needed without disrupting the next shift.

Machine life and tool life are further enhanced by operating the equipment at reduced speeds or reduced production rates. This concept is totally foreign to most American factories. The idea of less-than-full capacity operation suggests to us less-than-100-percent utilization. We always try hard to avoid this when in fact what we should do is worry about effective people utilization and let the machine utilization be whatever is needed to meet the demand.

SCHEDULING PM

Scheduling preventive maintenance (PM) is a task typically assigned to the industrial engineer. Production supervisors believe their manufacturing processes should not be shut down simply for PM, yet higher-level PM must be performed on schedule by the maintenance department. For this reason PM should be flexible within certain limits. Scheduling PM should be between the eight-hour shifts, in the four-hour time blocks, or on weekends if necessary. This presents some inconvenience for the maintenance engineers and specialists, however. Equipment can also be used on an alternate basis when overhaul maintenance is required. One machine can be removed from the cell and replaced with another, so that the necessary overhaul can be performed.

The pace of the manufacturing system in the entire plant is synchronized and output rates (cycle times, etc.) for a specific piece of equipment or cell are determined by the system needs. The machines are not run flat out. Furthermore, the entire eight-hour shift is not scheduled unless that is required to meet the daily production needs. Some time (15 minutes) at the start and end of each shift is allotted for routine repair and maintenance. If the entire eight-hour shift is scheduled, it is viewed as a serious problem and steps are immediately taken to correct this situation. In this way the equipment lasts longer and provides higher reliability. The idea is not to overtax the machine tools, the people, or the cutting tools. They are less likely to make mistakes or break down if they are not pressured.

Suppose you prepare a race car to run the Indy 500 but instead of running the car at 200 mph, you operate it at 100 mph—just sufficient to get you where you need to go on time with no waiting when you get there. The car will run much longer before it breaks down. The race is going to the steady and consistent, not the fastest.

Placing a cushion of time at the end of each shift (the shift is seven and one-half hours long) allows the line to be shut down for quality circle meetings. This helps make quality part of the operators' job. The first 10 or 15 minutes of the shift are dedicated to maintenance checks, machine warm-up, oiling the equipment, checking tools, and the like.

This methodology also gives additional flexibility to respond to changes in product demand because of the wide latitude it affords the cells. In order to increase the production rate, one can add workers to the cells and increase the operation rates of the machines when necessary.

WHAT PM MEANS

Preventive maintenance is designed to preserve and enhance equipment reliability. A correctly integrated PM program will provide a significant increase in production capability throughout the entire production system. The ideal PM program will prevent failure of all equipment before it occurs.

VALUE OF PREVENTIVE MAINTENANCE

People not exposed to preventive maintenance question its value. They believe that it costs more for regular downtime and maintenance than it costs to operate equipment until repair is absolutely necessary. However, one should compare not only the costs but the long-term benefits and savings associated with IPM. Without IPM, the following costs are likely to be incurred:

- Lost production time resulting from unscheduled equipment breakdown
- Variation in the quality of products due to deteriorating equipment performance
- Decrease in equipment service life
- Safety-related accidents due to equipment malfunction
- Major equipment repair and lost production time

The long-term benefits to be considered are as follows:

- If maintenance is a primary responsibility, operators are more familiar with the equipment, the way it operates, and its potential problems.
- Processes are in better control through IPM's machine and tool records, producing better quality.
- Quality, flexibility, safety, reliability, and production capability are improved.
- Reliable equipment permits inventory reduction.

Long-term effects and cost comparisons undoubtedly favor preventive maintenance. A carefully designed and properly integrated program requires a positive managerial attitude that will set the pace for a successful program.

Another preventive maintenance principle promotes the idea of performing housekeeping at an optimal level so that no machine breakdowns occur.

IPM INVOLVES THE INTERNAL CUSTOMER

IPM incorporates the idea that the operator is responsible for the machine/equipment in the manufacturing cell. This philosophy encourages the operator to take responsibility for the maintenance, operation, and performance of the equipment. If an operator is responsible for the repair of the equipment in the cell, that individual becomes more sensitive to the care and maintenance the machines may require. When the machines break down, it reflects on that operator's performance.

Machine operators should be trained to observe their equipment and to respond to their observations. If a piece of equipment needs special attention and the operator cannot perform the level of maintenance necessary, he or she should see that the proper maintenance specialist comes to the machine. Through preventive maintenance, production operators become more conscious of their performance and take pride in their work.

Operators need to realize the importance of an orderly and clean workplace and equipment. Housekeeping becomes a ritual in their everyday job performance. Routine cleaning familiarizes the operator with the machine, making it easier to understand the details involved in its operation. When operators have a sense of responsibility rather than just a duty to perform a specific task, they become enthusiastic about their jobs.

IPM emphasizes the significance of executing the correct procedures needed to operate all equipment in a manufacturing cell. When an operator runs the manufacturing cell in an incorrect manner, the irregularities in the processes will stand out. Problems are readily observed and may be prevented at earlier stages of the process.

MANUFACTURING ENGINEERING

Manufacturing engineers are responsible for the design, build, test, and implementation of manufacturing equipment. Maintainability should be considered in the design or selection of equipment for purchase. Simple, reliable equipment that can be easily maintained should be specified. In general, dedicated equipment can be built in-house better than it can be purchased. Many companies understand that *it is not good strategy simply to imitate or copy the manufacturing technology from another company and then expect to make an exceptional product using the same technology as the competitor*. The company must perform research and development on manufacturing technologies as well as manufacturing systems in order to produce effective and cost efficient products. However, an effective, cost efficient manufacturing system makes research and development (R&D) in manufacturing technology pay off. This is explained in Chapter 1.

Home-built equipment can offer some unique advantages:

- It is flexible, allowing rapid changeover for existing products and rapid modification for new products or model changes.
- It has unique capabilities.
- It offers maintainability/reliability/durability.
- Equipment and methods are designed to prevent accidents.
- It is easy to operate, has a fail-safe design.

The equipment is designed and developed with priority on the internal customer factors even though the factors affecting the external customer are the highest priority of manufacturing engineering. Although many plants lack the expertise to build machines from scratch, most have the expertise to modify equipment to give it unique capabilities. Modification of the equipment to prevent reoccurrence of a breakdown requires that management assign the highest priority to this work. The most skilled maintenance personnel must be given this task so that breakdowns in the L-CMS are eventually eliminated.

TOTAL PRODUCTIVE MAINTENANCE

The Japanese imported preventive maintenance from the United States over 30 years ago. Since that time they have improved and expanded it into what is now labeled *total productive maintenance (TPM)*. Seiichi Nakajima defines the developmental stages of TPM as follows:

1950s: Preventive Maintenance—establishing maintenance functions

1960s: Productive Maintenance—recognizing importance of reliability, maintenance, and economic efficiency in the plant design*

1970s: Total Productive Maintenance—achieving productive maintenance efficiency through a comprehensive system based on respect for individuals and total employee participation (Nakajima, 1988)

TPM includes the following five elements:

1. TPM aims to maximize the effectiveness and overall performance (efficiency) of the equipment.
2. TPM establishes a complete system of productive maintenance for the equipment's entire life span.
3. TPM is implemented by the departments responsible for design and manufacturing engineering, manufacturing systems, and maintenance.
4. TPM involves every single employee (associate), from top management to the production workers and operators.
5. TPM is based on the promotion of PM through quality circle group activities.

---

* (AKA, the manufacturing systems).

The word *total* in *total productive maintenance* has three meanings that describe the principal features of TPM.

1. Total effectiveness indicates TPM's pursuit of economic efficiency or profitability.
2. Total maintenance means designing equipment so that it needs less preventive maintenance and less corrective maintenance (has fewer breakdowns) and includes preventive maintenance of the existing equipment.
3. Total participation of all employees means developing autonomous maintenance devices. The operators working through small groups do much of this work. (Nakajima, 1988)

TOTAL PRODUCTIVE MAINTENANCE DEVELOPMENT

The objective of manufacturing improvement activities is to increase productivity by minimizing input and resources and maximizing output. Inputs to the system consist of energy, demand, information, and materials. The system is composed of machine tools, cutting tools, workholding devices, material-handling and storage equipment, and internal customers. The outputs are products (good and bad), information, and service to the external customer. In order to increase productivity, total productive maintenance should be correctly developed.

According to Nakajima, the five development activities of TPM are as follows:

1. Eliminate the "six big losses" and thereby improve the effectiveness of the equipment.

   Losses due to downtime:
   1. Equipment failure—from breakdowns
   2. Setup and adjustment—from exchange of die in molding machines, presses, and so forth

   Speed losses:
   3. Idling and minor stoppages—due to the abnormal operation of sensors, blockage of work on chutes, and the like
   4. Reduced speed—due to discrepancies between specified and actual speed of equipment

   Losses due to defects:
   5. Process defects—due to scrap and rework
   6. Reduced yield—from machine start-up to stable production.

2. Develop an autonomous maintenance program.

   The seven steps of autonomous maintenance are
   1. "Initial cleaning: Clean to eliminate dust and dirt mainly on the body of the equipment; lubricate and tighten; discover problems and correct them."

2. "Countermeasures at the source of problems: Prevent the causes of dust, dirt, and spattering of liquids; improve those parts of equipment that are hard to clean and lubricate; reduce the time required for cleaning and lubricating."

3. "Cleaning and lubrication standards: Establish standards that reduce the time spent cleaning, lubricating, and tightening (specify daily and periodic tasks)."

4. "General inspection: Follow the instructions in the inspection manual; quality circle members discover and correct minor equipment defects."

5. "*Autonomous inspection: Develop and use autonomous inspection check sheets.*"

6. "Orderliness and tidiness: Standardize the individual workplace control categories; thoroughly systemize maintenance control:

   - Inspection standards for cleaning and lubricating
   - Cleaning and lubricating standards in the workplace
   - Standards for recording data
   - Standards for parts and tool maintenance"

7. "Fully autonomous maintenance: Develop a company policy and goals for maintenance; increase the regularity of improvement activities. Record the mean time between failures (MTBF), analyze the results, and design countermeasures."

   These steps are based on the five basic principles of operations management. In the Japanese literature, they are known as the five S's: *seiri, seiton, seiso, seiketsu, and shitsuke*. A rough translation of the five S's means organization, tidiness, purity, cleanliness, discipline.

3. Develop a scheduled maintenance program for the maintenance department. This is usually done in cooperation with industrial engineering. The leveled schedule greatly helps the development of a regular maintenance program.

4. Increase the skill of operators and the maintenance personnel. The operators should work with the maintenance people at the time PM work is done on their equipment, discussing problems and solutions. Part of the operator's job is to keep records on the performance of the equipment, so the operators must learn to be observant.

5. Develop an equipment management program. A record of the use of machines and tools denoting how much they were used and who used them.

TOTAL PRODUCTIVE MAINTENANCE IMPLEMENTATION

Nakajima outlines 12 steps involved in developing and implementing a total productive maintenance program.

Step 1: Announce top management's decision to introduce TPM.
- State TPM objectives in company newsletter.
- Place articles on TPM in company newspaper.

Step 2: Launch educational campaign.
- For managers, offer seminars/retreats according to level.
- For general workers, provide slide presentations.

Step 3: Create organizations to promote TPM.
- Form special committees at every level to promote TPM.
- Establish central headquarters and assign staff.

Step 4: Establish basic TPM policies and goals.
- Analyze existing conditions.
- Set goals.
- Predict results.

Step 5: Formulate master plan for TPM development.
- Prepare detailed implementation plans for the five foundational activities.

Step 6: Hold TPM kickoff.
- Invite external customers, affiliated and subcontracting companies.

Step 7: Improve effectiveness of each piece of equipment.
- Select model equipment.
- Form project teams.

Step 8: Develop an autonomous maintenance program.
- Promote the Seven Steps.
- Build diagnostic skills and establish worker procedures for certification.

Step 9: Develop a scheduled maintenance program for the maintenance department.
- Include periodic and predictive maintenance.
- Include management of spare parts, tools, blueprints, and schedules.

Step 10: Conduct training to improve operation and maintenance skills.
- Train leaders together.
- Have leaders share information with group members.

Step 11: Develop initial equipment management program.
- Use MP design (maintenance prevention).
- Use start-up equipment maintenance.
- Use life cycle cost analysis.

Step 12: Perfect TPM implementation and raise TPM levels.
- Evaluate for PM prize.
- Set higher goals.

SUMMARY

Over 30 years ago, the Japanese learned about preventive maintenance from the United States. They have since developed and improved the preventive maintenance program into what they presently call total productive maintenance. The United States has also developed and improved preventive maintenance. The primary goal of preventive maintenance is to prevent failure of all equipment before it actually occurs. The objective of total productive maintenance is to increase productivity, improve efficiency, increase the percentage of time equipment is able to operate, and minimize the number of required steps by keeping it simple. The program requires heavy involvement with production workers. This is IPM.

CHAPTER
8

LEVELING AND BALANCING THE MANUFACTURING SYSTEM

Anything that does not add value is waste.

INTRODUCTION

As the level of inventory in the factory shrinks and the processes become more tightly linked, production rates need to become more closely coordinated. Ideally, the cycle time (CT) of each fabricated part and subassembly would be identical to the cycle times of the final assembly line. Balancing the CTs of the processes and final assembly also carries over to balancing labor and machines. In a traditional factory, balancing entails shifting people and tasks along the assembly line. This creates a somewhat balanced line. In the IMPS factory, this balancing extends upstream to subassembly cells and component parts–manufacturing cells.

As a production job shop converts to IMPS, different types of machines are rearranged into manufacturing cells. The machines in these cells are arranged to process parts conveyed between them one piece at a time. Inventory between machines disappears when only one part flows between machines. At this point, attention to machine setup time is essential.

144

BALANCING THE CELLS

The critical first stage of building an IMPS is cellular manufacturing. Machines are placed near one another, usually in a U-shaped design as shown in Figure 8-1. Cells consist of small, simple pieces of equipment. Operators walk a predetermined path on a precise time schedule. The cycle time for the cell is adjusted to match the cycle time of the final assembly line. The cell can now be synchronized with the assembly line. This means that the output of the cell over a short period of time is matched to the rate at which the parts are used by subsequent operations and ultimately by final assembly. Any mismatching of the production rate of the cell and the usage rate by subassembly (or final assembly) is absorbed by the kanban link between the two entities. The less the mismatch, the smaller the inventory link.

Suppose the cell is making two products, A and B, which are used by a sub-assembly cell in equal quantities. Half the time the cell is making A parts. While the cell is making A parts, there must be sufficient B parts in the kanban loop to keep the subassembly demand for B parts satisfied, *assuming there are no other problems* in the manufacturing cell.

Different parts in the family produced by a cell may not require all the machines to be utilized in the cell. The parts will usually require different amounts of machining time, but all the parts made in one cell should require labor times in the same general range. This is a general requirement so that a different number of workers is not required in the cell for each different part in the family. It should not be necessary to rebalance the tasks for each part in the family. This does not mean that the total machining time between the two parts must be balanced or equal. This is not necessary since MTs have been decoupled from the CT. The CT depends on the number of machines the worker visits on a trip around the cell.

Cell layout

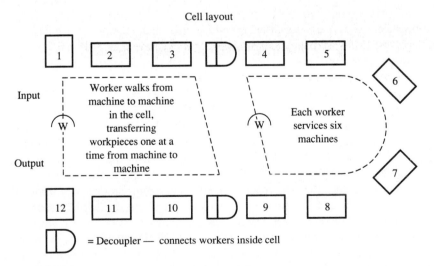

FIGURE 8-1
Manned cell with two workers making two parts, A and B.

The output rate of a cell can be adjusted by adding or subtracting workers. However, during a given fixed schedule period, the manning of the cells remains constant. When the scheduled period changes, personnel requirements may change. Occasionally the cell is redesigned and the number of machines included in the cell is changed. This will cause the work pattern in the cell to change. These changes are necessary so that the cycle times of the parts from the cell are matched up with the cycle times required by the new schedule for final assembly.

Workers who have performed only a single function or manufacturing personnel who have experienced only line balance problems with equipment fixed in place may find IMPS's rebalancing difficult to accept. Cells are designed with simple, single-cycle machines and equipment that has been modified for flexibility. A properly trained operator should be able to operate and set up every machine in the cell.

Supervisors are responsible for maintaining the data needed to determine how many workers are required for different cycle times in a cell. This job does not require large amounts of data, but rather a set of rules based upon past performance, trial and error, and perhaps a calculation or two. The industrial engineering department can be called on for assistance in complex balancing problems.

The balancing of a cell is easier when the required cycle time is greater than 30 seconds. If the needed cycle time is less than 30 seconds, then replication of the existing cell should be considered. This requires twice as much equipment, but since the machines are simple, single-cycle automatics, this should not require a large capital investment.

WORKER ALLOCATION

A very important principle of IMPS is that *the internal customers are the most important resource and will be the limiting factor*. Equipment is used to produce only the amount of product required. IMPS design concentrates on the utilization of the worker. Remember, using the equipment to produce more than is required violates the basic principles of IMPS. Overproduction means that eventually inventory builds up somewhere in the manufacturing system. This excess has to be stored, tracked, and retrieved—all wasteful operations.

Additionally, the minimum number of workers are used in IMPS. This is achieved by balancing the operations. Modifying the cycle time by replicating the cell may reduce the number of workers because balancing is easier. Elements of work are shifted from one worker to another until the operations are balanced. This may result in a situation in which a worker is no longer needed in the cell and can be assigned to another cell. This basic principle can be applied even if the cell cannot be divided. Figure 8-2 illustrates the general case for improving productivity through balancing in an assembly cell. The removal of worker G and the shifting of tasks (rebalancing) results in six workers, each having 0.875 minutes of work, or five workers each having one minute of work and the sixth having 0.25. Only one of the workers has idle time, and efforts could be made to eliminate these tasks so the worker can be shifted to another cell. This solution, however, brings the cell to full capacity, so additional improvements are necessary.

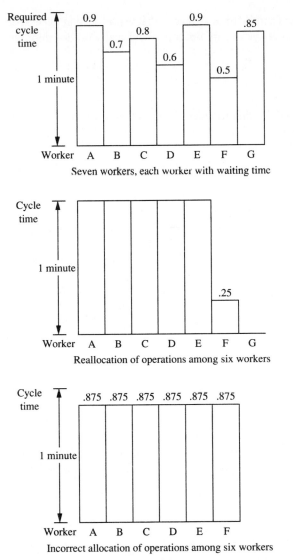

Seven workers, each worker with waiting time

Reallocation of operations among six workers

FIGURE 8-2
Worker allocation in assembly cells.
Incorrect allocation of operations among six workers   (*Monden, 1983.*)

What can be done at full capacity, if the production rate has to be increased (the cycle time lowered)? This presents problems because of the lack of flexibility at full capacity. A better approach would be to develop two cells, each with three walking workers, each worker producing a subassembly every 5.35 minutes or 11.42 parts per hour. Thus, five workers can produce 57–58 parts per hour, just a shade under the required 60 parts per hour. A little overtime permits the cell to meet the requirements. Notice that the objective of the improvement is not to reduce the cycle time. Reducing the cycle time is only necessary for meeting changes in the schedule. The objective is to minimize the amount of required labor while producing at a rate that yields the parts needed for final production. Changes that result only in excessive inventory stored in the manufacturing system are deceptive and really do not improve productivity.

THREE KINDS OF CELLS

Manufacturing cells are developed according to three basic strategies: process strategy, part geometry strategy, or product strategy. These strategies are not all the approaches available for cell formation, but rather some techniques from which some of the benefits of cellular manufacturing can be quickly achieved.

Process-defined Cells

Process strategy is useful when geometric information on the parts you wish to cellularize is not available or the parts appear to be geometrically dissimilar. This method assists in defining cells when understanding of manufacturing processes is limited.

Geometric data are not needed to create cells based on processes. Parts that all go to one key machine are selected, and the cell is built around that machine. Current routings are examined to find key machine tools and to select candidate parts that have common routings, then cells are developed for the part families.

Cells Defined by Part Geometry

Part geometry strategy is used when geometric information is available, the associated manufacturing processes are well known, and the parts look the same or very similar. In other words, geometry-based cells group parts based on common geometric characteristics. As with process cells, current production data are used to examine routings. However, new routings are then developed for the target part groups based on part feature analyses. Consideration is given to group tooling, machine loading, parts, and usage.

Cells Developed around a Product

Product strategy applies to cells intended to minimize inventory or cells that will be linked to an assembly line in support of just-in-time (JIT) manufacturing methods.

Product-focused cells are minifactories, dedicated to producing a product—that could be an assembly, a subassembly, or a finished primary part. The bill of materials details all the component parts that are going into the subassembly. Then a common routing is developed for these component parts. Often a factory within a factory results, incorporating both process- and geometry-based cells focused on a common assembly family.

The result of these strategies is the grouping of simple, flexible machines to meet required cycle times while eliminating inventory, floor space, transportation distance, and quality problems. Cells can compete with multistation high-speed automatic equipment because cells can be set up and debugged quickly, therefore providing manufacturing flexibility. When additional capacity is needed, the cell is replicated.

SYNCHRONIZATION

Balancing refers to making the times equal. *Leveling* refers to making the amounts of material equal over time. Leveling is also called smoothing of production. Another term, *synchronization*, refers to the process of timing the flow of material between cells or other operations. Even when the quantity of material has been leveled and balanced, unnecessary storage of in-process material can occur between unsynchronized operations. However, once the operations are leveled, synchronization is just a matter of efficient, integrated scheduling. Leveling must precede synchronization because leveling helps eliminate process delays that would make synchronization difficult.

EQUIPMENT AND PROCESS SYNCHRONIZATION METHOD

With the use of cams, microswitches, and similar devices, different types of machines can be synchronized to the same production rate by the following method:

1. At the completion of each machining cycle, the machine is stopped automatically. All the components and attachments of the machine are returned to the start position.
2. If there is space to hold a finished workpiece in the output (downstream) decoupler, the workpiece is automatically ejected from the machine to the decoupler. If not, the machine must wait until space is available. The empty decoupler provides a signal to the upstream machine to make another part.
3. When an unprocessed workpiece is available in an upstream decoupler, it is automatically fed to the machine, using guides to position it without human assistance.
4. When the unprocessed workpiece is located and clamped into the machine, the next machining cycle is automatically started.

Leveling quantities and synchronizing processes can significantly reduce delays, thus greatly reducing manufacturing throughput time. For example, using one-piece flow to eliminate lot delays for two serial processes reduces throughput time. The multiplier effect of eliminating process and lot delays by using one-piece part movement in cells may reduce the throughput time to as much as one-fiftieth when 10 processes are involved.

YO-I-DON SYSTEM SYNCHRONIZATION

Yo-i-don in Japanese means "ready, set, go" and is the name given to a method of synchronizing manual manufacturing processes or operations. This system is not used with a mechanical transportation mechanism such as a conveyorized assembly line. In these situations, the line paces the work. The yo-i-don system will be explained in an example that describes a body welding plant for an automobile manufacturer. The operation for the body plant may be divided into three primary areas such as underbody (floor pan) processes, side-body processes, and top-body (roof-body) processes (see

Process flow for body plant

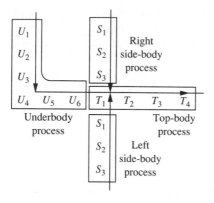

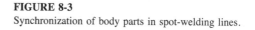

FIGURE 8-3
Synchronization of body parts in spot-welding lines.

Figure 8-3). The underbody and side-body processes can be divided into six and three subprocesses, U_1–U_6 and S_1–S_3, respectively. The top-body processes may be broken down into four subprocesses T_1–T_4. The top, two sides, and bottom pieces come together at T_1.

Suppose the final assembly line is turning out one unit every three minutes (the required cycle time of the factory). The operations of each subassembly area, processing area, and main assembly area must be completed in three minutes or some multiple of three minutes. Since each car needs a body, the car-body welding area produces one body every three minutes. The workers in each area must complete their tasks and pass the weldment to the next workstation by the end of the prescribed three-minute cycle time.

After completing his or her assigned tasks and passing the weldment downstream, each operator presses the job completion button. This button turns on a green light on the andon, indicating that a certain task has been completed (see Figure 8-4). The *andon* is a signalboard that hangs over the workplace. At the end of each cycle, a red light comes on informing everyone of incomplete tasks. When this happens, adjacent workers and supervisors provide assistance. Usually, the slow operation is completed in 10 seconds or less. However, the entire line comes to a halt when the andon red light comes on. When the task has been completed, the red light is turned off and the process cycle starts again, with all processes beginning together. This method synchronizes plant operations, getting them all to start together each cycle.

1/3		2/3		3/3	
U_1	U_2	U_3	U_4	U_5	U_6
S_1	S_2	S_3	S_4	S_5	S_6
T_1		T_2		T_3	T_4

FIGURE 8-4
Andon for the body shop—a signal board indicating progress at each stage of a system.

PLANT BALANCING

The steps for balancing the entire factory are

1. Balancing the production rate with the rate of consumption of the parts. The overall cycle times are the inverse of the production rates.
2. Adjusting the work content and cycle times at each cell or station until times match the system cycle time as nearly as possible.
3. Trying to off-load the work content of selected stations until they are no longer needed.

All the fabrication areas should be linked by the requirements of final assembly cycle time. The notion that there are no storage areas on the factory floor is incorrect, however. The idea is to minimize the material in these storage areas. The best place for the minimum storage area is near the point of use and close enough to the producing area so that operators have a visual signal of the parts' usage.

The linked cells and subassembly cells must be balanced to the final assembly cycle time. For example, if electric mixers are assembled with a cycle time of 120 seconds, then the mixer housings should have a cycle time of 120 seconds. Each mixer needs two blades, so blades have a CT of one minute.

Saying that a housing has a cycle time of 120 seconds is more involved than saying the part has a production rate of 30 per hour. Producing 30 parts per hour could mean producing at 30 parts per minute once each hour or even 240 parts in an hour, once each eight hours. A cycle time of 120 seconds implies a uniform rate of manufacture. In the factory, events rarely work out exactly to a predetermined plan. Therefore, a continual effort should be made to reduce the deviations between the rate set by final assembly and the production rates of the upstream elements. Real production improvements result from matching the upstream processes more closely to the rhythm set by final assembly.

Traditional line balancing refers to balancing the labor at each workplace, regardless of the CT. There is no attempt to achieve an overall factory balance. In traditional assembly line work and in IMPS, balancing the line or the plant also refers to balancing the material flow. In IMPSs, material flow balancing is done by the pull system of material control. Material balance and labor balance are not independent of each other. The primary signal that labor is out of balance is an excess or a shortage of material. The amount of WIP between cells results from unbalanced cycle times. The objective is to set the cycle times as required by the schedule and then to shift tasks and operations accordingly. As shown in Figure 8-2, this will result in less and less work for one operator, and eventually this worker can move to another area. It must be remembered that IMPS is a system designed to optimize the labor content as well as improve the labor efficiency.

Plant balancing is a dynamic, on-going process. Normally, a plant will have to be rebalanced whenever the production rate changes. The fear of losing line balance is the major reason for the reluctance to stop a balanced assembly line once it is running. This is also true of an entire factory. There are countermeasures to this:

- Visible signaling systems like andon allow the system to respond to temporary variations in parts usage rate and to changes in planned mix.
- The flexibility built into the cells permits the system to quickly adapt to requests for increased or decreased production rates or changes in the product mix.
- Less-than-full-capacity scheduling means keeping a little slack time, perhaps 20–30 minutes per shift, at each cell, so the system can respond to variations from the planned schedule. This adds flexibility to the system.

Since a plant's schedule changes periodically, the operations also may have to be changed. Manufacturing cells and subassembly cells can usually continue working without rebalancing if the cycle times required do not vary more than about 10 percent up or down. Cycle time variations beyond that usually require rebalancing. Detailed planning for production must take this into account.

LEVELING OR SMOOTHING THE MANUFACTURING SYSTEM

The definition for leveling is easy to comprehend. Leveling is the process of planning and executing an even production schedule. In an ideal situation, a factory would produce an even distribution of products every hour, each day. That is, items would be manufactured every day, and in the same way. Balancing is the method of setting the overall cycle time in order to synchronize the rate of production with the rate of consumption. The principle behind leveling and balancing is simply to regulate production output and final assembly in order to minimize the demand spikes. Final assembly should not pull products from the upstream subassembly cells, manufacturing cells, and production processes in a way that causes these elements to fluctuate or peak. Fluctuations cause production planners to set production rates on the upstream processes at the maximum level of the demand spikes. This, of course, results in overproduction and excess inventory—in other words, waste. On the other hand, it is desirable to have maximum flexibility in the final assembly lines. The trick is to produce to dealer orders and not to stock. This means that the manufacturing system must be flexible. For example, suppose an order normally needs to be filled four weeks after it is received. If the actual manufacturing lead time is two weeks, the system is able to change over to meet the customer's desires and easily fill the order.

SMOOTHING FINAL ASSEMBLY

IMPS companies have a yearly production plan that forecasts how many items they plan to produce in a given year. The yearly plan includes a *running two-month plan*. Product types and quantities are forecast two months before the month in question. A detailed plan is formulated one month before manufacturing starts. The amount produced daily is set from the monthly production plan. Leveling and balancing are important concepts incorporated into the daily schedule.

Leveling and smoothing tasks are based on averaged total production of a product per day and the averaged quantity of each variety of product in this total. For example, suppose a final assembly line produces model C. Monthly production is 10,000 C's. Then it is necessary to schedule and produce 500 model C's a day (10,000 units/20 days). The factory works two eight-hour shifts per day, separated by two four-hour time blocks. Each shift has 480 working minutes. Suppose that 300 variations (options) of model C are produced. It is absolutely necessary to balance the variations in the daily schedule. Continuing the example, suppose that three major types of models are produced. The daily average quantities of each type may be seen in Figure 8-5. The sequence on the final assembly is given in this figure. This is called a mixed-model final assembly line. There can be no setup time between models in this situation. The workers on such lines like to make at least one of each model every day so that they do not forget how.

The assembly line receives next month's schedule from the production control department in the latter part of the current month. Each model's daily average requirements are calculated. Once a manufacturing cell or process receives the monthly forecast of averaged daily usage of the parts it makes, the process must adapt its operations to the new schedule. For example, the load on a machine may normally be set at 90 percent of capacity (LTFC)[1], and each worker may operate up to 10 machines. When demand is increased, temporary workers must be hired and each worker will run eight machines. Machines that reach 100 percent utilization must be examined, and work must be off-loaded to less-utilized machines. The work must be simplified and standardized so that a new operator is able to achieve proficiency in three days. Short-term increases may be accommodated by overtime. The use of overtime can yield up to 37.5 percent increase in production. Process improvements that have netted slack time can be used to increase output if necessary.

The steps necessary to correct for a decrease in production are considerably more difficult. Temporary workers must be laid off in the manufacturing areas. Cell cycle times must be increased, which means each worker will operate more machines. Also, cycle times on the assembly lines will have to increase, again reducing the number of workers required. The extra workers are transferred to other areas of the plant or work reduced schedules. One of the important goals of IMPS is to operate the system with the minimum number of workers. On the other hand, it is not necessary to operate with a minimum number of machines. Having excess machine capacity means that when demand increases, only temporary workers are needed to effectively increase the production rate or the output.

[1] LTFC = less-than-full-capacity–See page 79

Model	Monthly quantity	Daily quantity	Tack time
Sedan	5,000	250	1.92 minutes
Hardtop	2,500	125	3.84 minutes
Wagon	2,500	125	3.84 minutes

Sequence: Sedan, hardtop, sedan, wagon, sedan, hardtop, sedan, wagon, etc.

CT = 480 min. × 2 shifts/500 = 1.92 min./car

FIGURE 8-5
Example of mixing the models on the line in order to smooth production.

The next step in the leveling and balancing of production, after the calculation of monthly and daily schedules, is the determination of the daily sequence. This schedule sets the assembly order of the various models through the assembly lines. For example the sequence may consist of vehicle type A, then B, then A, then C, and so forth. This sequence schedule is communicated only to the beginning of the final assembly line and not to any of the upstream processes or subassembly lines. This is the most fundamental aspect of the L-CMS information system. This important characteristic differentiates the L-CMS from other systems. The various upstream processes and subassembly lines receive only rough monthly forecasts. The supervisors of the upstream processes must schedule their work forces on the basis of this rough monthly schedule. Therefore, as the final assembly line builds a vehicle by pulling components from the kanban stores near the lines, the withdrawal kanban for these parts is detached and sent to the particular upstream manufacturing or assembly cell. The withdrawal kanban then signals the upstream process to produce more components in the exact quantities used and removed. Hence, upstream processes do not need detailed production schedules. Kanban informs the upstream processes of downstream needs as components are pulled toward final assembly (see Chapter 9 for details).

The workers on the final assembly line(s) need to know only what type of vehicle they must build next. This information is provided to them from the central computer via a printer or a computer monitor. Information about the type of vehicle to produce next is transmitted to the start of the assembly line via a computer terminal that also provides a label for each vehicle. The information on the label instructs workers on the assembly line to build a specific vehicle. This labeling system can also be used by the major subassembly lines such as the engine and transmission lines. Meanwhile, the other subassembly cells, manufacturing cells, and processes use kanban to control production quantities and rates.

Obtaining the best sequence schedule of mixed-model final assembly production is a difficult problem. The perfect model for sequencing would entail keeping the speed and quantity of withdrawal constant for every component. That is, the system needs to have the variation of consumed quantity of parts at the final assembly held to a minimum and the consumption rate of each component part maintained as constant as possible. This is obviously not possible for very complex assemblies, but the attempt to achieve such status should be made.

STANDARD OPERATIONS

Standard operations are designed to allow the manufacturing areas and assembly cells to use the minimum number of workers. The first goal of standard operations is to achieve high productivity through efficient work. This means working without wasted motions. A standard operations routine (SOR) is the standardized order in which various operations and tasks are to be performed by each worker. Each worker is expected to write down the operations, and this listing is compared with the standard operations routine. This procedure helps ensure that new workers are performing all the correct steps in the correct sequence. The SOR sheet is used for this purpose.

The second goal of standard operations is to achieve a balance among all the operations and processes in compliance with the final assembly cycle time. Final assembly cycle time is determined by the number of products to be produced in a given period. Therefore, the cycle time concept should be incorporated into the standard operations.

The final goal is that only the minimum quantity of material will be tolerated as standard quantity of work-in-process. In other words, the absolute minimum number of parts needed for the standard operations to be completed are kept on hand. This goal forces the elimination of excessive WIP inventories in the links. Therefore, standard operations must consist of cycle time, standard operations routine, and minimum quantities of material. Concurrently, the elimination of accidents, breakdowns, and defects is also a major component of standard operations.

COMPONENTS OF STANDARD OPERATIONS

Supervisors can determine the operations that should constitute the work at a machine, a process, a station, or a cell, provided the supervisor has received industrial engineering training in time-and-motion studies. Supervisors can also set labor hours. They are the people with the most knowledge of the work. It is essential for them to be able to teach their workers the best way to perform a particular job (i.e., the standard operations routine) and for the SOR to be maintained on a daily basis.

CYCLE TIME

Cycle time is the time span during which one unit of a product must be produced. The cycle time is determined by the following equation:

$$\text{Cycle time} = \frac{\text{effective daily operating time}}{\text{required daily quantity of output}}$$

It is not necessary to reduce the effective daily operating time by subtracting allowances for machine breakdowns, material shortages, rework, or personal breaks. It is wasteful to produce extra product to compensate for defective output. The cycle time is made longer to compensate for such problems (less-than-full-capacity scheduling), and therefore fewer workers will be needed because of the longer cycle time.

SUMMARY

Leveling and balancing are very important features in IMPS. These two basic elements smooth the rough peaks from the daily production schedule. Leveling and balancing regulate the upstream production to the final assembly rate. This is their most important function. Similarly, when leveling and balancing are applied to IMPS cells, they regulate (and may be used to reduce) the labor content. Synchronizing the system balances the individual processes to the rhythm of final assembly. A factory without production smoothing is often consumed by excess inventory and starved for parts—both at the same time! Upstream processes will see inventory overflow due to bottlenecks while downstream processes wither away waiting for stock to arrive. The proper application of leveling and balancing will remedy this situation and also provide a key building block for the factory with a future.

CHAPTER
9

INTEGRATED PRODUCTION AND INVENTORY CONTROL

Try to push a string and it piles up. Pulling a string makes it lean.

INTRODUCTION

Production control (PC) allows workers in the manufacturing system to know *where* material is to go (or come from), *when* material is to be *where* it is needed, and *how many* items are needed at that time. Inventory control (IC) allows workers to control *how much* material is at any given place in the manufacturing system. The production planning and control department has traditionally been in charge of PC and IC, which traditionally reside in the production system. To control the manufacturing system, the PC department issues a document called a *route sheet* or *traveler* that defines where the parts go in the manufacturing system and what processes are to be performed on the parts when they get there. Route sheets are usually prepared by production planners. The PC department also develops a schedule for the entire manufacturing system (defining when processes are to be done) and issues dispatches (telling when to initiate the processes). The amount of material moving through the manufacturing system is usually determined by the material requirements planning (MRP) methodology. MRP systems use the economic order quantity (EOQ) calculation to determine build quantities. Inventory levels are difficult to control because material is pushed into the manufacturing system by the material requirements plan, which is a planning document, not a control device.

IMPS uses a pull system for production and inventory control called *kanban*. There are many who think that an IMPS is nothing more than a kanban system, but this is not the case. Kanban is a production and inventory control subsystem for IMPS. It is a pull system for material management that goes with IMPS. Shigeo Shingo tells the following anecdote (liberally interpreted by the author).

> Now you might think that the Toyota Motor Company is just a company wearing a smart suit (referring to kanban), and you want to buy such a suit for your company. However, if you only buy the kanban subsystem, you soon discover that this suit will not fit your obese, fat body (your manufacturing system) and chaos soon results. (Shingo, 1981)

Just as JIT needs cells, kanban goes best with the L-CMS. Before implementing kanban, the CMS must be implemented to make the manufacturing system lean and hungry. The health of the manufacturing system is improved by eliminating waste. Kanban, therefore, is a method of production information management and inventory control, designed to achieve JIT objectives. A JIT manufacturing system can be run without using kanban, but this is not recommended.

KANBAN SYSTEM IN GENERAL

Kanban, literally translated, means "visible record" or "visible plate," but it is more generally taken to mean "card." The kanban system is a *manual* (and often visible) method of harmoniously controlling production and inventory quantities within the plant. The kanban system is frequently, though erroneously, equated with the Toyota Production System. The Toyota Production System is a manufacturing system, whereas kanban is the method used to *manage* this manufacturing system. While Toyota is undoubtedly a major supporter of the kanban system, it is not the only manufacturing company using such a pull system. Many American companies have adopted dual-card as well as single-card kanban versions of this system.

DUAL-CARD KANBAN SYSTEM

Figure 9-1a shows a kanban system within the context of an L-CMS. In contrast, Figure 9-1b shows a simple push system. The unique characteristic of the kanban pull system is that control information moves in the opposite direction of material movement. That is, downstream elements directly control upstream production rates. Material within a cell is called *stock-on-hand* (SOH). Material between cells in the links is *work-in-process* (WIP) *inventory*. The reason for this distinction will be shown later.

A kanban usually is a rectangular card enclosed in a vinyl sack attached to a container of parts. Sometimes the cards are made of plastic so that they can be reused. The containers are designed for each component (part) type and hold a precise quantity (generally small) of that part number. The two types of kanban cards are (1) the production-ordering kanban (POK) that signals an upstream cell or process to

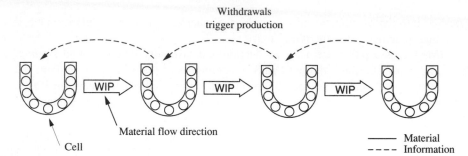

(a) Pull (kanban) system

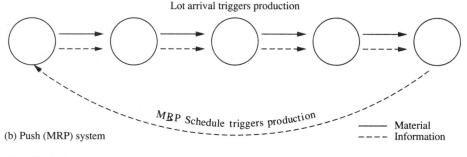

(b) Push (MRP) system

FIGURE 9-1
Comparison of pull to push systems.

produce a certain part; and (2) a withdrawal kanban (WLK) that serves to link two cells or processes. Figures 9-2 and 9-3 show examples of these two kanbans.

There is precisely one POK and one WLK for each container. They identify the part number, container capacity, the previous cell, the next cell or process, and other information. A WLK specifies the type and the quantity of a part number that a downstream process can withdraw from the upstream process. A POK specifies the type and quantity of the part that the next cell or process must produce. The beauty of this system is that it is simple and visual and the users understand how it works. Therefore, the users trust the system.

Store shelf no. Item back no.	Preceding process		
Item no.			
Item name			
Car type	Subsequent process		
Box capacity	Box type	Issued no.	

FIGURE 9-2
An example of a withdrawal kanban (WLK) for automobile manufacturing.

Store shelf no. Item back no.	Process
Item no.	
Item name	
Car type	

FIGURE 9-3
An example of a production ordering kanban (POK) for automobile manufacturing.

A modified version of the WLK is used to reorder raw materials (see Figure 9-4). Parts are withdrawn from the lot of 500 in containers of 100. When the stack of containers reaches the material requisition kanban, this kanban is used to requisition a coil of steel for the process (press #10 preceded by a shear). When the signal kanban is revealed, it is taken to the kanban post at press #10 and placed in the queue next to the material requisition kanban. These two kanbans combine to instruct the worker(s) at press #10 to make 500 left doors in containers of 100. The kanbans are reinserted in the stack of containers as shown in the figure. Table 9-1 lists some additional types of special kanbans.

Figure 9-5 demonstrates the container and kanban flow patterns for two cells. In this example, cell I supplies parts to cell II as well as to other cells in the plant. Cell I is serviced by stock point M, and cell II is serviced by stock point N.

Between the cells, material is moved in standard-size carts or containers. Each container holds the same number of parts. The carts or containers move in a loop (or on a circuit) from cell I to its stock point, then to the stock point of the next process. The material then moves into cell II for processing. Empty carts return to cell I for refilling. In summary, the WLKs circulate between the output side of cell I and the input side of cell II.

POKs move between the stock point for cell I and the supplying work cell. For each container, there is one POK and one WLK. Basically, the empty container is the signal to the manufacturing cell to make only enough product to refill that cart. Partially full containers are not allowed. The example shown in the figure begins at "start here," (found at the center of the figure):

1. At stock point N, a full container of parts is being moved into cell II. The WLK is detached from the container and placed in the kanban collection box for stock point N.
2. The most recently emptied container in cell II is returned to stock point N where a WLK is attached.
3. The WLK and the empty container are transported back to stock point M. (Stock points N and M are not usually side by side; they may be in different parts of the plant or in entirely different buildings.) The WLK is detached from the empty container and attached to a full container of parts. The full container with the WLK is returned to stock point N. (This is the withdrawing of material from the upstream cell by the downstream cell or assembly area.)
4. The full container (the one just removed from stock point M) had a POK attached. This POK was detached from the full container and placed in the collection box

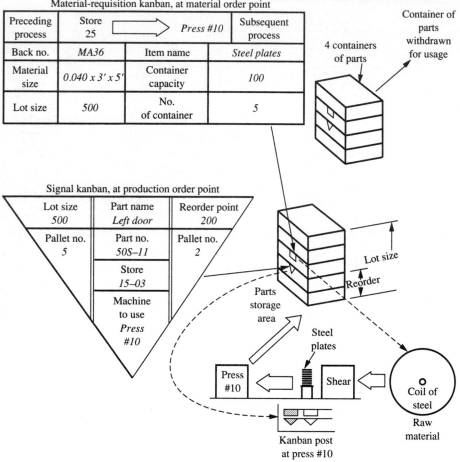

Material-requisition kanban, at material order point

Preceding process	Store 25	$\Longrightarrow$ Press #10	Subsequent process
Back no.	MA36	Item name	Steel plates
Material size	0.040 x 3' x 5'	Container capacity	100
Lot size	500	No. of container	5

Container of parts withdrawn for usage

4 containers of parts

Signal kanban, at production order point

Lot size 500	Part name Left door	Reorder point 200
Pallet no. 5	Part no. 50S–11	Pallet no. 2
	Store 15–03	
	Machine to use Press #10	

Parts storage area

Lot size

Reorder

Parts storage area

Steel plates

Press #10

Shear

Coil of steel

Raw material

Kanban post at press #10

FIGURE 9-4
How signal and material kanbans combine to make parts as needed.

for cell I. Then, and only then, can the container be removed from the stock point M and transported to stock point N.

5. Periodically, POKs are removed from the collection box and placed in the dispatch box for cell I. These POKs become the dispatch list for cell I, controlling the order of parts manufactured in the cell. These jobs are performed in the original order as received at stock point M.

6. The parts that are produced in cell I are placed in the empty containers taken from stock point M. The POK is attached to each container after it is filled. The container is then transported back to stock point M to be withdrawn by a downstream process when needed.

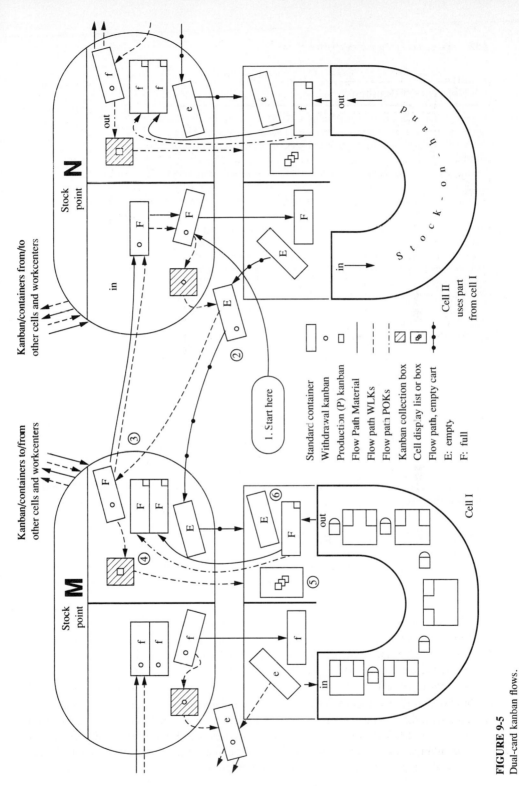

FIGURE 9-5
Dual-card kanban flows.

161

TABLE 9-1
Special types of kanbans*

Vendor kanban This type of withdrawal kanban is used specifically to request delivery of parts from a subcontracted supplier. Delivery times, receiving gate, and daily frequency of deliveries are indicated on a vendor kanban.

Emergency or special kanban This type of kanban is issued temporarily for defective work, extra insertions, or spurts in demand. Both a WOK and a POK exist. These kanbans are issued only for extraordinary reasons and are collected immediately after usage.

Signal kanban This type of kanban is used for lot manufacturing in job-order oriented production. It is a triangular form which is attached to a pallet or stack of containers at the reorder point. When containers are removed down to the reorder point, this kanban is removed and placed at the dispatching post to signal the need for the manufacture of additional parts (see Figure 9-4).

Material kanban This kanban is used in conjunction with the signal kanban. This kanban orders the raw materials for various processes within the plant. The material kanban is set higher than that of the signal kanban so that the material requirements will be fulfilled before manufacture of the desired part begins.

* For illustrations and a more complete explanation of each special type of kanban, see Monden, 1982.

This sequence is repeated many times during the day. Parts are produced as needed, that is, as withdrawn from the upstream cell.

Cell I may produce parts for cells or assembly lines other than cell II. All the other users operate in exactly the same manner. The carts are usually color-coded to prevent confusion.

DUAL-CARD KANBAN RULES

Rule l. The downstream cell or process should withdraw the needed products from the upstream cell or process according to the information provided on the WLK (the needed quantity at the necessary time).

While this may sound like motherhood, it is actually the realization of JIT: Parts should be withdrawn "just-in-time" as they are needed, not before they are needed and not in larger quantities than needed. The key points for enforcing this rule are as follows.

1. Any withdrawal without a WLK is prohibited. This prevents a large accumulation of excess inventory at the stock point that supplies the downstream process (stock point N in the example). The number of kanbans in the system is tightly controlled. (This will be discussed later as part of inventory control.) The withdrawal of any parts without a WLK undermines the control element of a kanban information system.

2. Any withdrawal greater than the number of kanbans should be prohibited. This is necessary for the same reason given above.

3. A kanban (either WLK or POK) should always be attached to the physical product, or its container, or should reside in a collection box. This key point eliminates the possibility of there being any unaccounted inventory in the system. If the number of kanbans in the system and the number of parts per container are strictly controlled, the amount of in-plant inventory can be determined and monitored at any time. This is the backbone of the kanban information system.

> **Rule 2.** The upstream process should produce products in quantities withdrawn by the downstream process or cell, according to the information provided by the POK.

This is the complement of Rule 1. If parts are withdrawn "just-in-time," then by complying with Rule 2, the parts will be produced "just-in-time." This is the cornerstone of IMPSs that utilize the JIT philosophy. The main points of this rule are:

1. Production greater than the number of kanbans must be prohibited. This prevents a large accumulation of excess inventory at the stock point for the upstream process (stock point M in the example) and eliminates the possibility of unaccounted inventory in the system.

2. When various kinds of parts are to be produced in the upstream process, manufacturing should follow the ordinal sequence in which each kind of kanban has been delivered. This helps to ensure that each type of part will be ready and available at the upstream process stock points whenever it is needed at the downstream processes or cells.

> **Rule 3.** Defective products should never be conveyed to the downstream process. If there is a defect, the line or cell should stop and immediately try to determine what corrective action should be taken.

One hundred percent quality control is necessary to achieve a truly effective kanban system. Based upon Rules 1 and 2, the parts are produced and withdrawn in the necessary quantities at the necessary times. If a defective part is sent to the downstream process, that operation may have to stop if there is no extra inventory (in the WLK loop) to replace the defective part. *In practice, the amount of inventory in the kanban link reflects the probability of a defect occurring in the upstream cell or process. Thus, downstream processes are not delayed unless all the inventory in the link is used up.* If this happens, then each of the upstream processes is stopped until the defective item is reworked, replaced, and the problem corrected. This rule is enforced by the practice of Integrated Quality Control and Autonomation in an IMPS.

> **Rule 4.** The number of kanbans can be gradually reduced in order to improve the processes and reduce waste.

This rule conveys the fact that inventory can be used as an independent control variable. The level of WIP inventory is controlled by the number of kanbans in the system at any given time. This number is initially the result of a management decision. Many companies opt for setting the initial number of kanban at about half of the existing number prior to the implementation of the pull system. The initial number of kanbans can be computed by the equation

$$K = \frac{DL + S}{a} \tag{9.1}$$

Where:

K = Number of kanbans or number of carts (K also equals the number of POKs or the number of WLKs)

D = Expected demand of parts, per unit time (per day)

L = Lead time (i.e., processing time + delay time + [lot delay and process delay] + conveyance time)

a = Container capacity (a fixed amount, usually ~10% of daily demand)

S = Safety stock (usually ~10 percent or less of DL)

Note from the equation the maximum inventory level (M) is expressed as:

$$M = aK = DL + S \tag{9.2}$$

The demand for parts is usually the daily demand, leveled from the monthly demand. The lead time takes into account the time needed to process a container of parts, the time to change over the cell and to process other items in the family, and the time to convey a container to the usage point, plus any delay times. Delay times include lot delay and process delay. Lot delay takes into account the fact that the first part produced cannot be conveyed (to the next cell) until the last item in the lot is produced. Smaller lots reduce the lot delay time. Process delay accounts for stoppages due to machine tool failures, broken tools, defective parts, and other manufacturing problems.

Suppose the cell is making a family of four parts, A, B, C, and D. Obviously there must be enough carts (or containers) in the loop of part A so that downstream processes do not run out of part A while the cell is making parts B, C, or D. This is a form of process delay that adds to the WIP inventory and is a tradeoff in flexibility. By designing the cell to be able to make a family of parts, a delay time for each member of the part family is being added.

Here is an example from Honda, in Marysville, Ohio, where they build the Accord. They have one stand of large presses that stamp out the sheet metal body parts for all the four-door Accords. This stand of presses manufactures 24 different sheet metal body parts in runs of 300 parts. (This is one day's supply of right rear doors.) The presses are changed over in about 10 minutes for the different parts. Obviously, enough right rear doors must be stamped out to last until the next quantity of right rear doors is stamped. Honda is constantly working to reduce the time required to change over these large presses from one part to another because this will permit them to further reduce the size of the run.

If lead time, L, is relatively small and the demand per unit time, D, is relatively constant, then the policy variable for safety stock can be small, resulting in a smaller inventory level. Therefore, the number of kanbans can be smaller. In practice, this policy variable is expected to approach zero, as will be discussed later. Lead times are reduced by eliminating setup times.

As the volume increases, more cells can become duplicated and dedicated. The inventory level between the cells can be further reduced. The smoothing of demand is achieved by smoothing production in the subsequent processes, as was discussed in Chapter 8.

> **Rule 5.** If there is no kanban card, there will be no manufacturing and no transfer of parts.

The WLK kanban card, as a production control device, should always be attached to the carts (or containers) unless they are in transit within the cell to order production. This rule reveals the visual control nature of the kanban card. The key manufacturing information is readily at hand. The removal of the kanban card prevents a cart from being transported and used.

> **Rule 6.** Kanbans should be used to adapt to only small fluctuations in demand (fine-tuning production by kanban).

Flexibility means the system can respond to changes in demand. There are three cases where kanbans can be used to fine-tune production, giving the system flexibility, with respect to changes in demand.

1. The first case is the result of changes in the product mix of the final assembly delivery dates and of small changes in quantities. There is no change in the daily total production load. The production schedule need only be revised for *final* assembly — the schedule for all the upstream processes will be revised automatically by transferring the kanbans.
2. The second case is the result of small, short-term fluctuations in the daily production load, although the monthly total load remains the same. Only the *frequency* of kanban movement will increase or decrease. The number of kanbans tends to be fixed despite the variation in demand.
3. This third case is the result of seasonal changes in demand or of increases and decreases in actual monthly demand. The actual number of kanbans in the system must be recomputed (increased or decreased) and the production lines must be rearranged (the cycle time must be recomputed and the number of workers in the cells must be changed accordingly).

These rules must be followed for the kanban system to be an effective management information system (MIS) that also can control the inventory process (level of WIP).

Kanban, as described here, is a relatively simple manual information system. Limitations for its use are as follows.

1. Goods must be produced in whole discrete units. Obviously, kanban is not applicable to continuous-process industries such as oil refineries and breweries.
2. Kanban should be a subsystem of an L-CMS system, using JIT philosophy. The use of a kanban system without the JIT philosophy makes little sense because Rules 1 and 2, regulating the use of kanbans, require the manufacture and withdrawal of the necessary parts in the necessary quantities at the necessary time.
3. The prerequisites for an IMPS (the design of the manufacturing system, standardization of operations within the cells, and the smoothing of production) must be implemented before an effective pull system can be implemented.
4. The parts included in the kanban system should be used every day (high-use parts). Kanban provides that at least one full container of a given part number is always available. There is not much inventory if the contents of the full container are used up the same day they are produced.

SINGLE-CARD KANBAN

Many companies have implemented what is known as a single-card kanban system that uses only the withdrawal kanban. The parts are produced or bought according to a daily schedule in the upstream process, and deliveries to the downstream process are controlled by WLKs. The previous example of the cells can be modified to show the cart and kanban flow of a single-card kanban system (see Figure 9-6). The stock point for cell I (stock point M) has been enlarged to accommodate production to a schedule, and the input side of stock point N for cell II has been eliminated because parts are delivered directly to the cell, as shown in the figure.

The standard cart moves on a circuit between the upstream process stock point and the downstream cell, then back to the upstream process or cell and finally back to the upstream stock point.

The WLK circulates between the stock point of the upstream cell and the process work center.

SINGLE-CARD EXAMPLE

1. The example begins as a container has just been emptied, and its WLK is placed in the kanban collection box at cell II.
2. At regular intervals, WLKs are gathered from the collection box. Full containers are delivered to cell II with WLKs (from a previous circuit) attached.
3. The empty containers are returned to cell I where they are filled with parts and taken to stock point M. Production quantities and part variety in cell I are controlled by the daily production schedule (push).
4. The WLKs are taken to stock point M, attached to full containers of parts, and delivered back to cell II on the next circuit.

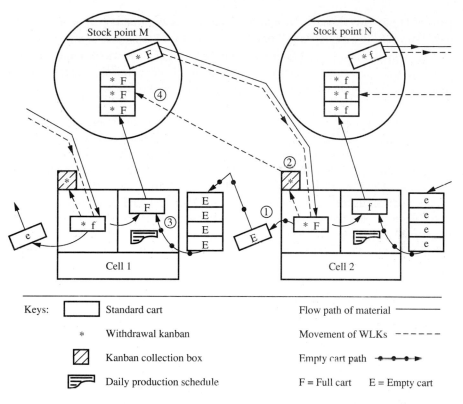

Keys:

☐ Standard cart		Flow path of material ———	
* Withdrawal kanban		Movement of WLKs – – – – –	
▨ Kanban collection box		Empty cart path •–•–•►	
▤ Daily production schedule		F = Full cart E = Empty cart	

FIGURE 9-6
Single-card kanban flows.

This process is repeated as many times a day as the parts are needed, just as with the dual-card system.

Single-card kanban systems have been equated with the "old two-bin system," where parts are reordered whenever the supply gets so low that the last box must be opened or the second bin must be used. Although it does work exactly this way, single-card kanban has some unique JIT elements.

1. Standard containers are used. Containers are designed for a specific part and hold a precise quantity of parts (as with the dual-card kanban system).
2. The number of containers is exact. There are exactly 11 containers in this link. Therefore, inventory is easy to count and to control.
3. The number of full containers at the point of use is usually one or two. Although inventory is allowed to build up at the upstream process stock point, this system controls the amount of inventory at the point of use.
4. The quantity in the container is small so that at least one container, and usually several containers, are used daily. If the container capacity is limited to about 10

percent of the daily demand, then at least one container of parts will be used every day. With the "two-bin system," one bin may last for several days or weeks.

5. The containers for the manufacturing cells hold small lots, which required prior action to cut setup times, thereby making small lots economical. Reducing setup time and producing in small lots are characteristics of an IMPS.

The advantage of a single-card push-pull system is that it is simple to implement. It can be expanded to a dual-card pull system later if it is deemed beneficial. A single-card kanban system strictly controls deliveries to the subsequent work center, never allowing a buildup of more than one or two containers of parts. It also eliminates the need for a stock point to supply the subsequent work center, thereby relieving the clutter and confusion around the point of use. Since production is controlled by a daily schedule, excess inventory is allowed to accumulate at the stock points for the upstream cell. For companies where it is easy to associate the required quantity and timing of parts with the schedule of end products, such as automobile companies, the accumulation can be small.

Very few companies have implemented a complete dual-card kanban system. The primary reason for this is that a dual-card kanban system requires a completely operational IMPS. A dual-card system controls both the use and the production of parts in order to have the necessary parts in the necessary quantity at the necessary time. Harley-Davidson is one company that has developed its own dual-card pull system.

MATERIAL-ORDERING KANBANS (MOKs)

A special kind of withdrawal card is often used to get material from vendors. An example of how these kanbans are used as material ordering kanban cards is shown in Figure 9-7. The information on the card is very similar to what is needed on a withdrawal card except that the card has detachable pieces that go to the user's accounts receivable department, as shown in Figure 9-8. A two-truck system is shown, but other systems are described in the chapter on vendor programs.

Here is how this simple system works.

1. At 8:00 A.M., a truck delivers MOKs and empty containers to the vendor.
2. Upon arrival at the vendor, the truck driver hands the MOKs to the vendor's store worker. The driver switches to a truck loaded with parts produced to the requirement of MOKs brought at 8:00 P.M. the night before. He drives back to the user's company and delivers the parts to the correct location within the plant.
3. At 8:00 P.M., the empty truck is returned to the vendor. More MOKs are given to the vendor and the full truck is taken back to the plant. One day's supply is carried in two trucks.
4. If the truck can be rapidly loaded and unloaded, only one truck is necessary. Many material transporting companies have already developed such systems.

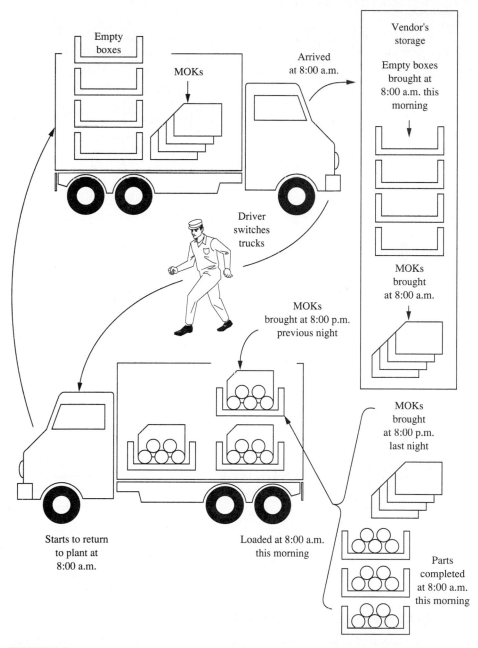

FIGURE 9-7
Movement of material-ordering kanbans (MOKs) between plant and vendor. (*Monden, 1983.*)

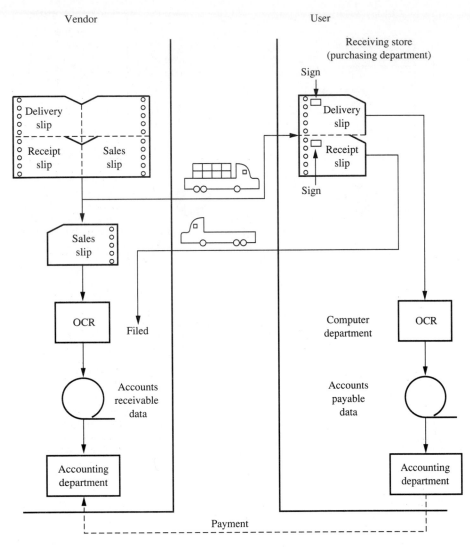

FIGURE 9-8
MOK voucher movement for two-truck system. (*Monden, 1983.*)

INTEGRATED INVENTORY CONTROL

The most powerful analogy presented in Japanese literature, by Shingo (1981), is the now-famous "rocks in the river" (see Figure 9-9). In this simple analogy, rocks are equated to problems, and the river is inventory (material) moving through the plant. The level of the river is equivalent to the work-in-process (WIP) inventory that flows through the factory, just as the river flows between its banks. When the river level is

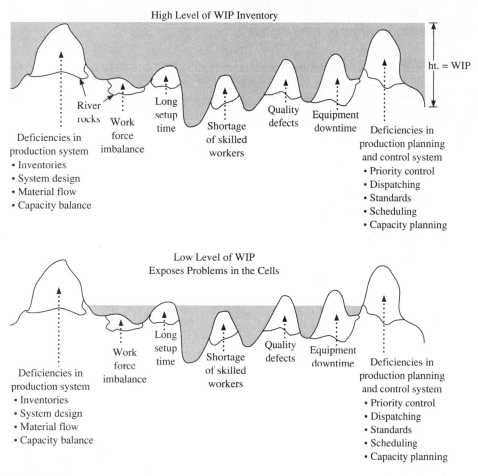

FIGURE 9-9
Lowering the level of inventory uncovers the problems.

high, the rocks, which represent hazards to safe navigation, are covered. (See Table 9-2 for a listing of problems and traditional solutions.)

Now it might be asked, "Isn't that good?" Hasn't inventory traditionally been used to circumvent the problems of poor quality, machine tool breakdowns, long setup times, shortages of parts, and many other deficiencies in the manufacturing or production systems? True, but there are errors in this way of thinking. Covering up the problems is the wrong approach. Inventories are wasteful and expensive to carry. Low-cost, high-quality manufacturing will never be achieved when WIP levels are high. Besides, the inventory, if not controlled, may suddenly drop because of factors outside of one's control, revealing some problem in the system at the most inopportune time and throwing the entire plant into disarray.

TABLE 9-2
Problems and solutions in the workplace

Problems in the Workplace (rocks in the river)
   Machine failures (wait for repair)
   Bad raw materials (poor incoming quality)
   Tool failure (fractured, worn, or missing tools)
   Workers absent or late
   Changeover from one part to another
   Waiting for parts
   Waiting for material handling
   Waiting for inspector/setup/or maintenance person

Typical Western (USA) Solutions
   Lots of inventory and buffer stock
   Backup machines or material-handling equipment
   Supermachines (large and expensive automation)
   Extra tools and materials
   Extra repair parts
   Extra workers (expediters and dispatchers)
   Elaborate information systems (computerized)
   Robotize and automate (expensive)

INVENTORY: AN INDEPENDENT CONTROL VARIABLE

IMPS alters the nature of inventory completely, changing it from a dependent variable in the classical push system to an *independent control variable* in the pull system. Taking the rocks in the river analogy a step further, the river has some volume of flow that represents capacity. River flows are described in cubic feet per minute. The materials that flow in continuous processing manufacturing such as chemical plants and refineries are also described in ft^3/min. Continuous processing manufacturing systems represent the ideal in terms of efficient manufacturing with the minimum WIP and therefore represent the "vision" of IMPS. However, in order to make the discrete parts flow like water or oil, one must reduce the setup time and lot sizes and eliminate the defective products and machine breakdowns in the systems. Inventory flow rate is, therefore, an independent variable that can be described as follows:

River flow rate (ft^3/min) = IMPS capacity = depth × width × velocity

Depth of river level (ft) = Amount of WIP

Width of the river (ft) = Number of manufacturing systems (No. of final assembly lines.)

Velocity (ft/min) = Throughput rate or production rate of the system (units/hr)

   In our classical systems, we have concentrated on the production rate with little regard for the level of inventory. *In IMPSs, the depth of the river is also controlled.*

That is, the inventory levels are deliberately raised or lowered, even though lowering the inventory level will expose problems. When this happens, the inventory is restored (temporarily) in order to ease the pain to ourselves or our customers, and the problem is attacked and eliminated; the rocks are removed from the river.

How is the inventory level controlled? By the use of kanban. Kanban allows for specific amounts of inventory to be added or extracted from the flow, thus changing the depth.

The flow rate can be changed by altering the production rate or the number of workers in the manufacturing cells. The production rate in units per hour is the inverse of the cycle time in hours per unit. Cycle time is controlled by other means, such as varying the number of workers in a manufacturing or assembly cell—the more workers, the lower the cycle time and the greater the production rate.

Getting back to the analogy, the river level can never be lowered completely to the riverbed, because flow stops completely. *There is no such condition as zero inventory.* A certain minimum amount of inventory must always be in the system. The power of the analogy is that the more rocks removed, the lower the river level can be run safely, without interruption.

In the same way, the level of WIP between the cells reflects the progress that has been made in removing setup time, eliminating defective products, eliminating machine breakdowns, and standardizing the cycle times (eliminating the variability). The nearer the system gets to perfection, the lower the WIP level can be and still flow smoothly.

USING INVENTORY AS A CONTROL VARIABLE

Dual-card kanban systems have a unique productivity improvement feature that neither push systems nor single-card kanban systems have. Foremen or supervisors have the authority to remove kanban from the system to reduce inventory and thus expose problems. To do this, they do not have to remove the container from the system; all they do is gather a pair of kanbans from a full container. The container cannot be moved without a kanban attached to it. Even though workers and foremen are upset when the removal of inventory from the system causes delays in the schedule, this gives them a chance to uncover some problems in the upstream cell. The inventory can be released by reinstating the cards. Meanwhile, the problem can be corrected. Once a solution is in place, the inventory level can be lowered again and another round of problem solving begins. Productivity and quality are continuously improved. This feature makes the dual-card kanban system very effective.

The dual-card system is particularly effective for small-lot mass production of complex assembly items in which there is the potential for delays caused by the compound effect of

1. Large number of parts (wide variety)
2. Variable usage of the parts
3. Multiple stages of manufacture/assembly

In order to avoid running out of parts when delays occur, huge buffer stocks are normally carried. However, the dual-card pull system signals the manufacture of each part number to match the up-and-down output rate of downstream production stages. The inventory between the cells is continually reduced by the removal of carts (see Figure 9-5). Suppose you begin with 12 carts between the two cells. Suppose each cart holds 20 parts. The maximum inventory between the two cells is therefore 240 parts. The removal of a cart lowers the maximum inventory level to 220 parts. If no problems occur, another cart is removed. The process continues until finally no more carts can be removed without serious delays occurring due to lack of available parts. Let us say that this occurs when there are six carts remaining. (This number will often depend on how close one cell is to another and on the length of setup times between different parts).

Now the number of parts in each cart can be cut in half (10) and the number of carts restored to 12. Thus, the level of inventory is the same, but the frequency of lot production is increased. The flow is smoother (smaller lots produce smaller demand spikes in the system). The problem of setup reduction will become immediately apparent since cutting the lot size increases the setup frequency. Once setup time has been reduced, inventory levels can again be reduced by holding kanban cards.

This method of inventory control is integrated because it is operated entirely by the people who run the manufacturing system. Eventually the users get the inventory level as low as possible without causing major disruptions to the manufacturing system. The system will require upgrading and automation to go to the next level. This kind of automation is usually easy to justify.

KANBAN PULL SYSTEM COMPARED TO MATERIAL REQUIREMENTS PLANNING (MRP)

In this section, various features of the pull system will be compared to MRP, inventory levels, and production philosophy. The pull system will be compared to the push system.

At its initialization, kanban should be a *manual* information system utilizing cards. This helps familiarize everyone with the system. The capital investment in a kanban system alone will not be large compared to the costs of changing the manufacturing system itself.

Material requirements planning, on the other hand, is a computer-based system. Because the existing manufacturing system and MRP are so complex, MRP is *not* manageable without computer assistance. The capital investment in an MRP system is extensive. In 1980, the average cost to the company for MRP installation was $375,000. This included labor, software, hardware, and training for the development of the system. The eventual cost could rise to over $600,000 for a fully-developed MRP system.

MRP systems take a long time to implement. At a conference in Canada, I spoke with a material manager who had just spent two years implementing the company's MRP program. I asked him how many people were in his company. "500 workers and 200 others," he replied. I asked him how many of those people *understood* the

MRP system. After a long pause, he estimated three. I wondered how any system can function well when only three people understood how it was supposed to work. People will not use a system they do not understand. Material is the lifeblood of the manufacturing system. To not understand how it is controlled is bad engineering.

In addition, MRP is a material requirements planning system that uses built-in EOQ calculations. Therefore, quantities will vary considerably. It is better to have fixed small quantities and vary the frequency of the parts. The system was developed for planning in the job shop, not for control of the material moving through the plant.

A dual-card kanban system is truly a "pull" system of parts ordering and control. The ordinal production schedule is issued *only* to the starting point on the final assembly line and not to any other process. The production schedule for each of the preceding processes is determined by the transfer of the parts and withdrawal kanbans looping between the processes in the system. Therefore, the parts are actually pulled through the system from the end of the line to the start.

The single-card kanban system is a combination of a push-and-pull parts ordering system. The manufacturing aspect in a single-card kanban system is a push system because parts are produced according to a daily production schedule rather than for immediate needs as in the dual-card kanban system. Coupled with this push system for manufacturing is a pull system for deliveries. Parts are delivered using withdrawal kanbans only as they are needed by the downstream processes.

MRP is a push system of parts ordering and control. A push system is simply a schedule-based system in which a multiperiod schedule of future demands for the company's products is prepared. The computer breaks down the schedule for manufacturing and develops a production schedule for each work center based upon the master schedule. Then the parts are delivered throughout the system without regard to the actual immediate need. The connection between the planned schedule and reality may not exist.

Companies using pull kanban systems have less delay or lead time between parts manufacture and use, so they have only hours' or minutes' worth of materials in inventory. An MRP system carries days', weeks', or months' worth of material in inventory because the parts are produced to cover the demand for a week or longer.

A kanban information system is a logical extension of an IMPS. The elimination of setup time makes small lot sizes economical. Making all lots equal in size or as small as possible plus redesigning the manufacturing system, standardizing the operations, and smoothing the manufacturing system are all integral parts of the pull system.

An MRP system produces parts in *large* lot sizes in order to cover the demand of a single period. This system has *not* adopted the concept of small economical lot sizes through eliminating setup time and streamlining the operation. In MRP, lot sizes vary considerably, so production cannot be smoothed.

The crucial factor of determining which information system to use is the ease of associating requirements for parts with the schedule of end products. Figure 9-10 shows the relationship between the ease of associating the requirements and the type of information system used. This will affect the size of the inventory level, as discussed earlier.

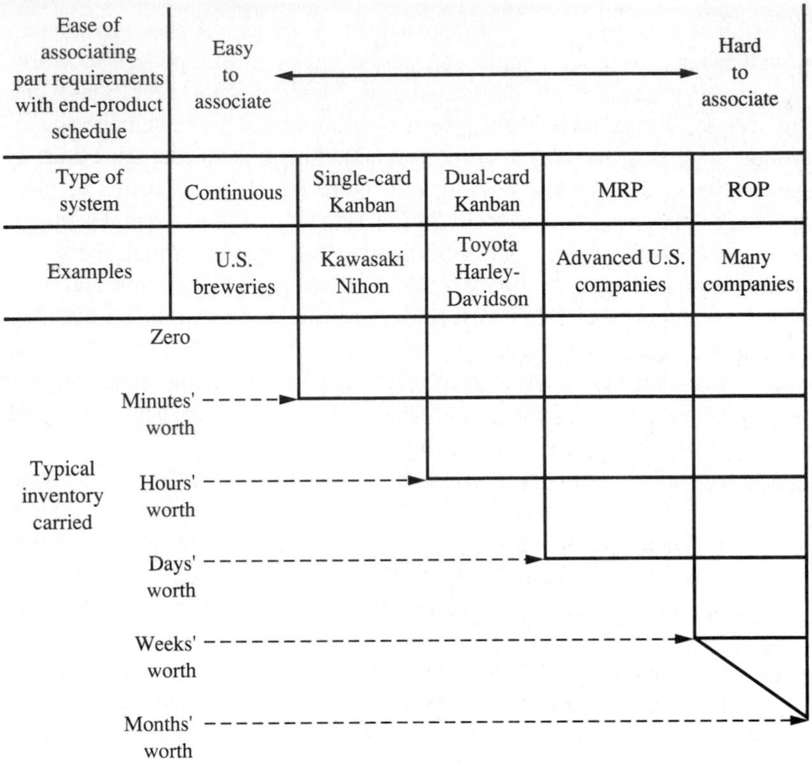

Ease of associating part requirements with end-product schedule	Easy to associate				Hard to associate
Type of system	Continuous	Single-card Kanban	Dual-card Kanban	MRP	ROP
Examples	U.S. breweries	Kawasaki Nihon	Toyota Harley-Davidson	Advanced U.S. companies	Many companies

Typical inventory carried

Zero
Minutes' worth
Hours' worth
Days' worth
Weeks' worth
Months' worth

FIGURE 9-10
Manufacturing inventory systems. (*Schonberger, 1982.*)

The major distinguishing factor between the pull system and the MRP system is the ability of the former to accurately associate the component part requirements with the end-product schedule. The dual-card kanban system is able to associate accurately because it manufactures and withdraws parts according to the actual needs of the system. Production control is truly integrated into the manufacturing system. The MRP system does not have as high a degree of association or integration because of error introduced into the part requirements as the result of changes in the actual end-product schedule. Although MRP correctly calculates the part requirements by precisely associating them with the master schedule of end products, long lead times and large lot sizes erode the close association between the part requirements and the end-product schedules. The way to make MRP a truly effective information system would be to reduce setup time to make small lot sizes more economical. This would reduce the error inherent in the MRP part requirements calculation. However, if the setup time is reduced in order to make MRP more effective, MRP is not needed for material control in IMPS, since pull systems are preferable.

THE PAPERLESS FACTORY OF THE FUTURE

Dinosaurs ruled during the age of reptiles. The biggest dinosaur, the swamp monster *Brachiosaurus*, was too large to support its own weight on land. It needed the buoyancy of water to stand. It might be said that manufacturing systems have their "dinosaurs" and their "endangered species." The principal one is the production job shop, a manufacturing system kept afloat (by the ingenuity of people and by oceans of inventory) long after it has reached a size and complexity that should have caused its utter collapse. Clearly the time has come for the invention of a new manufacturing system. What motivated Taiichi Ohno, then vice-president of Toyota, to develop this system, and why does the system have the characteristics that it does?

After World War II, Japan was known as a nation that made junk. The Japanese wanted to develop full employment in their country through industrialization. To do this, they needed to learn how to build quality products—products other nations would buy. They thought that we in the United States knew how to do this, so they learned about quality control from us (the now-famous trips of Deming and Juran). Initially, quality control techniques were taught to the engineers and managers. Then the Japanese did something very different—something not done in the U.S. factories. Most surprisingly, the workers were taught quality control techniques. Next, the workers were given the responsibility for quality and the authority to stop the processes if something went wrong. Toyota and its suppliers began to develop early versions of linked-cell manufacturing systems for the manufacture of (families of) parts. In these early cells, they learned to eliminate setup and to work together to eliminate defective parts. The workers became multiprocess, so that they could operate different processes. But these events do not explain why this unique system came to be.

This question probably lies in the very nature of the Japanese language. In his seminars, Richard Schonberger tells of not being able to find a typewriter on his travels to various Japanese companies. As a language, Japanese is very difficult to use for written communication. The classical, large production job shop requires a very sophisticated information system to deal with the complexity of the manufacturing system and its interface with the production system. Since Taiichi Ohno could not change the language, he had to find a way to simplify the manufacturing and production systems to eliminate the need for communication. He began to eliminate all kinds of unnecessary functions. In contrast, manufacturers in the United States tried to computerize and optimize the functions.

The Toyota system was created by trial-and-error processes within an environment where the language would not permit them to construct a written communication system (information system) that could control a large, complex manufacturing system. So Toyota developed a manufacturing system that was simple to operate and control with a very simple information system, one now known as kanban. This is a pull system of production and inventory control and it is unique. Kanban uses visual cards for information transfer and inventory control. The manufacturing system is redesigned such that only the final assembly line needs to be scheduled. What could be simpler? In fact, the long-range goal of the system is to eliminate the need for kanban by directly linking the processes. This means that the output from each cell goes to only one customer. Note that this defines *what* the cell or process is to make. Moreover, one of the system's operational characteristics is the gradual *elimination of its primary information document*, the kanban cards.

Thus, the proper path to get us to the paperless factory of the future is evident. We must begin today to eliminate the manufacturing system called the production job shop and replace it with cellular manufacturing systems linked with kanban. We also must redesign our flow line manufacturing systems so that they have the same characteristics as the cells, particularly regarding flexibility (ability to react quickly to changes in demand or changes in design).

The trick is to begin to implement integrated manufacturing production systems concepts immediately in every plant. Notice I said IMPS, not CIM (computer-integrated manufacturing), or CAD/CAM, or FMS. Do not computerize the existing system. Plugging the advanced technologies (computers, robotics, automated guided vehicles, automatic storage racks, etc.) into the "batch-building" production job shop will lead to automated economic dinosaurs. These are expensive solutions, and if they simply eliminate a direct laborer or two, the gains will be negligible. The correct approach is *to change the manufacturing system*, get rid of the PJS, implement IMPS and then computerize, robotize, and automate *to solve production problems*.

SUMMARY

In conclusion, the kanban system accurately associates the part requirements with the end-product schedule. Part usage and manufacturing in all the upstream processes are determined by the actual need of the end-product assemblies through the transfer of withdrawal and production kanbans. These parts are manufactured "just-in-time" (the necessary products, in the necessary quantities, at the necessary time).

The system, being manual at the outset, is easily understood by all its users, something that cannot be said for many of the computerized systems used in the job shop. All employees understand how their actions influence the entire system and that they can make the system better.

Large lot sizes, long lead times, and changes in the schedule make it difficult for an MRP system to associate accurately the part requirements with the end-product schedule. If inexpensive kanban can achieve better estimates of part requirements than computer-based MRP systems, the money saved is better spent on implementing IMPSs to improve quality, lower costs, reduce inventory, and facilitate an inventory control system. After all, the most expensive system is not necessarily the best.

CHAPTER 10

INTEGRATING THE VENDOR INTO IMPS

The external customer is always right.

INTRODUCTION

IMPS purchasing is a program of continuous, long-term improvement. The company and its vendors work together to reduce lead times, lot sizes, and inventory levels. Both the vendor and the company become more competitive in the world marketplace. Extending IMPS to the vendors requires that the IMPS company develop a program that educates and encourages suppliers to develop a manufacturing system that produces superior quality at the lowest possible cost, delivers on time, and is flexible. The vendors essentially become remote cells from which materials and subassemblies are withdrawn just as they are pulled from cells within the plant.

Purchasing in the Job Shop: Where We've Been

- Multisourcing
- Weekly/monthly/semiannual deliveries
- Long lead times (weeks/months)
- Safety stock
- Quantity variances
- Late/early deliveries

- Inspection of incoming materials
- Inconsistent packaging
- Expediting

IMPS Purchasing: Where We're Going

- Daily/weekly/quarterly deliveries
- Shorter lead times (days/weeks)
- Less safety stock
- Specified quantity
- On-time deliveries
- Bypass incoming quality inspection
- Standard packaging
- Less expediting

CHARACTERISTICS OF IMPS PURCHASING

Single sourcing. One vendor, the best vendor, will be selected to be the sole source for each part, component, or subassembly used by the company. This reduces the variability between parts (improves the quality), since all the parts are coming from the same manufacturing process or system. This approach replaces the strategy of multiple vendors competing against each other and helps to eliminate the adversarial relationship between the vendor and the customer.

Advantages of Multiple Source

- Hedge against vendor problems
- Consistent quality by incoming inspection
- Some vendors cannot handle all of a division's work
- Competitive advantage

Advantages of Single Source

- Divisional resources can be focused on selecting/developing/monitoring one source rather than many
- Volume buys are higher, leading to lower cost
- Vendor is more inclined to do special favors for the customer since the customer is a large account
- Easier to control and monitor for superior quality
- Tooling dollars are concentrated in one source rather than many (save money)

Longer term contracts. The company and the supplier develop long-term contracts (18- to 24-month) that enable the vendor to take the long range view and plan ahead. Contracts are renegotiated every 6 to 12 months with very short lead time.

1. The company supplies updated forecasts every month (good for 12 months).
2. The company commits to long-term quantity and eventual excess material buyout.
3. Delivery specified by mid-month for the next month.

Advantages of Long-Term Contracts

- Builds schedule stability. No "jerking" up and down of vendors' build schedule; smooth increase or decrease.
- Better rapport. Monthly, or more often, communication between buyer and vendor.
- Better visibility. The vendor sees one year's worth of forecasted needs as soon as the company sees it, instead of a limited lead-time view.
- Less paperwork. Fewer (none, if possible) change orders to run through the system. Good for the company and the vendor.
- Inventory elimination. Initially at the company, followed by vendors as lead times are reduced.

Very frequent delivery. The vendor will be expected to deliver materials to the company daily or weekly, depending on the type of part or subassembly. Most parts can be categorized according to an ABC analysis, as shown in Figure 10-1. "A" parts are critical, high-cost parts, but are few in volume. "C" parts are low-cost, but numerous. "B" parts are in between, but are critical for other reasons. For example, many companies classify bulky parts like packaging materials and sheet metal as "B" parts. They are not very expensive but they take up a lot of space.

100% good quality. The vendor should be taught how to implement the IMPS strategy so that the vendor can deliver the correct quantity, on time, with no incoming inspection. In short, move toward becoming a JIT vendor.

Engineering aid to the vendor. Often the vendor will be a much smaller company, unable to afford engineering expertise in the manufacturing and quality areas. The vendor and the customer work together to improve the vendor's manufacturing processes, efficiency, and quality. The customer should visit the vendor's plant at least once a year (more often if there are problems), and the vendor should visit the customer so that the vendor sees how the components are used in the customer's products.

	A	B	C
# Parts	Low to moderate	Low to moderate	Very high
Volume %	Low	Low to moderate	High
Cost %	High	Low to moderate	Low
Receipt frequency	Daily	Daily to weekly	Monthly or 2-4 times/yr
Strategy	Inventory Management	Space	Service Level

FIGURE 10-1
ABC analysis for parts from the vendors.

Local sources when possible. While it is not absolutely necessary (or even possible) that all the vendors be located close to the customer, the closer the vendor is to the customer or the company, the easier it is to provide the customer with daily deliveries. Every day material spends being transported adds to the amount of stocked material inventory.

Freight consolidation program. Materials from vendors can be consolidated onto one truck for transportation to the customer. If a company has three vendors in the same town who deliver daily, one truck and driver can pick up daily from each vendor and deliver to the customer.

Standard packaging in fixed quantities. This means the containers are standardized in terms of size and quantity. Never ship a half of a container. Tables 10-1 and 10-2 summarize the customer and vendor relationships.

WHAT IT ALL MEANS TO THE VENDORS

The big companies must rely on their suppliers and vendors to deliver the materials and subassemblies they need. The supplier who is first to grasp the new process control and management techniques that the customer wants will survive. The small company, on the other hand, does not have the expertise to make sweeping engineering changes, but does have the advantage of being small and less encumbered. That is, the small company is able to adapt to the new IMPS ideas quicker. The small companies had better be ready to climb on board. The big companies are reducing the number of vendors and going with those closer to home. The vendor must be ready to adapt to IMPS and all it stands for. If he does not, he will not be chosen as a sole source vendor. What this means is that the vendors simply cannot become a "ship from stock" operation to satisfy the JIT needs of the customer. The vendor must cut the manufacturing lead time. Then the vendor won't need stable forecasts of demand since it will be able to alter production rates quickly.

TABLE 10-1
Summary of what the customer expects from a vendor

Parts that consistently meet print requirements with no
   incoming inspection required
On-time shipments
Short, constant lead times
Full service vendor
Long-term relationship
Fair dealings
Daily shipments (if justified)
Control of processes (changes with the permission of
   the customer only)
Cost reductions passed on to the customer (mutual
   engineering)
Parts packaged in issue quantities

TABLE 10-2
Summary of what vendors want from the customer

Customer satisfaction
Fair profit
Long-term business arrangements
Fair return on investment
Enough time to plan
Accurate forecasts
Specifications called out correctly
Parts designed to match vendor's process capability
Smooth order releases
Minimum number of order changes (dates/prints)
Prompt payment of invoices

With respect to vendors, here are the JIT results at the Greeley (Colorado) Division of Hewlett Packard one year into the implementation of IMPS.

- Inventory reduced from 2.8 months to 1.3 months
- 50 percent space savings in stockroom
- 20 vendors supplying 45 parts now deliver on JIT basis
- All employees trained and aware of program
- Task force is addressing JIT systems needs
- Several lines now converted to continuous flow manufacturing
- Many production efficiency and quality problems have been exposed and solved

CHAPTER 11

AUTOMATION OF MANUFACTURING CELLS

Routine for the machine, exceptions for the human.

INTRODUCTION

The word *automation* was first used in the early 1950's to mean automatic material handling. As automation technology progressed, the term was used in a wider sense. Today automation refers to both services performed and products produced automatically and to information handling tasks. According to Webster's New Collegiate Dictionary, automation is "The technique of making a process or system automatic."

Table 11-1 provides a yardstick for automation. The order of automaticity is based on the human attribute mechanized or automated into the manufacturing process.

All work requires both energy and information, and these two elements must be provided by some source, either a human being or a substitute. As a machine assumes higher levels of human attributes, it advances to the next stage of automation. The more human attributes performed by a machine, the higher it is in "order of automaticity." Automaticity is thus defined as the self-acting capability of the device. In this classification, it is observed that 10 levels are sufficient to describe all the present machines and all those that will be invented in the future.

An A(0) represents hand tools and manual machines. No human attribute is mechanized. This process is without self-action properties. It does not replace human energy or any basic control but may include built-in guides and measurements. A(0) tools include all hand tools. Hand tools and manual machines increase worker efficiency but do not replace human functions and include all muscle-energized machines

TABLE 11-1
Yardstick for automation

Orders of automation	Human attribute replaced	Examples
A(0)	*None:* lever, screw, pulley, wedge	Hand tools, manual machine
A(1)	*Energy:* muscles replaced	Powered machines and tools, Whitney's milling machine
A(2)	*Dexterity:* self-feeding	Single-cycle automatics
A(3)	*Diligence:* no feedback	Repeats cycle; open-loop machine control; automatic screw machine; transfer lines
A(4)	*Judgment:* positional feedback	Closed loop; numerical control; self-measuring and -adjusting
A(5)	*Evaluation:* adaptive control deductive analysis; feedback from the process	Computer control; model of process required for analysis and optimization
A(6)	*Learning:* by experience	Limited self-programming expert systems
A(7)	*Reasoning:* exhibits intuition; relates causes from effects	Inductive reasoning; AI
A(8)	*Creativeness:* performs design unaided	Originality
A(9)	*Dominance:* supermachine; commands others	Machine is master (Hal from "2001, A Space Odyssey")

Source: Amber & Amber, *Anatomy of Automation*, Prentice-Hall, Inc., Englewood Cliffs, N.J., 1962. Used by permission of Amber & Amber.

(machines that give mechanical advantages but do not replace man's energy or control). Some examples of A(0) machines are a lever, an inclined plane, a wheel and axle, a screw, a pulley, and a wedge.

An A(1) machine is a powered machine or tool. The human attribute mechanized is energy. Muscles are replaced by the basic machine function. Machine action and control are completely dependent upon the operator. These tools or machines use mechanical power (windmill, waterwheel, steam engine, electric motor) but the operator positions the work and machine for desired action.

An A(2) machine is a single-cycle automatic or a self-feeding machine. The human attribute mechanized is dexterity. These machines complete an action when initiated by an operator. The machine feeds a tool to the workpiece by power. These machines include all single-cycle automatic machines. The operator must set up, load, initiate actions, adjust, and unload.

An A(3) machine is an automatic machine that repeats the cycle. The human attribute mechanized is diligence. These machines carry out routine instructions without human aid. They start cycles and repeat the actions automatically. The machine loads, goes through a sequence of operations, then unloads to the next station or machine. They are open loop (not self-correcting) and obey internal (fixed) or external (variable) programs, such as cams, tapes, or cards. These machines include all automatic machines including many transfer machines and classical "Detroit" automation.

An A(4) is a self-measuring and -adjusting machine with feedback. The human attribute mechanized is judgment. These machines measure and compare results to the desired size or position and make adjustments to minimize any error. Although feedback control of the actual surface of the workpiece is preferable, positional control of the machine table or tool is of great value too. A process may use more than one A(4) subsystem operating independently. See Figure 11-1 for examples of A(1) through A(4) machines.

An A(5) machine has computer process control or has automatic cognition. The human attribute mechanized is evaluation. These machines are cognizant of multiple factors on which the machine or process performance is predicated, and they evaluate and reconcile such factors by a computer model (analysis) to determine the proper control action. Any process or problem that can be expressed as an equation can be computer controlled. Such a control system can adapt to variations in materials, in process conditions, and in the job. Limited-purpose, on-board computers are used to accomplish A(5) computer control. A(3), A(4), or A(5) control systems are superimposed on A(2) machines to reduce the dependence on operator skills.

An A(6) machine has limited self-programming capability. The control algorithm contains an expert system. The human attribute mechanized is learning. These machines may be set up to try subroutines based on the general program. By remembering which actions were most effective in obtaining the desired results, the machine "learns by experience," or by trial and error.

An A(7) machine relates cause and effect or has artificial intelligence (AI). The human attribute mechanized is reasoning. These machines have the ability to forecast trends, patterns, and relationships from incomplete facts. They exhibit "intuition" by going beyond available data. The control software is infected with artificial intelligence models. Other strategies may be the basis of operation. Inductive reasoning A(7) is not the same as the deductive reasoning of A(8) machines. Analysis requires deduction; synthesis requires induction.

An A(8) machine has originality. The human attribute mechanized is creativeness. These machines have the ability to originate work to suit human tasks and preferences. They do not copy, imitate, or follow plans and instructions. A program for an A(8) machine only designates the general form of the desired action and eliminates clashes, discords, and disharmonies. The actual result is original.

An A(9) machine commands. The human attribute mechanized is dominance. These machines govern the actions of men, machines, and other systems. They act as a "commanding general" or as a "dictator" to achieve results. The machine is no longer a servant but the master. An A(9) supermachine is capable of superior energy, dexterity, diligence, judgment, evaluation, learning, reasoning, and creativeness (that

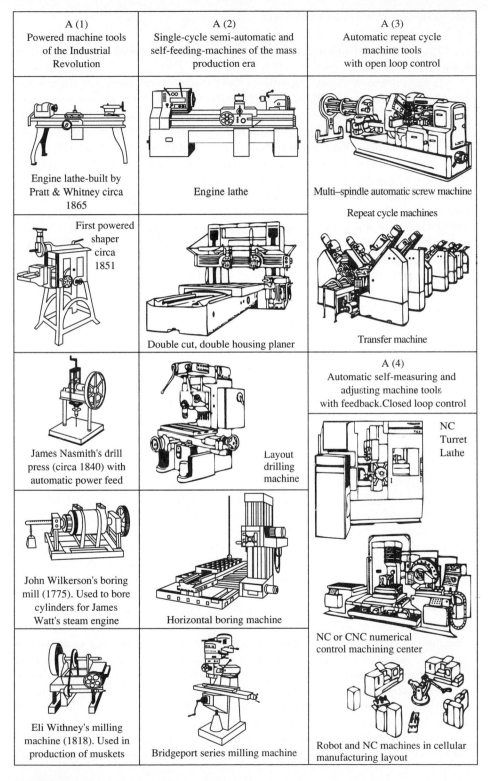

A (1) Powered machine tools of the Industrial Revolution	A (2) Single-cycle semi-automatic and self-feeding-machines of the mass production era	A (3) Automatic repeat cycle machine tools with open loop control
Engine lathe-built by Pratt & Whitney circa 1865	Engine lathe	Multi–spindle automatic screw machine
First powered shaper circa 1851	Double cut, double housing planer	Repeat cycle machines Transfer machine
James Nasmith's drill press (circa 1840) with automatic power feed	Layout drilling machine	A (4) Automatic self-measuring and adjusting machine tools with feedback.Closed loop control NC Turret Lathe
John Wilkerson's boring mill (1775). Used to bore cylinders for James Watt's steam engine	Horizontal boring machine	NC or CNC numerical control machining center
Eli Withney's milling machine (1818). Used in production of muskets	Bridgeport series milling machine	Robot and NC machines in cellular manufacturing layout

FIGURE 11-1

Machine tools of the first industrial revolution (A1), the mass production era (A2), and examples of A(3) and A(4) levels of automation. (*DeGarmo, 7th ed.*)

is, all the human attributes replaced by the other levels of automation) and would be able to dominate man.

In the current levels of automation, A(4) machines are computer numerically controlled and are commonplace on the factory floor. A(5) machines are adaptive control machines. A(5) machines make use of mathematical equations and problem solving capabilities as part of their control system. This is based on the fact that most processes can be mathematically modeled. The control system tries to optimize some aspect of the process. For example, the metal removal rate per unit force may be maximized by varying feed or depth of cut. At the A(6) level, an expert system is incorporated that allows the computer control system to learn by experience (become more expert). The next stage requires the computer software to have artificial intelligence (AI) or the ability to reason (to suggest causes based on the effects observed by sensors in the process or system). The computer logic for levels A(5), A(6), and A(7) are still in the developmental stages. Very few machines with adaptive control are found on the factory floor, although they exist in other areas of human endeavor. Machines that use expert systems and artificial intelligence in their control logic are found mostly in research laboratories.

AUTOMATION IN IMPS

To obtain maximum benefits from automation, the manufacturing system has to be redesigned into an IMPS. The restructured system is further refined through continual improvement efforts. Once the system is running at peak efficiency, it can be automated to give maximum return on the investment in complex, sophisticated equipment. This is because improvements in the efficiency of the processes will have a stronger impact on the bottom line when the system is at peak efficiency. Within the JIT philosophy, automation is not buying supermachines (machines capable of producing thousands of parts every day), but is instead optimizing the use of existing equipment and improving its efficiency through preventive maintenance. Actually, just as the process of converting the factory to IMPS is best done in stages, the process of automating the plant is basically an evolutionary or incremental process, initiated by the need to solve a problem in quality or capacity (eliminating a bottleneck). It can begin with mechanization of simple operations like loading, unloading, inspecting, and clamping, and move toward emulating the human attributes of sensing and correcting problems.

In an unmanned cell, the material handling is done by a robot, conveyors, gravity chutes, or perhaps an AGV. Simple operations like picking, loading, and unloading a machine are the preliminary operations that can be automated. For these simple operations, robots can be employed. After a certain level of efficiency is reached in performing these simple tasks, the robots will need to be able to perform more intelligent tasks, such as picking up the correct size bar stock or checking the surface finish of the product. These are difficult tasks for robots to perform at this stage of robot development.

Let us compare a manned cell to an unmanned (robotic) cell. A manned cell comprises conventional or programmable machines and multifunctional workers. A manned cell is typically U-shaped. In an unmanned cell, all the machines are programmable (CNC or other automated equipment) and there are no workers in the cell. Unmanned cells are typically U-shaped or circular in design to allow the robot to access the equipment. A typical example of an unmanned cell is shown in Figure 11-2. The full range of motion of the robot is required so it can reach all the machines. At each machine, the robot is called upon to do critical unloading and loading tasks. This requires that the robot have a certain level of accuracy and repeatability. This is called *robotic process capability* (RPC), and it must be known prior to designing the cell.

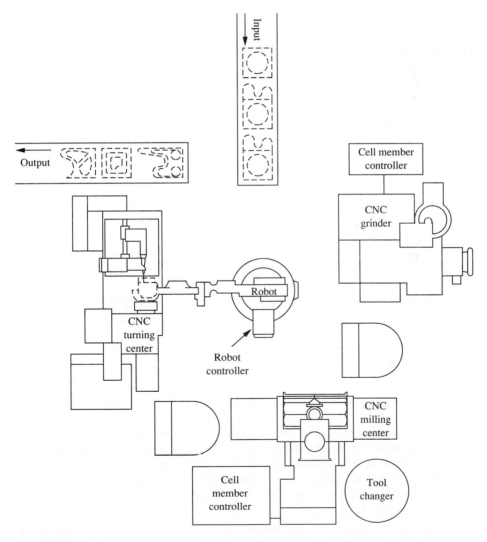

FIGURE 11-2
Example of unmanned robotic manufacturing cell with decoupler.

As stated earlier, for both manned and unmanned cells, flexibility is the most important functional design characteristic (functional requirement). In manned cells, flexibility was not difficult to maintain since the human was available to perform many varied tasks. The operator in the cell unloaded, inspected, deburred, manipulated (reoriented), and loaded parts into the machines, one after another. The operator performed setup when parts were changed, changed tools as needed, and maintained the equipment. Clearly the multifunctional worker was the most flexible element in the system. In unmanned cells, the worker is replaced by a robot. It is not an easy task to replace human flexibility. To deal with this problem, a new element, called a *decoupler*, can be introduced into unmanned cell designs to increase the capability and flexibility of the system.

DECOUPLERS IN MANUFACTURING CELLS

When machines are placed next to each other in a cell, the processes become functionally dependent on each other. The worker services many machines. The decoupler breaks the dependency of the processes on each other in a cellular environment. Decouplers hold one part and have specific input and output points. The simplest type of decoupler exists in a manned assembly cell—the kanban square. Figure 11-3 shows an electronic assembly cell with kanban squares between each work station. The squares provide for production control within the cell, controlling the timing of the operations and creating flexibility in the staffing (manning) of the cell, which provided flexibility in the cell production rates (CTs). The decouplers hold only one part. Do not confuse decouplers with buffers. Buffers are used just to store parts. The decoupler performs many of the various functions that a worker in a manned cell performed routinely, imparting flexibility back into the system. Decouplers can perform the following functions in unmanned cells.

1. **Functionally Decouple the Processes.** Decouplers separate or decouple processes so that they are not dependent on each other. This relaxes the need for precise line balancing when the work in the cell is redistributed. Also, decouplers can overcome the problem of process (machine) time variability.

2. **Pokayoke Inspection.** A decoupler can check critical dimensions of parts. The feedback signal from sensors is sent back to the process controller so that only good parts are pulled to the next station. This is an example of 100 percent inspection. Figure 11-4 shows a decoupler for inspection. This decoupler is designed for handling a family of parts that the cell is producing. Suppose the family has three basic sizes of parts—small (S), medium (M), and large (L). Just as the machine tools must have flexible fixtures to handle the different sizes of parts and the robot's gripper must adapt to different sizes of parts, the cell must have flexible decouplers to handle a family of parts. This flexible decoupler chute is designed for a family of three parts (S, M, L).

3. **Freedom of Movement for the Robot.** This is the most important function of the decoupler as far as automation of the cell is concerned. In manned cells, the

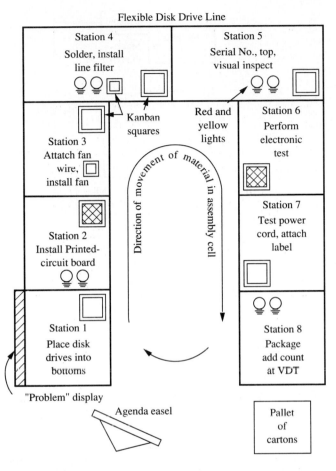

FIGURE 11-3
A manned assembly cell designed with kanban squares (decouplers). (*Black, 1988.*)

addition of the decoupler allows the human worker to move upstream, which is opposite to the direction of part flow. That is, the decoupler allows the worker to move in any direction within the cell. The same is true for the robot. Remember, most robots have only one arm and cannot walk, so compared to a human, robots are severely handicapped workers.

4. **Part Manipulation.** In an unmanned robotic cell, decouplers can handle a family of parts and can locate a part for the robot gripper. Often parts must be manipulated or reoriented for insertion into the next machine. Figure 11-5 shows a simple decoupler designed for part reorientation. The robot places a part in slot A. Before rotation, surface 1 is at the top. After rotation, surface 2 comes to the top so that a new orientation is obtained. The wheel holds four slots, one slot for each part in the family of four parts.

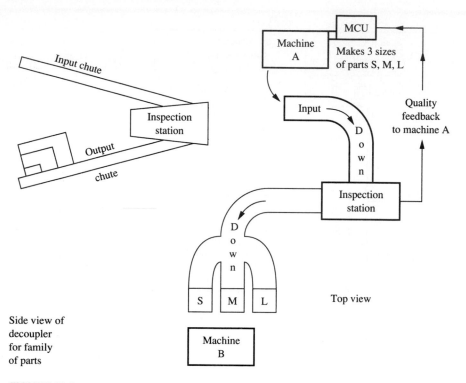

FIGURE 11-4
Decoupler for a family of parts, with inspection station.

5. **Intracell Transportation.** Decouplers in the form of gravity slides or chutes can transport parts from process to process within the cell. This eliminates the need for precisely locating the part on the input side of the decoupler. Precise location on the output side ensures correct repeatable registration of the part for the gripper of the robot. The transportation process can be automated. Figure 11-6 shows a decoupler chute that transports and reorients the part.

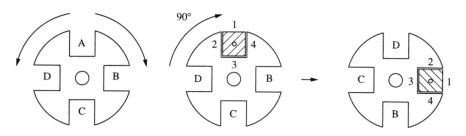

FIGURE 11-5
Decoupler reorients by rotation of the part.

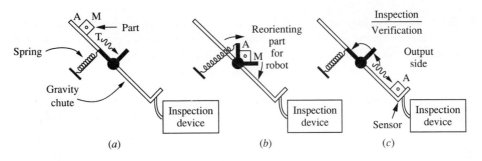

FIGURE 11-6
Decoupler reorients part and inspects part with feedback to previous process, detecting the part's presence or absence as part of inventory control of cell.

6. **Handling a Family of Parts.** In a cell, handling a family of parts will require flexible decouplers along with flexible workholders. A decoupler designed with a family of chutes, as shown in Figure 11-4, allows parts to pass each other in the cell or to skip a process altogether. The simple rotary device shown in Figure 11-5 can handle a family of parts, while providing part reorientation.

7. **Automatic Production Control.** Decouplers can act as automatic production control devices between two automatic processes by automatically shutting off the upstream machine that cycles faster than the downstream machine. An example of a decoupler performing this function is shown in Figure 11-7. In this figure, the decoupler consists of an inspection station, a gravity chute, and a limit switch. The limit switch automatically stops the operation of machine A when three parts are in the chute. One part has been inspected, the second part is being inspected, and the third part is ready for inspection. No additional parts are made by machine A until they are needed and the controller for machine A receives a signal from the decoupler that the previous part passed inspection.

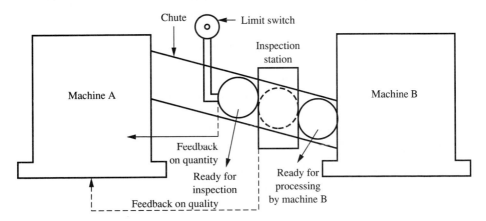

FIGURE 11-7
Automatic process control function of a decoupler, combined with quality control.

8. Branching. We have seen examples of manned cell designs where two (or more) machines are being fed by one machine or one machine is being fed by two (or more) machines. This is called *branching*. When this happens in unmanned cells, a decoupler is needed to control the branching function.

Looking at the various functions a decoupler can perform, it can be observed that decouplers are needed to replace all the functions that an operator performs in a manned cell, functions that neither the machines nor the robots can adequately perform. For example, decouplers for performing setup or decouplers for removing sharp, possibly dangerous burrs left on the part after machining are also feasible. Therefore, it is obvious that, in order to convert a manned system into an unmanned system, decouplers are an essential element.

AUTOMATING THE IMPS

Before proceeding from simple mechanization to complex, programmed automation, we need to consider exactly what automation is designed to achieve. Automating just to avoid human processing of products is not the objective. As the ninth step in the IMPS strategy, automation is developed when it becomes clear that further progress in efficiency by manual means is impossible. To establish a factory with linked automation is not easily accomplished. Trivial matters never considered in a manned system can create serious problems in unmanned cells. Automating the IMPS requires three things:

1. Development of the manufacturing system to move materials as quickly, precisely, and efficiently as possible from raw material to finished product. If this aim is accomplished, whether tasks are performed manually or automatically is secondary. In fact, tasks designed for the robot are easily performed by humans.
2. Proper preparation for the advancement to the next higher stage of machine automation by previewing the potential problems. Incremental, continuous improvements rather than radical changes must be made.
3. Maintaining proper roles for people and machines. Automation should not degrade people. In other words, the machines should be used in such a way that the operators remain fully utilized and involved. Progressively building the level of automation requires revising the interaction of the workers, machines, and materials that make up the manufacturing system. Once modifications to old equipment no longer create viable returns, the system itself will automatically tell the users what modifications are needed.

Buying a machine having more capability than needed can be wasteful. Here are some guidelines for the selection of equipment:

1. Purchase or build flexible equipment (low-cost, small) or equipment capable of being modified and maintained in-house.

2. Purchase or build equipment that can be easily moved or linked. This way, no area or process is locked out from development.

3. Remember that the quality, flexibility, and reliability of the equipment, the processes, and the people are important.

ROBOT PROCESS CAPABILITY

The lack of adequate robot process capability (RPC) can lead to the failure of the robot installation. It is very embarrassing to have to remove a robot from an assembly line or manufacturing cell because the robot was not able to accomplish the desired tasks. Manufacturers and users need more effective techniques for measuring robot process capability so that they can evaluate a robot's ability to perform required tasks and to select a robot that best meets the company's needs. Robot tasks or processes that require process capability measurements include assembly, insertion, spot welding, inspection, and loading and unloading parts. In unmanned cells, equipment is placed anywhere within the reach of the robot, but the ability of the robot to perform the task within its reach is highly variable.

DEFINITION OF PROCESS CAPABILITY

Machine tool process capability has been defined as the natural capability of the process, that is, the machine's ability to consistently perform a job with a certain degree of accuracy, precision (repeatability), reproducibility, and stability.

In machine tool process capability studies, which traditionally have been performed on metal-cutting machine tools, the parts made on the machine can be examined to determine the machine tool's process capability. However, in many robot tasks (for example, material handling or assembly), there is no product or output that can be directly examined or measured to determine the robot's process capability. Therefore, the problem of how to measure RPC is not trivial.

Robot process capability refers to the positional accuracy, repeatability, reproducibility, and stability of the robot during its operational cycle. RPC is a function of move speed, move position, arm orientation, and the weight being moved. Robot process capability must therefore be determined by a method that provides an independent measurement of the spatial location of the robot's end effector at any given time under a variety of operating conditions.

Although the terms *accuracy*, *repeatability* (*precision*), *reproducibility*, and *stability* seem clear, disagreement exists about their proper meanings. This discussion uses the following definitions.

Accuracy	The robot's ability to move to an exact point that was programmed offline the first time, and to hit what is aimed at. It is the degree of agreement between independent measurements and the target value being measured.

Precision (process variability) or repeatability	The robot's ability to return to an exact point from the same starting point. It is the degree of mutual agreement between independent measurements under specific conditions.
Stability	The robot's ability to return to a point and hit what is aimed at over time without drifting off target. It is measured as percent error in a given period of time.
Reproducibility	The robot's ability to return accurately to a point from different starting points. In general, the farther away the end effector is from the end point, the poorer the reproducibility.

Generally, one or two of the operational characteristics of the process will dominate or have the strongest influence on process capability. Process capability measurements must therefore reveal both dominant and interactive characteristics. For example, a manufacturer should specify not only a robot's weight-handling and velocity capabilities but also the relationship between weight handling and arm velocity. If the relationship is mutually interactive, changes in either factor will affect the robot's subsequent positional accuracy, precision, and reproducibility accordingly.

IMPROVEMENT AND MEASUREMENT TECHNIQUES

Most manufacturers provide specifications for static or extreme conditions but not for the robot's process capability of performing specific tasks. Both users and manufacturers need acceptable techniques for measuring and improving robot process capability to achieve quality control objectives. Techniques that are currently available are contact sensing devices and noncontact sensing devices. Some robot process capability measurement and improvement techniques are compared in Table 11-2.

CONTACT SENSING DEVICES

Contact sensors are one way to measure robot process capability. Perhaps the simplest low-cost method is the use of three dial indicators as shown in Figure 11-8. The robot holds a block of known size and moves it into the desired location where the dial indicators can measure deviations. This method works for point-to-point measurement over a limited range.

Another contact method for measuring the positional accuracy and precision of industrial robots is shown in Figure 11-9. Here is a one-dimensional extensible ball-bar with 6 cm of travel that is monitored by a built-in electronic transducer with 2.5 μm (0.0025 mm) resolution. On each end of the bar is a precision steel sphere. One sphere is magnetically attached to a socket located within the robot's work zone. The other sphere is mounted on a universal joint attached to the robot end effector. The transducer installed in the ball-bar measures the radial displace-

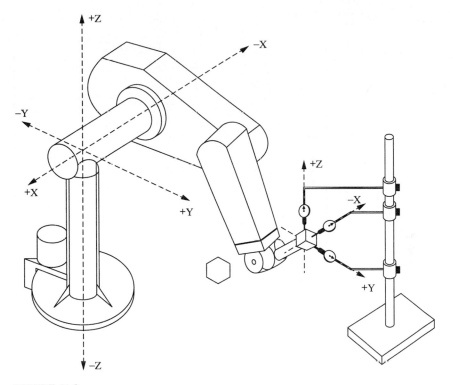

FIGURE 11-8
Dial indicator setup for 3-D measurement.

ment between the two spheres. Tests conducted with this device (to measure errors on commercially available robots) include point-to-point teach-mode test, wrist rotation test, circular movement test, and drift test (to measure the robot's thermal stability). Although it is a reliable and economical instrument, an extensible ball-bar is limited to one-dimensional measurements.

NONCONTACT SENSING DEVICES

The noncontact sensors locate a robot's position by detecting changes (electrical, optical, or acoustic) from a known reference location. Acoustic-based, optical-based, and electromagnetic-based systems are the most common types of noncontact systems. An advantage of using a noncontact sensing device is that the measuring devices do not touch the object to be measured. Therefore, measurement error is reduced because the measuring device remains stationary.

Acoustic-Based System

Acoustic systems work on the principle of time domain or sonar. High frequency sound is transmitted in pulses to the object whose position is to be measured. A receiver is positioned to receive the reflected pulses. When the velocity of the sound waves in

TABLE 11-2
Summary of measuring techniques

Method	Resolution	Accuracy	Repeatability	Advantages	Disadvantages
Contact sensing					
Dial indicator	0.0025 mm	n/a	n/a	a. low cost b. easy to setup for one-dimensional measurement	a. for point-to-point (PTP) only b. measuring range limited by the dial construction c. difficult to set up for accuracy test
Extensible ball bar	5×10^{-6}m	32×10^{-6}m	20×10^{-6}m	a. simple in operation b. both positioning and path accuracy can be measured	a. limited to one dimensional measurement b. measuring speed is limited
Latin square	n/a	n/a (depends on the probe type)	±0.15 mm	a. experimental setup is defined by statistical procedure	a. slow speed b. for PTP test only c. velocity must be very slow when the probe contacts the tooling balls
LVDT sensor	0.0025 mm	n/a	n/a	a. both position and orientation can be measured	a. slow speed b. for PTP only c. measuring range is limited (2 mm)

TABLE 11-2 (*continued*)

Method	Resolution	Accuracy	Repeatability	Advantages	Disadvantages
Noncontact sensing					
Acoustic-based system:					
Acoustic-range sensor	0.2 mm	n/a	n/a	a. uses lightweight sensor b. can improve accuracy (reduce background noise) by using ultrasonic sensor	a. environmental effects are likely
Optical-based systems:					
Active-video system: SELSPOT and WATSMART	12 bits (1:4096)	1 mm	point: 0.005% path: 0.01%	a. high speed (4700 Hz) multiple markers b. can be used for both PTP and continuous path (CP) c. presurveyed calibration frames are available	a. lighting environment should be controlled to avoid reflection b. LED position may cause inaccuracy c. high temperature due to extensive usage may cause inaccuracy
Theodolite	13×10^{-6}m	n/a	n/a	a. simple algorithm and operational procedure b. system capability is good enough for industrial robots	a. method very slow (about 1 point/min.) b. manual operation could cause eye fatigue for a long period of operation c. for PTP only
Proximeter	25×10^{-6}m	n/a	n/a	a. can measure both position and orientation	a. linear measuring range is limited (2mm) b. for PTP only c. difficult to set up for accuracy test

199

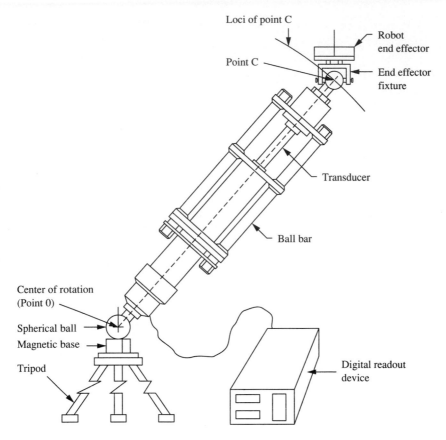

FIGURE 11-9
Extensible ball-bar method.

air and the time taken to hit the object and reflect back are known, the distance can be computed. Special electronics are built into the transmitter and receiver to account for inertia. Two or more of the transmitters and receivers are used to measure the 3-D location.

Optical-Based Systems

The operating principle of optical-based systems is as follows. The optical sensors are positioned to detect the light sources placed on the end effector and thereby determine its coordinates. The optical sources may be light-emitting diodes (LEDs), infrared rays, or ambient light. Optical-based systems can be categorized into active and passive sensing systems. Active systems are those that have active communication between the sensors and the light generators. Passive systems usually work in ambient light.

Active video systems are those that send pulses or other forms of signals (infrared, laser, fiber optic light, etc.) to the sensing and measuring unit. SELSPOT and WATSMART belong to this category. SELSPOT's robot check system and Waterloo spatial motion analysis and recording techniques (WATSMART) are the commercially available systems for 3-D noncontact digitizing active video techniques.

The robot to be monitored is fitted with a number of infrared markers or light emitting diodes (LEDs). Each marker is attached to a distributor (strober) through wires and is activated for a brief period of 65 μs by the controller. For 3-D recording, two cameras are used simultaneously. The camera lens focuses an image of the marker on a two-dimensional photosensitive sensor called the lateral effect photodiode. The resulting signals are amplified, converted to 12-bit digital values in the camera, and transmitted to the camera's controller board in the system cabinet. Here, the data is transformed into 3-D coordinates by a direct linear transformation (DLT) technique. A computer (for example, an IBM PC/AT) drives the camera and strobing controllers. A schematic of the camera setup is shown in Figure 11-10. The calibration frame is used to precisely determine the location of the camera with respect to the space being observed.

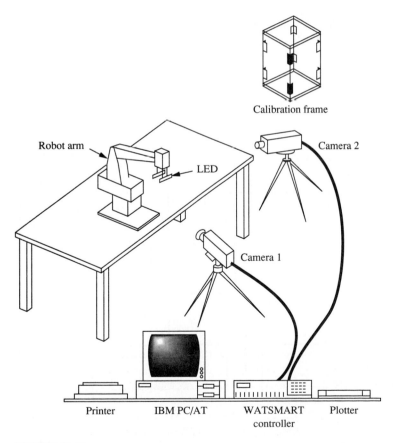

FIGURE 11-10
SELSPOT and WATSMART systems setup.

Laser Systems

In this method, reflected laser beams are detected by a sensor, and the resulting data are used in computations to determine positional and orientational accuracy. Laser-based systems demonstrate higher accuracy and faster measurements than other noncontacting systems.

There are five techniques available for measuring distance or coordinates by using a laser system. (1) the time-of-flight technique involves the emission of a pulse, which is made to reflect from the target and return to the measuring device; (2) the phase modulation technique involves a collimated laser beam that is modulated to produce an amplitude varying wave; (3) the triangulation technique involves the measurement of angles via a camera or a laser probe; (4) the optical encoder technique involves passing laser light through an encoder and then measuring the encoder's angular position; and (5) the interferometry technique is based on the interference of waves that are made to travel different paths. The time-of-flight and phase modulation techniques yield low measuring resolution, while interferometry and triangulation techniques have the best accuracy and precision.

The laser interferometry technique is based on the phenomenon of phase change caused when light waves are made to travel in different paths. By recombining these waves, an interference pattern (in Doppler signals) is produced from which the number

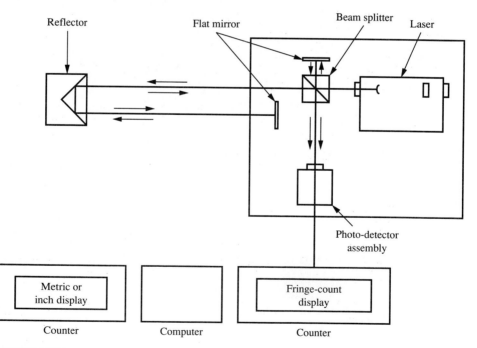

FIGURE 11-11
Laser interferometer (*Harry N. Norton, Sensor and Analyzer Handbook* ©1982, p. 104. Reprinted by permission of Prentice-Hall, Inc., Englewood Cliffs, NJ.)

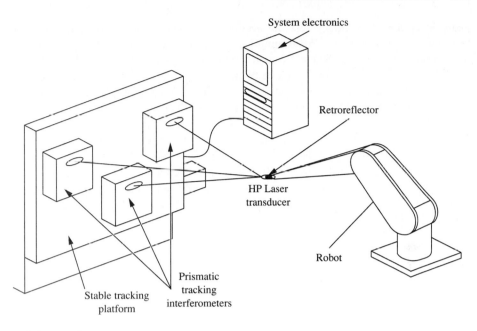

System electronics

Retroreflector

HP Laser
transducer

Robot

Prismatic
tracking
interferometers

Stable tracking
platform

FIGURE 11-12
Multiple-beam laser tracking system. (*Courtesy of Chesapeake Laser Systems, Inc.*)

of quarter waves of path differences can be counted as the target is moved. By analyzing this interference, the exact location of the end effector can be determined. A schematic diagram of a laser interferometer is shown in Figure 11-11.

The National Bureau of Standards (now NIST) developed a single beam 3-D laser tracking system. This system is commercially available. This system consists of a single beam, laser interferometer system for distance (length) measurement and an encoder system for angle measurement. By combining the distance and angle measurements, a robot's position can be determined.

Another commercially available 3-D laser tracking system employs three laser beams (called "trilateration") to track a retroreflector that is attached to a moving target (the arm of the robot). With multiple beams, no angular information is required to determine the exact 3-D location (see Figure 11-12). Resolution of this laser system is limited by the range over which the device can operate and the wavelength of the light selected. Although such a laser-based system can measure robot process capability characteristics with accuracy and speed, the high cost of the system may deter its use for routine robot process capability checks.

Testing Procedure

To determine a robot's accuracy and precision before installing the robot in the workplace, a test procedure was developed by the Robot Assessment Program of Ford Motor Company that included the manufacturer's specification verification test, a repeatable placement accuracy test, an accuracy of playback to commanded position test, and a stabilization test. Positioning was determined with noncontact eddy current measurement system equipment (Kaman Sciences Corporation Model KD-4358 with Model 15U1 sensors) arranged in three planes. Data recording and storage involved a data acquisition and monitoring system, a chart recorder, a power monitor, a stylus, and other peripherals. Maximum and 50 percent payload, arm reach, and speed were reported and statistically analyzed for the robot process capability information. Although the test considered several critical variables affecting robot process capability, the testing and measuring processes were slow and partially conducted manually.

In 1986, the Robot Assessment Program developed a modified robot testing procedure that included a point-to-point test, path control tests, continuous path tests, and cycling tests. The Industrial Technology Institute reported a similar testing procedure. The Robot Assessment Program testing system was also modified to use the Selspine Robot Check System (Selcom Selective Electronics Inc., Troy, Michigan), which included two cameras, a micro-PDP 11/23 computer, LEDs, a control unit, a calibration fixture, and a plotter. This optical-electronic, motion-analysis vision system uses active light sources to determine the actual positions of moving objects in space. These positions can be presented in Cartesian coordinates and used to calculate speed and acceleration. Unlike other vision systems that process an object's entire image, this system records and processes data by detecting the LED locations, which decreases processing time because only the required data is retained while unnecessary image processing is deleted.

PROCESS CAPABILITY
VERSUS CALIBRATION

Studies have proven that robot positioning errors can be significantly reduced with calibration techniques. However, a calibration study is intended to develop no-load data, whereas a process capability study is intended to determine operational or performance characteristics. Furthermore, in a robot process capability study, the measurement system must be independent of the robot. Calibration systems, however, can be part of the robot, which can cause intrinsic errors to occur.

MEASUREMENT EQUIPMENT
REQUIREMENTS

To conduct periodic process capability checks (ideally before robot installation), companies require access to low-cost, high-speed robot process capability measurement equipment and a simple, effective checking procedure. In selecting measuring equipment, the following factors should be considered:

- Processing speed—the measuring system's processing speed is usually limited by the computer's processing speed. For example, a commercially available high-speed camera can take thousands of pictures per second, but the fastest computer can only process up to 50 frames per second.

- Precision and accuracy—the measurement device should be 10 times more precise than the variability to be measured and 10 times more accurate.
- Linearity—this refers to the calibration accuracy of the measurement device over its full working range. Is it linear? What is its degree of nonlinearity? Where does it become nonlinear and what is, therefore, its real linear working region?
- Stability—how well does this device retain its capability over time? Does it drift off target and need realignment?
- Resolution—this refers to the smallest dimensional input that the device can detect or distinguish.
- Magnification—this refers to amplification of the device's output portion over the actual input dimension. The better the resolution of the device, the greater the magnification required of the measurement so that it can be read and compared with the desired standard.

A trade-off exists between measurement system performance and cost. For example, a low-resolution, low-speed video-based system may cost a few thousand dollars, while a sophisticated laser-based system may cost hundreds of thousands. Selection of measurement equipment should be based on the robot performance and task requirements. Unfortunately, most measurement systems are expensive or do not have sufficient accuracy for use in measuring RPC of different robots. Future research should be directed toward developing a low-cost, high-speed, portable system to measure robot process capability.

FINAL ASSEMBLY

Most products involve some assembly before the product is ready to be shipped to the marketplace. However, final assembly lines have resisted automation for many years. One of the reasons assembly processes have not been automated is because of the design and quality of the manufactured components.

If individual components get to final assembly and are defective, then it is necessary to inspect and rework these defective parts. This situation is correctable by making the parts correctly the first time and every time (that is, by integrating quality control).

Designing the product for final assembly eliminates a high percentage of direct labor. Innovative product and process designs for assembly can bring a new level of flexibility to the manufacturing system. A design that accommodates automation is able to perform a greater variety of manufacturing steps without delay or unnecessary handling of the product in process. The functional requirements of an automated final assembly are

- Uniqueness and creativity necessary to develop technical competitiveness
- Flexibility and adaptability to product changes
- Responsiveness
- The number of (assembly) steps can be minimized by the integration of components and simplification/standardization of product design

- One step, one machine (small, special, simple machines)
- Multiple functions at each step
- The size of equipment be minimized

The only good method to achieve automated assembly is to study each specific product component in detail. A product designed for automated assembly must have component parts of consistent quality. Parts of nonuniform character and widely varying dimensions must be assembled by hand. Thus, the manufacturing methods used are critical. Parts produced or assembled in machines are usually less variable than parts produced by hand.

SUMMARY

Automation in an IMPS means converting manned cells into unmanned cells. This is an evolutionary process where automation is used to solve problems in setup, part loading, quality (inspection), or capacity (eliminate a bottleneck). Automating the entire manufacturing system is not easy. It may not even be possible. However, automating the manufacturing system without first redesigning it into a highly efficient manned IMPS is not advisable.

Automating an IMPS does not necessarily mean buying highly sophisticated equipment with greater capacity than actually required. The emphasis should be on integrating the best abilities of the machines and the people in the system. The rule is *routine for the machine and exceptions and improvement for the human.*

The task of automating any manufacturing system involves automation of all elements—product design (CAD), process design (CAPP), product manufacture (CAM), material handling system (AGV), and final assembly. Conversion of manned cells into unmanned cells requires devices performing all the functions a worker performed in the manned cell. A decoupler is such a device. Decouplers separate the processes when they are functionally dependent on each other. Hence, they are one of the most important elements for maintaining the flexibility of the unmanned cell.

The ultimate goal of automation in any system is to achieve the highest possible level of automation, that is, to infuse attributes such as evaluation and reasoning (human characteristics) into the machine. The main obstacle for implementing adaptive control into a process may not be the unavailability of the technology but a lack of knowledge about the process that needs to be adaptively controlled.

CHAPTER 12

COMPUTERIZATION
OF
IMPS

Computers don't make mistakes, people do.

INTRODUCTION

Linked-cellular manufacturing systems have proven to be simple and effective designs for a factory with a future. Although there are many different names for these designs, many of their results are the same: the processes are standardized and well understood; automation is added only after the processes are stabilized; critical control functions are well integrated; inventory is decreased; setup time is reduced; the system is flexible; the manufacturing lead time is shortened; waste is eliminated; and superior quality products are produced.

Fundamental to all these results is the restructuring of the manufacturing system prior to the automating and computerizing that took place over a period of time. Finally, as the last step, the production system functions are computer integrated with the manufacturing system functions in order to have the manufacturing system and production system (management) closely aligned. The linked-cell system provides the proper structure for computerization.

Computerizing the IMPS links it to the other parts of the company and produces a computerized integrated manufacturing production system (CIMPS). CIMPS is the extension of the IMPS with computerized data communication links. The most important aspect of computerization is a well-designed IMPS. Isn't it strange that everyone accepts the idea that the product must be redesigned in order to manufacture it with automation, but they think that the manufacturing system can be automated and computerized without redesigning it? The bottom line is that it is far easier to computerize the integrated system than the conventional job shop. So a distinction is being made between CIMPS and computer integrated manufacturing (CIM). Perhaps we should write it as IMPS,C!

Computer integrated manufacturing is still a concept rather than a proven technique in most companies. CIM is aimed at the integration of several methods and techniques that are now being applied independently at various stages in the overall manufacturing process. The concept of CIM represents the attempt to integrate all computer applications within a company into a coherent whole. These existing areas of computerization, such as CAD, CAPP, and CAM, are often islands of automation, unable to communicate with each other because they do not have a common data base. CIM has not focused on the basic manufacturing system but rather on how to use new techniques like robots and computers to do the dirty work such as loading/unloading, line balancing, inventory control, or process planning. The manufacturing system design is still a job shop.

CIMPSs use manufacturing and assembly cells coupled with a JIT philosophy to simplify the entire system and to integrate the critical control functions into the manufacturing system. The IMPSs can operate efficiently without computers for complicated process planning and floor control. The purpose of the computerization of IMPS is to share information between design, engineering, manufacturing, and the various other support groups, thereby becoming a factory with a future (FWAF).

INTEGRAL ELEMENTS OF CIMPS

An unmanned manufacturing cell in a CIMPS consists of CNC-type machine tools equipped with automated workholding devices and automated toolholders. The cell will need decouplers and automated material transfer devices (usually robots). The material flow system and the information flow system are integrated into the manufacturing system. The cells are controlled by host computers that are linked to a systems level computer, which supervises the entire manufacturing system. The systems level computer provides the schedule to final assembly, as well as a short range forecast to all other departments of the factory. This forecast is simply a forecast, nothing more; it is not controlling material movement. This is done by the kanban links.

The manufacturing systems level computer contains a factory simulator that can emulate the performance and behavior of the entire factory. The factory simulator contains a model of each of the cells, subassembly areas, and final assembly, as well as the inventory links between the entities. This computer also communicates with computers performing design and process planning functions, including manufacturing programming (CNC programming).

COMPUTER-AIDED DESIGN (CAD)

CAD can be defined as any design activity that involves the effective use of the computer to aid in the creation, modification, or documentation of an engineering design. CAD often uses an interactive computer graphics system, simply called a

CAD system. There are several important reasons for using a CAD system to support the engineering design function.

1. To increase the productivity of the designer
2. To improve the quality of the design
3. To improve design documentation
4. To create a manufacturing database
5. To reduce time and effort needed to change and update designs

CAD is now so widely used for both drafting and design that over 100 commercial packages are available, ranging from simple two-dimensional drafting packages to three-dimensional solid modeling software programs that can virtually do anything to the objects, from color shading to 360° rotation. Key to the CAD design is a database that can be used by all other functions and people in the system. Each relevant detail of an individual part is stored in the CAD database so that other departments or suppliers can access these details for their own use.

A typical CAD system consists of one or more design workstations, a central processing unit (CPU), secondary storage, plotters, printers, and other output devices. The relationship among the components is illustrated in Figure 12-1.

The design workstation is the interface between the CAD system and the designer. The input devices for a CAD system typically include an alphanumeric keyboard, electronic keypad, and other devices for inputting special graphics functions,

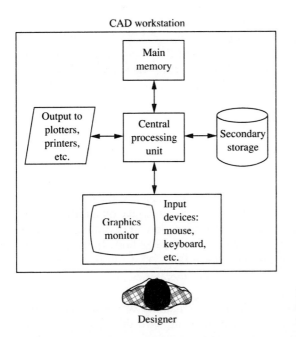

FIGURE 12-1
Configuration of the typical structure of a CAD system.

and a cursor control device (a "mouse," light pen, etc.). The graphical design output is accomplished by a graphics display monitor.

The CPU is the CAD system computer. The processor performs the mathematical calculations required for geometric modeling, engineering analysis, and other data processing calculations.

There is a trend in computer-aided design toward small CAD systems in which many of the functions and capabilities of a full computer-aided design system can be accomplished on a personal computer (PC). The PC-CAD systems can be used as stand-alone systems. They are popular with small firms that cannot afford a large CAD installation that requires a mainframe computer. The PC-CAD modules can be interconnected to a mainframe and to other PC-CAD systems using a local area network (LAN). Access to the mainframe permits the designer to tackle applications that require a more powerful computer than the PC or to exchange data between CAD workstations on the network.

COMPUTER-AIDED MANUFACTURING (CAM)

CAM is the use of computers to aid in the planning, management, and control of manufacturing processes. The primary function here is the preparation and delivery of numerical control programs to the CNC machine tools, machining centers, material handling equipment (the robot), and other supporting equipment (decouplers, flexible programmable fixtures, etc.). Most of this hardware is now controlled by software and this control software often becomes the limiting factor in the operation of the system. The software can be as complex, expensive, and difficult to implement (debug) as the hardware. This is why cells should be designed to be as simple to operate as possible. However, some CAM functions include those in which the computer is used indirectly to support manufacturing (that is, there is no direct connection between the computer and the process). The computer is used "off-line" to provide information for the effective planning and management of manufacturing activities. Included here might be computer analysis of the final assembly line to try to determine the effects of schedule changes on inventory levels.

Another developing area of CAM application is concerned with computer systems for implementing manufacturing inspection and control functions. This might be called CATI (computer-aided testing and inspection). On-line quality monitoring, factory floor control, and process monitoring (reliability of machine tools) are all included within the scope of this function.

With the development of unmanned manufacturing cells and the elimination of stand-alone requirements, direct numerical control (DNC) will take on a different role in the FWAF. One DNC central computer can service a variety of dissimilar machines within the cell. Therefore, the DNC computer becomes the cell host. It can store data on production needs, tool wear, and machine down-time. This information can be used by management for improved decision making, thereby enabling the FWAF to operate effectively at high utilization.

An important factor in unmanned cells is the reliability of the cell host computer. Plans must exist to ensure continuity of manufacturing if this computer should fail. One approach is to create distributed or star-type networks, so the intelligence of the cell is distributed among all the elements in the cell. An alternative strategy is to maintain a standby computer. This computer must be in constant touch with the cell host computer and be ready to step in if a malfunction is detected. The standby computer also can be used for software development. The low cost of computers makes this a reasonable alternative.

COMPUTER-AIDED PROCESS PLANNING (CAPP)

Computer-aided process planning (CAPP) represents the bridge between design and manufacturing in a CAD/CAM system. In a traditional job shop, people plan the processes that are going to be used to make the parts. This requires thinking (that is, planning), so this task should not be completely computerized. Process planning in the job shop involves

1. Selection of specific processes and operations in the proper sequence
2. Identification of the necessary resources (equipment, materials, people, tooling)
3. The routing of the job through the shop
4. The time needed for each process setup

The majority of CAPP programs are based on variant process planning using GT; only about 10 percent permit the process plan for relatively new individual parts to be automatically generated. However, in the FWAF, it is clear that certain processing sequences will exist and new parts will have to be designed to take the existing sequences into account. The process capability of the cells as well as the sequences will be known to the designer.

CAPP systems in CIMPS can be based on the principles of group technology and classification and coding systems. Parts having similar process plans define part families. Part families can be used to identify machine groups and ultimately to design the manufacturing and assembly cells. State-of-the-art CAPP systems are capable of applying process knowledge and planning logic to a given part description.

In the FWAF, a pull system is used. Only final assembly is planned (scheduled) with repetitive operations and mixed-model scheduling matching manufacturing with customer demand. Excessive inventory, which results from mismatches between forecasted demand and actual usage, is avoided. This is not a simple task (see Chapter 9). The kanban system linking the cells provides parts as needed, without guesswork, and defines the sequences of operations and processes. New or redesigned parts must use the existing sequence, although individual processes can be skipped and modified. The system has sufficient flexibility to accept new or redesigned parts without major restructuring.

In a full CIMPS environment, feedback from the manufacturing system can be routed directly to the CAPP system to further enhance its performance. CAPP is thus an essential bridge between CAD and CAM, taken in conjunction with a GT philosophy. It is also a necessary and integral part of CIMPS in which all design and manufacturing functions are linked together by means of computer communication systems.

COMPUTER NETWORK AND INTERFACE

The various computers and computer-controlled devices within the CIMPS must be able to communicate with each other. CIMPS is achievable only by an integrated computer system operating throughout the plant. The lowest level computers control the machines, the processes, the material handling equipment, and the decouplers. The next level computer controls the cell. Traditionally, computers are connected to each other by either hierarchical or heterarchical architectures or structures. Major characteristics of hierarchical organizations include centralization, global information, and tree structures. Most of the multiple machine control systems for manufacturing in current usage are hierarchical. In hierarchical cells, there exists a master-slave relationship between a central supervisor and the lower-level cell resources as shown in Figure 12-2. As the number of levels in the hierarchy increase or as the number of slaves per level increases, system complexity tends to increase.

Heterarchical control systems are characterized by distributed computing and local autonomy. All processors are treated equally, as shown in Figure 12-3. There are no master-slave relationships or central supervisors. Supervisory activities are conducted by the processors as a group in a cooperative and distributed manner. Decision-making is located at the level where the information originates by the use of autonomous processes. The objectives are to modularize the control system, reduce the control system complexity, increase flexibility (so it is easy to add and delete equipment to the network), and increase fault tolerance (so that one computer can pick up the tasks of another), ensuring system robustness.

CELL WITH HIERARCHICAL CONTROL

For hierarchical cell control, the computer network consists of a cell host computer and control computers for machines, robots, and other cell hardware (decouplers). Control of part movement is performed by the cell host computer. Each part is coded and the code specifies the routing required to process the part, thus ensuring that the part is being pulled through the prescribed path within the factory. The cell host also contains information on the status of each machine and each part in the cell. When a request from assembly is received by the cell host computer, this computer directs the cell to make a part or parts.

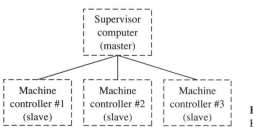

FIGURE 12-2
Hierarchical control architecture.

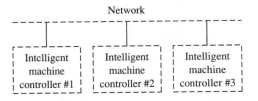

FIGURE 12-3
Heterarchical control architecture.

CELL WITH HETERARCHICAL CONTROL

In the heterarchical cell control system, the cell host is eliminated by distributing its supervisory functions throughout the system. This distributed system is easier to analyze than the hierarchical system. Each CPU or computer in the heterarchical system has identical control software implementing the same algorithm. The control algorithm for the CIMPS is based on a pull system. In this pull control system, no work station within a manufacturing cell can accept a component part until the downstream decoupler requests that part. Assume the cell is making parts to meet the demand of a subassembly line. When part processing is complete in the last machine in the cell, a request message is broadcast on the network to the upstream decoupler. The part in that decoupler is pulled to the last machine. This creates a message to the next upstream machine, and that machine will start to make another part. Information flow is upstream and the parts are moving downstream. Each machine/decoupler pair communicates with the upstream machine and decoupler. This arrangement leaves the robot to fend for itself. Note that most of the control systems developed so far have been push control with hierarchical control strategies.

LOCAL AREA NETWORKS (LAN)

A local area network (LAN) is a nonpublic communication system that permits the various devices connected to the network to communicate with each other over distances from several feet to several miles. Factory devices attached to the network include computers, programmable controllers, CNC machines, robots, data collection devices, bar code readers, and vision systems. There are three common configurations used in local area networks: star network, ring network, and bus network (see Figure 12-4).

The network preferred for communications in many manufacturing cells is the bus network. In the bus network, all the individual devices are attached to a single main transmission line. Any device or station can communicate with any other device in the network by sending a message through the bus with the address of the desired recipient. This main transmission line can be laid out as a circle that corresponds closely to the layout of the manufacturing cells in the factory. The robot can communicate with any other device in the cell and vice versa. In addition, the end of this line is connected to the cell host computer in order to control the entire cell.

In the bus network, there must be a method for controlling the message transmissions between stations. This is done using schemes by which the devices can gain access to the network. One of the popular access methods for LANs is token-passing.

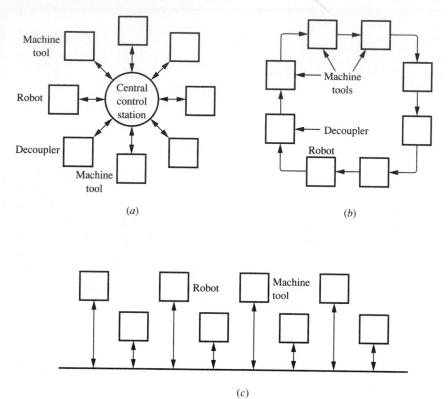

FIGURE 12-4
Three common network configurations:
(a) star; (b) ring; (c) bus.

In token-passing, a special code (the token) is passed along the network at high speeds from one device to another in a predetermined sequence (upstream for pull cells). The sequence can be designed to allow devices with higher priority to have greater access to the network. In operation, a device can transmit messages to some other device only when it possesses the token. In this way, access to the network is controlled and coordinated.

MANUFACTURING AUTOMATION PROTOCOL (MAP)

Because the format and interpretation of pulses differ from one computer-based device to the next, a set of formalized procedures is used by each device in the computer network whenever data are exchanged between them. Such procedures (or handshaking between devices) are called communications protocols. One such protocol standard, designed for use in the factory local area networks (such as the hierarchical structures described), is called the manufacturing automation protocol, or MAP.

ISO layer	Task	MAP specification
Layer 7: Application	Service interface for users	MMFS/EIA 1393 A ISO-CASE-subset ISO-FTAM-subset MAP-messaging MAP-directory-service MAP-network-management
Layer 6: Presentation	Conversion/ammendment of formats, code, etc.	Null
Layer 5: Session	Link synchronization and management	ISO-session-kernel
Layer 4: Transport	Reliable end-to-end links	ISO-transport-class 4
Layer 3: Network	Protocol coordination between different networks, routing	Currently null
Layer 2: Datalink	Error discovery, transfer between topologically adjacent nodes, media access	IEEE 802.2 LLC Type 1 IEEE 802.4 token-bus
Layer 1: Physical link	Encodes and physically transfers messages between adjacent nodes	IEEE 802.4 token-bus-broadband

FIGURE 12-5
Communication in automated production using MAP as of 1988.

MAP was developed by General Motors to solve communications problems in the factory. It is a communications protocol based on the International Organization for Standardizations's (ISO) Open Systems Interconnect (OSI) reference model.

Figure 12-5 shows the MAP communication specification. That is, MAP is essentially a seven-layer, broadband, token-bus communications specification for the factory floor. It is a hierarchical system. Each layer provides communications-related services to the layer above except for layer seven, which provides services to the device's program. The first four layers in MAP are concerned with interconnection functions, and the top three layers are concerned with interworking functions.

COMPUTERIZING THE UNMANNED
MANUFACTURING CELL

In an unmanned manufacturing cell (UMC), the cell host computer is the most important component. To reduce the hardware and software costs, a microcomputer can be used as the cell host. In the UMC, a hierarchical control system with a port controller (multiplexer) can be implemented to control the cell members. Also, a data communication architecture for this control system can be designed, and algorithms of the pull (or push) system for file transfer and cell control can be developed.

Let us assume, as shown in Figure 12-6, the factory is composed of manufacturing cells, subassembly cells, and final assembly lines all linked with a pull system for material control. The signals can be kanban cards or any device that provides a message to the upstream processes. Critical system control functions are integrated directly into the manufacturing system.

An unmanned manufacturing cell consists of computer numerical control (CNC) machine tools, a robot or robots to transport parts, a host computer (cell host) to control the cell, and decouplers. When the multifunctional workers are removed, decouplers are placed between the processes within the cell to improve flexibility and replace lost capability. This is the simplest or lowest level UMC. It has very little intelligence.

The cell host simultaneously releases commands to and receives messages from the machines, decouplers, and robots. In addition, the cell host communicates with computers that control the rest of the manufacturing system and with the other peripheral equipment. Thus, the cell host needs sufficient data communication capacity to meet the system's multiple needs. Therefore, minicomputers with powerful and efficient input and output (I/O) capacities have been used as cell hosts. If saving money is the objective, a microcomputer can also be used as the cell host in the UMC design.

To evaluate the ability of a microcomputer as a cell host, physical simulation can be used. Physical simulation is an important tool for studying unmanned cell behavior. Although digital simulation can evaluate problems related to cost, efficiency, and time, this technique cannot address problems in data communication, control software, and robot process capability. Physical simulation can address such problems in simulated time and find ways to overcome them.

CELL HOST PROBLEMS

In using a microcomputer as the cell host for a UMC, several problems arise.

Problem 1: System Philosophy

What will the system philosophy be when the microcomputer is the cell host? Can this system philosophy meet future developments? How do we modify this system to develop the manufacturing automation protocol (MAP)? The system philosophy is a hypothesis for constructing a UMC. A system philosophy should be selected that meets current and future needs.

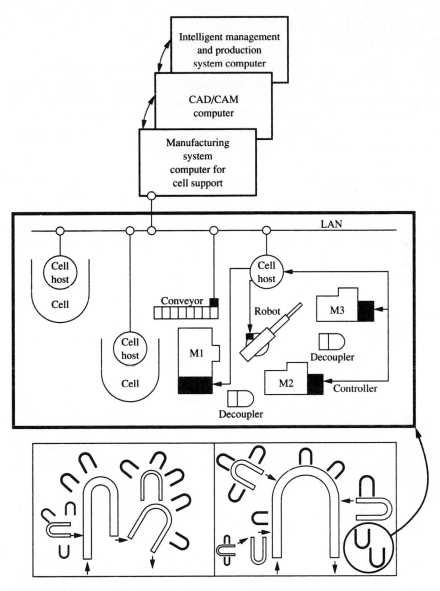

FIGURE 12-6
Unmanned (robotic) cell showing hierarchical computer structuring. LAN = local area network.

Problem 2: Data Communication Architecture

What is the physical medium of this data communication architecture? What are the algorithms of the file transfer and cell control? The physical media chosen will determine the data communication capacity needs for the cell host and the cell members. The algorithms' efficiency for file transfer and cell control will determine the cell efficiency.

Problem 3: Capability of the Cell Members' Controllers

Can these controllers communicate with the cell host? Do the manufacturers provide hardware and/or software support? How can the cell members be modified if they cannot meet the data communication needs? Data communication problems arise when the cell members lack communication capabilities or when the cell members have the data communication capabilities but are incompatible with the cell host. So the data communication device must be modified to communicate with the cell host.

Problem 4: I/O Capacities of the Microcomputer

Unlike the minicomputer or super-minicomputer with powerful I/O capacities, today's microcomputers have limited I/O capability. Although some special expansion I/O capacities are available, more efficient and better organized I/O capacities are needed.

A PROPOSED MANUFACTURING SYSTEM

A proposed unmanned L-CMS includes a manufacturing system computer (MSC), MAP, several UMCs, and some material-handling devices to link the cells. In the manned L-CMS, kanban links the cells. In an unmanned CMS, these links also must operate. The MSC's tasks are to get job orders from the sales department, dispatch the job orders to the design department, obtain the design information from a computer-aided design (CAD) subsystem, convert this information into a bill of materials for the manufacturing cells in the L-CMS for parts manufacture, schedule final assembly by advising all cells of any changes requiring resources and shipping capacity changes, supervise all the manufacturing cells, and release the instructions to the cell host of each manufacturing cell. The MSC communicates via MAP and LANs with the CAD subsystem, the manufacturing cells, the computer-aided process planning system, and the material-handling subsystems.

A manufacturing cell within this system manufactures a family of parts. It receives specific manufacturing instructions from the MSC via the MAP links. Meanwhile, the manufacturing cell reports its current manufacturing status to the MSC via the cell host.

Figure 12-7 shows the control methodology for a manufacturing system composed of UMCs. This model has four control levels: designing, authorizing, distributing, and processing. Designing, the control system's highest level, controls and coordinates several authorizing control systems on the second level through the MSC. The second level includes the cell host computer, the CAD subsystem computer, and other subsystem computers. The authorizing systems control distributing, the third level. The control units in the distributing level are multiplexers with data buffers to collect messages from the cell members. The lowest level, processing, controls the machine tools, I/O switches, decouplers, workholders, and other peripheral equipment. The processing computers control the CNC machines or the microcomputers that control the auxiliary equipment. Microcomputers are used for intelligent machine controllers.

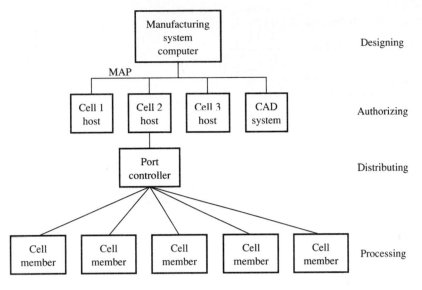

FIGURE 12-7
Block diagram of control system.

In this control system, a mixed-type control methodology implements the manufacturing system. A heterarchical control model in the upper level for designing and authorizing increases the flexibility of plugging in and unplugging the UMCs. The hierarchical arrangement for the lower level increases the speed of distributing control information to the processing levels.

In this manufacturing system scheme, the UMC in Figure 12-8 was constructed in the Manufacturing Systems Modeling Laboratory (MSML) in the Advanced Manufacturing Technology Center (AMTC) at Auburn University. A PC was used as the cell host. Other cell members include:

1. Milling machine I
2. Milling machine II
3. Vision system
4. Decoupler
5. Robot (instructional)
6. Conveyor (input parts)
7. Rotary table (output parts).

Three IBM PCs (processing computers) were connected to milling machine I, the robot, and milling machine II, respectively, for communication between the cell host and machine tools. A port controller distributed the commands to and collected messages from the cell members. Cell activities include transferring files and sys-

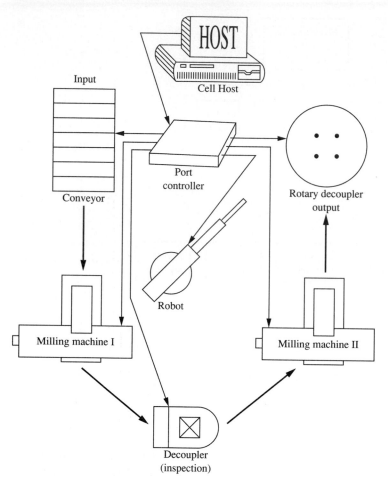

FIGURE 12-8
Layout of unmanned manufacturing cell using hierarchical control system.

tem commands, machining parts, decoupling, and operating workholding devices (air vises).

The cell host receives the production order and data files and the manufacturing data from the MSC via MAP. When the cell host has stored all the production data on its hard disk, it transfers the data command files via the distributing computer to each cell member. These data command files include CNC commands for milling machine I and machining data for milling machine II.

When the file transfer is finished, the cell host issues the manufacturing commands to each cell member to manufacture the parts. These commands determine the parts sequence.

DESIGN OF THE DATA COMMUNICATION ARCHITECTURE

Figure 12-9 shows the cell's data communication architecture. In this tree structure, the cell host is the root and the port controller is the first level of the node. This port controller, however, is the only node at this level. All the cell members are nodes at the second level.

The port controller controls and buffers data from different cell members. One host port and eight slave ports compose the data communication links of the port controller.

There are six different modes of operation for the port controller. The first operation mode transmits data from the cell host to a specific cell member by assigning a port identification number. The port controller buffers all the data from the cell members. When the cell host retrieves the data, the port controller assigns the data a port identification number. The second operation mode multiplexes messages from cell members. Data are buffered until a terminating character is received or until the buffer is full. The data are then sent to the cell host. The third operation mode uses the same transmitting method as the second mode, but sends data to the cell host only when a command is received requesting a message.

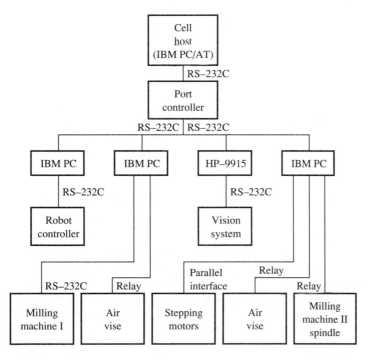

FIGURE 12-9
Data communication architecture of UMC.

The fourth and fifth operation modes are the same as the first and second modes for transmitting data from the cell host to cell members, but send data to the cell host only when a command with port selection is received. The last operation mode automatically multiplexes data from cell memory by continuously scanning all ports for characters in the receiving buffers. If a receiving buffer contains data, the port controller attaches a port identification code to the front of the data and transmits the data to the cell host. Transmission continues until the buffer is empty or until the entire data block length is transmitted.

DISCUSSION OF UMC

An unmanned cell with a port controller is an economical method to implement UMCs in an L-CMS. This method is easy to implement using the current hardware. As long as a machine has a serial port and a remote host mode, the machine can be used as a cell member. These constraints are very important in industry where very few of the existing machines have MAP capability.

Unsophisticated software restricts the capability of the hardware. For example, the software for milling machine I did not give any feedback after executing a statement. The alternative, hardware handshaking, limits the number of statements that can be used. Any statement taking more than 65535 milliseconds to execute results in a data communication error. The hardware and software of all the cell members must be able to communicate with the processing computer.

DESIGN-MANUFACTURE INTEGRATION

With CAD/CAPP/CAM, a direct link is established between product design and manufacturing engineering through process planning. It is the goal of CAD/CAPP/CAM not only to automate certain phases of design, process planning, and manufacturing, but also to automate the transition from design to manufacturing. Without redesigning the manufacturing system so that it can readily accept automation, this final integration will be excessively difficult and costly.

In the ideal CIMP system, it will be possible to take the design specification of the product as it resides in the CAD data base and convert it into a process plan for making the product, this conversion being done automatically by the system.

A large portion of the processing will be accomplished on computer numerically controlled machine tools. The numerical control (NC) part programs would be generated automatically by CAD/CAPP/CAM. The CAD/CAPP/CAM system would then download the NC program directly to the machine tool. So under this arrangement, product design, NC programming, and physical manufacturing can all be implemented by computer. These implementations are still in the future—the factory with a future.

MAN-MACHINE INTERFACES

CIMPS have the objective of integrating the functions of design, development, planning, manufacturing, and marketing by providing comprehensive information and user-specific solutions. The performance of the man-machine interface (human-computer or user interface) is a major factor that determines the quality and adaptability of CIMPS for practical applications.

A man-machine interface may be visualized as a medium through which data and control are passed back and forth between computer and user. Graphics is the most powerful medium of communication between man and machine. It has been reported that almost 70 percent of all information received by the human brain comes from visual input through the eye. Thus, graphics enhances our problem-solving ability. There is a growing expectation that in the future, all computer programs will present an elegant, user-friendly graphical interface.

A FACTORY WITH A FUTURE

After the computerization of the IMPS, the manufacturing and assembly cells will be linked together by computers and linked to the production system. Will these unmanned manufacturing cells be able to produce 100 percent perfect quality with no defects? Will all the processes have computerized adaptive control? Will the system have a very short lead time and low unit cost? Will machines run perfectly and never break down? Will all setups be eliminated? Will all the material be transferred one at a time from process to process automatically? Of course not! This is Valhalla. No factory can operate that way, but perfection can be a goal to work toward. Continuous improvement of the products and processes are certainly within reach, and the better the manufacturing system prior to automating and computerizing, the better it will be afterward.

The kanban method used in IMPS is still valid in CIMPS; only the computer monitors the progress of materials and bar codes substitute for the kanban card. AGVs (automated guided vehicles) replace the kanban carts because they can be controlled by computer and are flexible. Methods for transferring parts between devices are still being worked out along with flexible fixtures and decouplers to handle the diverse mixture of products made in the FWAF. However, trouble lights will still be flashing in the FWAF and warning beeps from the monitoring computers will be notifying the maintenance personnel something went awry. Things will continue to go wrong for years to come.

Information systems in the FWAF will have the capacity to interpret data in more than the conventional data processing sense. Instead of merely performing repetitive calculations on the data, the system will be able to understand the inherent relationships in the data. For example, an engineering design change related to a given product would be automatically propagated throughout the various databases that are affected by the change. New process plans and tooling are automatically brought into the manufacturing system. Ultimately, changes in flexible fixtures needed to accommodate the process change would be made automatically. The characteristics of a linked cellular manufacturing system are summarized in Table 12-1.

The FWAF has substituted machines for human workers. The implications for employment in factory operations are clear. As automation is implemented, there will be a shift from direct labor jobs to indirect labor jobs. Human workers will

TABLE 12-1
Characteristics of a linked-cellular manufacturing system

Characteristic	Linked-cell system
Typical size of facility	Varies; floor space used efficiently.
Scale economics	Large; plant level.
Potential for learning improvements	Substantial and continuous.
Type of equipment	Simple and customized. Usually all single-cycle automatics that can complete the machining cycle unattended, turning themselves off when done with a machining cycle.
Capital intensity	Varies; moderate investment.
Definition of capacity	Cell capacity (the cycle time) can be quickly altered to respond to changes in customer demand.
Additions to capacity	Incremental over a wide range.
Bottlenecks	Bottlenecks are easy to identify because everyone understands how the cell functions.
Speed of process (units/time period)	Moderate; very flexible.
Control over work pace	Equipment and process design.
Setups	Short; frequent; one touch.
Run lengths	Flexible; can be long or short. System runs small lot sizes.
Process changes required by new products	Often incremental; system reacts quickly.
Rate of change in process technology	Moderate.
Labor content (value added)	Varies; labor used very efficiently.
Job content (scope)	Varies; depends on market demand and cell content.
Worker skill level	Multi-functional; respected.
Work force payment	Hourly or salaried.
Wage rate per hour	Moderate. Although workers are multifunctional, tasks have been simplified to avoid "skilled" worker requirements.
End of period push for output	It is not required since flexibility and reduced lot sizes enable manufacturing to run leveled/mixed production.
Work training requirements	Very predictable; uses monthly and daily information supplied to vendors.
Control over suppliers	Very high. Suppliers are remote cells, part of the team. Daily multiple deliveries for all active items are expected. The vendor takes care of he needs of the customer, and the customer treats the vendor as an extension of his factory.
Vertical integration	Some backward, often forward.
Raw material inventories	A liability; every effort extended to minimize.
Work-in-process	Minimized; controlled.

TABLE 12-1
(continued)

Characteristic	Linked-cell system
Finished goods inventory	Ideally, only goods required by the final customer are produced.
Responsibility for quality control	Direct labor in each cell.
Production information requirements	Moderate; communication between cells uses kanban technique.
Information systems	Integrated into system with the kanbans.
Scheduling	Varies with customer demands. L-CMS is flexible enough to meet demands without expediting.
Staff needs	Process control and coordination with emphasis on decentralization.
Stock-on-hand	Material in the cell.
Importance of forecasting	Important in any system, including L-CMS using kanban, which assumes leveled/mixed model scheduling.
Work force management tasks	Training and supervision.
Response to business downturns	Reduce number of employees in each cell.
Challenges	Process design improvements; continue to reduce lot sizes and WIP. Approach one-touch setup on all equipment. Approach zero defect maintenance system.

not be participating directly in the manufacturing and assembly processes, but will be required to manage and maintain the processes. This will require more highly educated people. Education is a keystone to survival of a manufacturing nation. Included in that education must be an understanding of technology and manufacturing systems.

This is the dawning of a new era in manufacturing systems. Already new manufacturing giants have emerged (Honda and Toyota), fueled chiefly by the development of integrated manufacturing production systems. These are the Factories with a Future.

REFERENCES

Black, J T., "Cellular Manufacturing Systems—An Overview," *IIE Journal*, Nov. 1983, p. 36.

Black, J T., and Schroer, B. J., "Decouplers in Integrated Cellular Manufacturing Systems," *Trans. ASME,* May 1988, p. 77.

Burbidge, J. L., "Production Flow Analysis for Planning Group Technology," Oxford Science Publications, 1989.

Crosby, Philip, *Quality is Free: The Art of Making Quality Certain*, McGraw-Hill, New York, 1979.

DeGarmo, E. P., Black, J T., and Kohser, R. A., *Materials and Processes in Manufacturing*, 8th ed., MacMillan, New York, 1988.

Hall, R. W., "Kawasaki U.S.A, A Case Study," APICS, 1982.

Hall, R. W., and APICS, *Zero Inventories*, Dow Jones-Irwin, Homewood, IL, 1983.

Ham, I., Hitomi, K., and Yoshida, T., *Group Technology—Applications to Production Management*, Kluwer-Nijhoff Publishing Co., Boston, MA, 1985.

Hayes, R. H. and Wheelwright, S. C., *Restoring Our Competitive Edge*, John Wiley, New York, 1984.

Hirano, H., *JIT Factory Revolution*, with English editing by J T. Black, Productivity Press, Cambridge, MA, 1988.

Kanban and Just-In-Time at Toyota, (Book based on seminars by T. Ohno et al.), Ed. Japan Management Association, Trans. D. J. Lu, Productivity Press, Cambridge, MA, 1986.

Kusiak, A., *Intelligent Manufacturing Systems*, Prentice Hall, Englewood Cliffs, NJ, 1990.

Mitrafanov, S. P., "Scientific Organization of Batch Production," *AFMS/LTV Technical Report TR-77-218, Vol. III*, Wright Patterson AFB, OH, Dec. 1977.

Monden, Y., *Toyota Production System*, IIE Press, Norcross, GA, 1983.

Nakajima, S., *Introduction to TPM*, Productivity Press, Cambridge, MA, 1988.

Naisbitt, J., *Megatrends*, Warner Books, New York, 1984.

Nof, S. Y., Meier, W. L., and Deisenroth, M. P., "Computerized Physical Simulators Are Developed to Solve IE Problems," *IR*, Oct. 1980.

Ohno, T., *Toyota Production System*, Productivity Press, Cambridge, MA, 1988.

Ouchi, W. G., *Theory Z*, Avon Books, New York, 1981.

Ranky, P. G., *The Design and Operation of FMS, Flexible Manufacturing Systems*, IFS (Publications) Ltd, UK, and North-Holland Publishing Company, New York, 1983.

Ross, P. J., *Taguchi Techniques for Quality Engineering*, McGraw-Hill, New York, 1988.

Rubenstein, M., *Patterns of Problem Solving*, Prentice Hall, Englewood Cliffs, NJ, 1975.

Schonberger, R. J., *Japanese Manufacturing Techniques*, Free Press, New York, 1982.

Schonberger, R. J., *World Class Manufacturing*, Free Press, 1986.

Shingo, S., *A Revolution in Manufacturing: The S.M.E.D. System*, Productivity Press, Cambridge, MA, 1985.

Shingo, S., *Study of 'Toyota' Production System from Industrial Engineering Viewpoint*, Japan Management Association, Tokyo, (Also available from Productivity Press, Cambridge, MA), 1981.

Shingo, S., *Zero Quality Control*, Productivity Press, Cambridge, MA, 1986.

Stockless Production, Hewlett-Packard Co., Greeley, CO, Videotape.

Suh, N. P., Bell, A. C., and Gossard, D. C., "On an Axiomatic Approach to Manufacturing and Manufacturing Systems," *J. of Eng. for Ind., Trans. ASME*, Vol. 100, 1978, p. 127.

Suh, N. P., *Principles of Design*, Oxford University Press, New York, 1990.

Suzaki, K., *The New Manufacturing Challenge*, The Free Press, New York, 1987.

Taguchi, G., "Introduction to Quality Engineering," Asian Productivity Center, 1986.

Taguchi, G., Elsayed, E. A., and Hsiang, T., *Quality Engineering in Production Systems*, McGraw-Hill, 1989.

Taguchi, G. and Wu, Y., "Introduction to Off-line Quality Control," Tokyo, Central Japan Quality Control Association, 1980.

Wantuck, K. A., *The Japanese Approach to Productivity*, APICS Conf. Proceedings, 1983.

Wright, P. K., and Bourne, D. A., *Manufacturing Intelligence*, Addison-Wesley, Reading, MA, 1988.

Young, R. E., Campbell, J. A., Morgan, J. A., "Physical Simulation: Use of Scaled-down Components to Analyze and Design Automated Production Systems," *Computer and Indus. Eng.*, Vol. 8, No. 1, 1984, pp. 73–85.

Zelenovic, D. M., "Flexibility—A Condition for Effective Production Systems," *Int. J. Prod. Res.*, Vol. 20, No. 3, 1982, p. 319.

INDEX